T0138666

WIRELESS CRIME AND FORENSIC INVESTIGATION

OTHER INFORMATION SECURITY BOOKS FROM AUERBACH

AUERBACH PUBLICATIONS

WIRELESS CRIME AND FORENSIC INVESTIGATION

GREGORY KIPPER

Auerbach Publications
Taylor & Francis Group
Boca Raton   New York

Auerbach Publications is an imprint of the
Taylor & Francis Group, an informa business

Auerbach Publications
Taylor & Francis Group
6000 Broken Sound Parkway NW, Suite 300
Boca Raton, FL 33487-2742

© 2007 by Taylor & Francis Group, LLC
Auerbach is an imprint of Taylor & Francis Group, an Informa business

No claim to original U.S. Government works
Printed in the United States of America on acid-free paper
10 9 8 7 6 5 4 3

International Standard Book Number-10: 0-8493-3188-9 (Hardcover)
International Standard Book Number-13: 978-0-8493-3188-6 (Hardcover)

Visit the Taylor & Francis Web site at
http://www.taylorandfrancis.com

and the Auerbach Web site at
http://www.auerbach-publications.com

Dedication

For Grant

Author's Intent

Before the final idea of this book was fully visualized, I spent a lot of time thinking about what investigators and security professionals would need tomorrow, next year, and on, into the future; content that really needed attention but that was not widely covered. My thoughts kept coming back to conducting forensics in a wireless environment.

First, there is a need. I wanted to get some good material out to investigators on this particular type of forensics. Second, it is important. Mobile devices are changing the very dynamics of our society, and those changes will continue to evolve as people live and work, and as our children grow into adults. Crime will, of course, continue to be a factor, as well as the growth of new, inventive ways of carrying it out. My goal is that by the time you've finished this book, you will know a good deal more than you now do and that you'll be able to effectively apply this knowledge to your work.

Who Should Read This Book

For those of you who have read my first book, *Investigator's Guide to Steganography*, you will notice a similar style and organization in this book. I did my best to make this book readable for anyone, but it is, of course, tailored to the forensic investigator, the private investigator with technical skills, and the IT security professional. The flow of the book is designed to take you from basic to advanced understanding. It does not necessarily have to be read in order, but that is probably the best approach to take if you're a beginner or haven't looked at the technology in a while. I'm a big believer in keeping information in context: showing where technology came from and why it is being used, before approaching the subject of forensics. The book is crafted along those lines of thought.

Acknowledgments

First and foremost, I would like to thank Amber Schroader for her contributions to this book. Quite simply, without her support and that of the Paraben engineers and developers, this work would not have seen the light of day. I would also like to thank Ken Ammon, John Sleggs and NetSec, as well as Eoghan Casey from Knowledge Solutions, for contributing their insights and expertise. Their assistance and research added greatly to this endeavor. I'd also like to recognize all of my technical editors — Eric Cole, Amber Schroader, and Joe Tomasone — for their time, expertise, and personal contributions to this book. Additionally, I'd like to thank Dave and Lisa Stafford, Spike and Ruth, Cody McKinney, Rich O'Hanley, Kimberly Hackett, Rachael Panthier, and the Taylor & Francis crew. Additionally I'd like to acknowledge James Briggs for his great work on all the graphics that went into this book.

Greg Kipper

About the Author

Greg Kipper has been active in the field of IT security and information assurance for the past 12 years. Through his experiences in the intelligence community and IT security, he moved into the emerging field of digital forensics. The last six years of his career have been spent working on the future of technologies and their impact on the process of forensic evidence gathering. He is also the author of *Investigator's Guide to Steganography* and continues to contribute to the fields of security and digital forensics through participation in numerous conferences and organizations. Mr. Kipper is currently working in the greater District of Columbia area as a private consultant in the field.

Technical Editors

Amber Schroader

Amber Schroader has been involved in the field of computer forensics for the past 16 years. During this time, she has developed and taught numerous courses in the computer forensic arena, specializing in the field of wireless forensics as well as mobile technologies. She is the CEO of Paraben Corporation and continues to act as the driving force behind some of the most innovative forensic technologies. As a pioneer in the field, she has played a key role in developing new technology to help investigators with the extraction of digital evidence from hard drives, e-mail, and handheld and other mobile devices. Her extensive experience includes dealing with a wide array of forensic investigators, ranging from those at federal, state, and local levels to corporate. With an aggressive development schedule, she continues to bring new and exciting technology to the computer forensic community worldwide and is dedicated to supporting the investigator through the new technologies and training services that are being provided through the Paraben Corporation. Ms. Schroader is involved in many different computer investigation organizations including the Institute of Computer Forensic Professionals (ICFP), High Technology Crime Investigation Association (HTCIA), the Computer Forensic Tool Technology (CFTT) program, and Federal Law Enforcement Training Center (FLETC).

Eric Cole

Eric Cole is a renowned Thought Leader with over 15 years of experience in the network security consulting market space. Dr. Cole is currently chief scientist and director of cyber security for Lockheed Martin Information

Technology (LMIT). Cole continuously executes high-end consulting services with Fortune 500 companies, financial institutions, international organizations, and the federal government. As a recognized industry expert, he is a frequent keynote speaker at security events around the world, including the Systems Administration Network Security Institute, and has been interviewed by CBS News, *60 Minutes*, and CNN. Cole is a member of the HoneyNet project and the *Common Vulnerabilities and Exposures* (CVE) editorial board, and has authored several books, including *Hackers Beware, Hiding in Plain Sight, Network Security Bible,* and *Insider Threat.* Dr. Cole contributed to the development of several of the GIAC certifications.

Joe Tomasone

Joe Tomasone is the senior network security engineer for Fortress Technologies. With more than 15 years in the IT industry, he has extensive practical experience in networking and security, and has briefed local, state, and federal agencies such as the Pentagon, the White House Communications Agency, the National Security Agency, the U.S. Air Force, U.S. Navy, and U.S. Army, plus numerous Fortune 1000 companies on wireless and wired security. In his current role, he is responsible for educating potential customers and partners on wireless security matters as well as the features and benefits of the company's Air Fortress family of products. He is a frequent speaker on these topics at conferences and to industry groups such as ISSA and Infragard.

Introduction

My in-laws just came to visit, and when they walked in the door, they were amazed at how much my five-month-old child had grown. They had not seen her in about two months and were astounded at how much she had changed. My first reaction was, "You really think she has changed that much?" As I see her every day, I do not notice the changes because I adapt and grow as she grows, which introduces an interesting problem. Although my daughter has been growing rapidly, because I am constantly around her, the day-by-day or hour-by-hour changes are so subtle that I fail to realize how significant the change has been until I look back at a picture when she was born, compare it to how she looks now, and realize that miraculous growth has occurred.

Similarly, we can all relate to this phenomenon with our children, but the same metamorphosis has been occurring with technology. Those who work with technology on a daily basis may be less aware of the dramatic growth. We do not always recognize or understand the change until a significant time period has elapsed or until others have pointed it out to us. Probably the one area in which this phenomenon has been most pronounced is wireless technology.

Wireless impacts everything we do and has become an integral part of our lives. Although I could fill pages talking about wireless, the focus here is on wireless data transfer in regard to computers. I am using the term *computers* in the liberal sense, indicating any device that has some processing and storage capability. For many people, one of their last activities before they go to sleep at night — and one of the first things they do in the morning — is utilize a wireless device. Whether it is a home computer or a BlackBerry to check on the status of a company and make sure no last-minute e-mails have arrived, wireless is all around us. And if you think they are everywhere now, you have not seen anything yet. Many of those who actively utilize wireless capabilities may think there is no scope left for practical development; the current technical boundaries often limit our perspective on creative ideas for the future. A perfect example is that many people five years ago thought cell phones were pretty sophisticated, but since then that technology has been taken to an entirely new level. Similar advancements will continue to occur.

As we move into the future most, if not all, critical data at some point between source and destination is going to go over a wireless link — if not several. As homes and offices, towns, cities, states, and countries continue to increase their bandwidth and connectivity, a natural solution to the problem is wireless. It is easy to install and does not require significant changes to operate. Let us start with the smallest example, a house. As technology advances, houses are going to have an increased need for bandwidth for home control systems. If you decide to install all new wiring to support a home control system you, in essence, will need to replace all Sheetrock® and walls in your house to support the number of wires that would be needed. Or in very strategic locations, you could install a few wireless access points, and have the same connectivity and benefit at a fraction of the cost and for a fraction of the time it would take to set up the network. Now take this example and scale it up to a town, city, or country. The problem with wires only gets worse, and the tremendous benefit provided by wireless only increases.

Therefore, in the next several years we can almost guarantee that critical data is going to be routed over wireless links. The efficiencies are too great to be ignored, and the functionality benefit will only continue to rise. As new, complex solutions of data transfer continue to occur, wireless, in most cases, is going to be the only reasonable solution to this problem.

Although wireless solves many problems, it creates a huge number of issues. The biggest problems with wireless is control, which leads to security problems. Wired connections are controlled, and if you cannot get access to the wires to either tap them midstream or at the demarc points, you are not able to intercept the signal. However, with wireless, anyone within a certain area is able to intercept the signal. Whether they can actually process or interrupt the signal is a completely different problem, but they can at least see the signal, which makes the attacker's problem much easier than if it was a wired situation. Many of you might think I am stating the obvious; however, obvious or not, this is a concept that many people either forget about or ignore in implementing solutions.

Now for the really bad news. The problem of controlling and securing wireless is not a linear problem; it is an exponential problem in terms of complexity. This means the longer we allow functionality to increase, the problem of securing those wireless networks increases at a much steeper pace.

As most organizations traditionally do after they implement a solution, they assume it is secure, and after it is compromised or they see the potential for compromise from other organizations, they slowly address the problem. We have readily observed with viruses, worms, and other problems that this reactive measure does not work and does not scale. With a problem space as big and as complex as wireless, proactive measures must be put in place, and they must be put in place immediately. Organizations can either pay now, or they can pay later. However, one problem is that wireless is like a high interest rate credit card. If you pay off the debt now, you no longer have any debt to worry about, but if you pay later by paying the minimal each month, you will probably never be able to pay it off because of the compound growth of the problem. Even if you do manage to pay it off, you will end up paying much more than you needed to.

General security is also a concern with any new technology, and when we think security we typically think of stopping an attacker from breaking in or gaining access. However, based on the broad reach of wireless, stopping someone from passively listening in is just as critical. Therefore, all current disciplines need to be applied to the wireless arena. Intrusion detection systems, firewalls, and forensics are just a few of the key areas that one must understand and apply to proactively solve the wireless problem.

Dr. Eric Cole

Contents

Chapter 1

Overview of Wireless Technologies and Security

A Brief History of Wireless

On December 12, 1901, Guglielmo Marconi was on Signal Hill in New-foundland when he heard the three dots of the letter "S" come through in Morse code from 2000 mi away in Cornwall, England. This signal proved beyond doubt that wireless communications could travel tremendous distances and even around the curvature of the Earth. Marconi was awarded the Nobel Prize in Physics for this achievement in 1909.

As the century progressed, the first voice over radio transmission was heard in 1914. Between 1920 and 1940, mobile receivers were installed in Detroit police cars, and by 1940 the majority of police radio systems converted to the frequency modulation (FM) standard.

A mobile phone was interconnected with the standard public telephone system for the first time in 1946. By 1979 NTT/Japan deployed the first cellular communication system. In 1991 the U.S. Digital Cellular phone system was introduced, and by 1997 the number of cellular telephone users in the United States exceeded 50 million.

Figure 1.1 Guglielmo Marconi.

The Benefits of Modern Wireless Technology

The impact of wireless technology today has been huge, to say the least. To grasp how rapidly things are changing, consider all the things you can do today that would have been difficult or impossible just a few years ago. Even looking at the most basic of devices, such as the television remote control, one doesn't have to ponder for long to see the tremendous impact wireless in all its forms has had on everyday life.

People now have anytime/anywhere access to data and information. Large wireless networks have created an ever-expanding coverage area, allowing users to communicate on the move. New technologies have improved responsiveness and efficiency in both personal and business communications, reduced costs for setting up computer networks, and permitted unprecedented flexibility for the infrastructure of those networks.

And the future will have even more to offer by:

- Making wireless work everywhere by having hotspots that connect all devices and all types of information, creating what could be called a *wireless fabric*.
- Unwiring the home and living room. Phones and digital media from music to video will be linked together wirelessly.
- Using wireless to cross the last mile. Wireless will allow broadband access to areas that may not have the wired infrastructure to support DSL.

- Converging with the cell phone. By using Wireless-Voice-over-IP (WVoIP), calls will be far cheaper because they will travel over the Internet rather than a phone network.

Unfortunately, with most things this usable and flexible there is always a downside. What one can use for good another can use for bad, and it's the latter aspect that the rest of this book focuses on. I do this not to detract from the usefulness of wireless and wireless technologies but to stay focused on the factors and issues surrounding wireless forensics.

The New Risks Created by Wireless Technology

Before we look at some of the threats associated with wireless technology, I think it's important to cover the new risks that have been "created" by the widespread use of this technology. First, wireless is a shared and largely uncontrolled medium. When *shared* and *uncontrolled* are used to describe a condition, it is almost always a recipe for risk; and when you add millions of users to the risk equation, it becomes an even bigger issue.

Next, wireless is a promiscuous technology. Simply put, the next evolution of information technology is about connectivity, not information. The information revolution was over almost 20 years ago and in that time individuals, industries, and countries haven't been trying to get more information, they've been figuring out how to manage the vast sea of data that already exists. Connectivity is becoming the next revolution.

Third, mobile devices are transient. They are not permanently located in one fixed location and tied to fixed physical infrastructure. They move into, out of, and around the wireless coverage areas at will, adding a complicating factor for detecting and locating suspicious activity and the forensics that accompany a security incident. Attacks that used to originate from the public side of the firewall can now take place from the LAN inside the firewall, requiring security professionals to reorient their thinking and their threat analysis of their internal networks. However, the same lessons that common carriers learned in moving to cellular telephony from wired telephony largely apply here; chief among them is that ironclad authentication and location capabilities are crucial to mitigating and responding to security concerns. The fourth risk problem is ease of use. Ease of use creates familiarity, which encourages user indifference, which in turn exposes them to risk. This is not an uncommon phenomenon, however. There are people who are mortally afraid of flying who think nothing of getting in their cars and driving, although driving is statistically the most dangerous activity we engage in on a regular basis.

And fifth, wireless is simply easier to attack. It's one thing to contain a signal in a copper wire or phone cord, and it's quite another when an omnidirectional device is sending and receiving those same signals. Wireless networks have made war-driving and war-chalking possible, just to use a simple example. Wireless networks are also easier to attack because they can be deployed quite easily. A *Computerworld* survey estimated that at least 30 percent of business networks have rogue wireless local area networks (WLANs). So now this means not only do you have to watch out for the wireless networks you have deployed, but you have to watch out for the ones you haven't deployed as well.

Overview of Modern Wireless Technology

In this section I'll quickly outline the modern wireless technologies in use today. I have kept this extremely brief as I expect anyone reading this to already be somewhat familiar with these technologies. However, rather than leave them out completely, I did want to provide an overview should you need to reference something quickly. There are, of course, mountains of books and articles available in print and on the Internet should you need to research any of these areas further.

Personal Area Networks

Wireless personal area networks, or WPANs, are a combination of technologies used within short distances (less than 10 m) to connect computers and peripherals and transmit data at high rates of speed. WPAN technology is being developed to be easily integrated into existing wired and wireless networking technologies without adding too much complexity.

Bluetooth

Bluetooth is a wire replacement peer-to-peer and mesh standard designed to allow the automatic networking of computer peripherals such as keyboards and mice, or personal peripherals such as wireless phone headsets. It is common for PDAs and, increasingly, cell phones, to have Bluetooth functionality. From a security standpoint, it is important to understand the technology as well as the security risks these devices could pose, either personally or on an enterprise's network. For example, even though a device, like a PDA, may not connect to an internal network directly, sensitive information could be stored on that device that could be retrieved by an unauthorized user through a weak Bluetooth configuration.

Figure 1.2   Bluetooth symbol.

InfraRed

Infrared (IrDA) is a line-of-sight short-range technology that is predominantly used on laptops and PDAs for file transfers and basic networking. IrDAD, or IrDA-Data, is a point-to-point, ad hoc data transmission standard with a limited operating distance of 0 to 2 m. The big security weakness of IR is that it is very easy to use and available on almost every computing device. Often it is assumed that owing to the line-of-sight operational nature of IR-to-IR communication, the communication stream is secure. However, it is possible for a third party to capture information from the data stream by detecting reflected light and filtering out the surrounding ambient noise.

Ultrawideband

Ultrawideband (UWB) is a superfast wireless networking solution that can be used for wire replacement between multimedia equipment. UWB uses no underlying carrier wave. Instead, UWB modulates superfast pulses in precisely timed sequences over a large continuous band of spectrum. UWB is a technique to deliver data over an extremely wide spectrum.

ZigBee

ZigBee is a home area network designed specifically to replace the proliferation of individual remote controls. ZigBee was created to satisfy

Figure 1.3 ZigBee Alliance logo.

the market's need for a cost-effective, standards-based wireless network that supports low data rates, low power consumption, security, and reliability.

Wireless USB

Universal serial bus (USB) technology has been a popular method of connecting devices to PCs for a number of years now. Wireless USB is the next iteration of this technology. WUSB is intended to provide a wireless connectivity interface to host and device at less than 10 m range. WUSB will operate at 480 Mbps initially, with future versions moving to 1 Gbps, allowing for the transmission of rich multimedia content, including audio and video, as well as high-rate streaming.

Wireless Local Area Networks

802.11

802.11, known as Wi-Fi, is a family of specifications for WLANs developed by a working group of the Institute of Electrical and Electronics Engineers (IEEE). 802.11 applies to WLANs and provides 1 or 2 Mbps transmission in the 2.4 GHz band using either frequency hopping spread spectrum (FHSS) or direct sequence spread spectrum (DSSS). Appendix D outlines the remaining flavors of 802.11.

900 MHz Packet Radio

Early wireless networking projects employed the 900 MHz frequency range. Radios using this range were designed to provide a 10Base-T interface data port and were designed to transport IP-based data. Cordless phones, pagers, medical equipment and other products also use the 900 MHz ISM (Industrial, Scientific and Medical) band. It is possible to experience interference while using this band. Interference can prohibit data transmissions and can result in poor or unreliable communication rates.

Metropolitan Area Networks

A metropolitan area network, or MAN, is a network designed to provide broadband connectivity to a densely populated geographic area. Examples of such areas include cities, counties, and campuses. MANs are sometimes referred to as *"last mile solutions."*

Microwave

Microwave links are point-to-point network connections that cover line-of-sight distances and use licensed frequency bands. Microwave MAN technology is basically high-powered AM radio. Microwave MAN technology broadcasts at much-higher-frequency signals, so much so that they effectively function as point-to-point communications. The most significant benefits to using Microwave MANs are cost and ease of deployment.

Free Space Optics

Free Space Optics (FSO) is another point-to-point network connection that uses a laser instead of a specific radio frequency, allowing for very high data rates. FSO is a high-bandwidth MAN solution that incorporates the security of fiber-optic cables. Instead of transmitting lasers across glass strands, FSO transmits a line-of-sight laser between two points. This technology first appeared over 30 years ago when the U.S. military used FSO for data communication between ships at sea.

Ricochet

Ricochet is a wireless Internet service provider (ISP) network solution for a specific geographic location. Ricochet allows portable wireless clients to move throughout a coverage area and access the Internet.

WiMAX

WiMAX (Worldwide Interoperability for Microwave Access), the 802.16 standard for 2 to 11 GHz, is a wireless MAN technology. WiMAX is designed for long-range networking and is capable of very high throughput on the order of 70 Mbps. WiMAX is the next step on the road to a wireless world, extending broadband wireless access to new locations and over longer distances, as well as significantly reducing the cost of bringing broadband to new areas.

Wide Area Networks

Unlike personal or metropolitan network technologies, which are used in a specific area and have limited range, wireless wide area networks (WANs) are intended for communications between mobile and fixed devices nationwide.

Satellite

Satellite transmissions use radio frequencies in the same fashion as radio or other wireless technologies. Satellite includes television, global positioning systems (GPS), satellite ISPs, satellite telephony, and satellite radio (XM Radio).

Cellular

Cellular technology has been around for some time in the United States, yet has only become affordable, and thus widely used, within the last 15 years. Below is a list of the most common types of cell phone technology:

- *Cellular Digital Packet Data* (CDPD) uses unused cellular channels in the 800–900 MHz range to transmit data packets.
- *Global System for Mobile Communications* (GSM) uses a narrowband TDMA method to allow eight simultaneous calls on the same radio frequency.
- *Third-Generation Global System for Mobile Communications* (3GSM) will support multimedia applications such as full-motion video, videoconferencing, and Internet access.

- *General Packet Radio Service* (GPRS) is a common standard that enables high-speed wireless Internet and other data communications offering theoretical data speeds of up to 115 kbps.
- *Code Division Multiple Access* (CDMA) uses a spread spectrum technique to scatter a radio signal across a wide range of frequencies. CDMA is a 2G technology.
- *Time Division Multiple Access* (TDMA) is a technology used in digital cellular telephone communication to divide each cellular channel into three time slots to increase the amount of data that can be carried.
- *Advanced Mobile Phone Service* (AMPS) operates in the 800 MHz band using frequency division multiple access (FDMA) technology.

BlackBerry

BlackBerry devices are portable two-way text-messaging units that allow users to access corporate e-mail, or send peer-to-peer messages or files between other BlackBerry users. These devices are providing mobile employees with services previously limited to Internet-connected desktop PCs.

The BlackBerry devices offer the following services:

- Wireless e-mail — ability to send/receive e-mail
- Voice and SMS — ability to "instant-message" other BlackBerry users, and also use the BlackBerry as a cellular phone
- Mobile data service — ability to access remotely stored data
- Wireless calendar — ability to remotely synchronize calendar
- Wireless Internet — ability to remotely access the Internet
- Attachment service — ability to read e-mail attachments
- Paging — ability to send and receive pages

Paging

Paging technology has remained the same for many years. This includes both one- and two-way text messaging. Paging technology has remained popular because of its reliability: it can consistently reach pagers inside buildings and in remote areas. With the popularity of cellular phones increasing, paging has lost some of its appeal.

Other Technologies of Note

iMode

iMode is NTT DoCoMo's mobile Internet access system. iMode is an overlay over NTT-DoCoMo's ordinary mobile voice system. iMode is *packet switched*, meaning that in principle it is *"always on."*

Short Message Service (SMS)

SMS is a service for sending messages of up to 160 characters (224 characters if using a 5-bit mode) to GSM mobile phones. SMS messages can also be sent to digital phones from a Web site equipped with PCLink or from one digital phone to another.

VoWiFi

Stands for *Voice over WiFi*; allows voice calls to be broken down into IP packets and transmitted seamlessly through a wireless network.

Intel Centrino

Intel Centrino mobile technology is a WLAN capability that enables wireless connectivity from Wi-Fi WLAN networks. Intel plans to incorporate Wi-Fi into the motherboard chipset, which will allow laptops to easily connect to Wi-Fi networks without the use of additional hardware.

Bibliography

Anderson C., The Wi-Fi Revolution, *Wired Magazine*, May 2003.

Arora R., State of Affairs of Wireless Networks, SANS Institute, January 2003.

Cox, J., The WLAN Standards Alphabet Keeps Growing, *Network World*, January 2004.

Dawson, F., FSO: The Next Generation, *Xchange*, September 2001.

Farely, T., Mobile Telephone History, Privateline.com, March 16, 2006.

Farely, T., Basic Wireless Principles, Privateline.com, January 3, 2006.

Fisher, J. and Wang, R., Wireless Wide Area Networks, pdaFN.com, November 2005.

Galeev, M., Home networking with Zigbee, Embedded.com, April 2004.

Geier, J., 2.4GHz vs. 5GHz Deployment Considerations, Wi-Fi Planet, January 2003.

Griffin, E., 11g — The New Mainstream, Wi-Fi Planet, November 2002.

Grinsven, L., Bluetooth goes Mass Market in Phone, Car, and Fridge, *InfoWorld*, June 2002.

IEEE Standards Association, IEEE 802.11 Standard, May 2005.

Infosecsys, Cellular Communications and Security, www.infosyssec.org, 2005.

Jones G., Wireless makes waves 100 years on, CNN, December 12, 2001.

Karygiannis, T. and Owens, L., Wireless Network Security NIST Special Publication 800-48, National Institute of Standards and Technology, November 2002.

Kleinrock, L., The Birth of the Internet, www.lk.cs.ucla.edu/LK/Inet/birth.html, August 1996.

Kolic, R., An introduction to Wireless USB (WUSB), Deviceforge.com, February 2004.

Meurling, J. and Jeans, R., *The Mobile Phone Book: The Invention of The Mobile Phone Industry*, Communications Week International, London, on behalf of Ericsson Radio Systems, 1994, p. 43.

Network Computing — Network Design Manual, Wireless Broadband and Other Fixed-Wireless Systems, TechWeb, 2005.

Ricochet Networks, Ricochet — About the Ricochet Network, www.ricochet.com/about.aspx, 2006.

Shea, J., Brief History of Wireless Communications, January 2000.

Shim, R., GPS Owners Play High-Tech Hide-And-Seek, *CNET News*, January 2001.

The Aerospace Corporation, The Global Positioning System, Jan. 2003, Los Angeles.

Thomson, A., *Satellite Vulnerability: A Post Cold-War Issue?*, Space Policy (ISSN 0265-9646) February 1995, Washington, D.C.

U.S. General Accounting Office, Critical Infrastructure Protection: Commercial Satellite Security Should Be More Fully Addressed, Washington, D.C., August 2002.

Voorhis, N., Security on Internet Satellite — Any Different than Wired or Wireless?, SANS, June 2005.

Chapter 2

Wireless Threats, Vulnerabilities, and Security

Introduction

Currently, it is estimated that 75 percent of the United States' wireless computer networks are vulnerable to attack. However, in spite of this statistic, the fact that wireless use is so widely prevalent illustrates that the benefits of the technology, for now, outweigh the risks. These risks may become more problematic as the nation's critical IT infrastructure, namely, corporate America, emergency services, and Government agencies, are becoming more and more tied to the Internet. This leads to an even bigger concern: the Internet is being accessed more and more frequently by wireless links connected to networks with inadequate security, which makes auditing and forensics all the more difficult.

To counter or prevent the effects of these types of computer attacks, it is always best for organizations to ensure they are complying with basic network security guidelines. Although convenient and easy to deploy, wireless local area networks (WLANs) require proper planning, training, and an ongoing awareness of the security risks introduced by using wireless devices and networks. In this chapter we're going to cover threats, vulnerabilities, and security solutions related to Wi-Fi, PDAs, and cell phones as a review before diving deeper into conducting forensics on these devices.

Wireless LANs

Wireless Network Security Threats

The security risks in WLANs extend beyond those in a wired network to include the additional risks introduced by weaknesses in wireless protocols. The security threats posed by WLANs are considered in the following subsections.

Eavesdropping

Intercepting information that is transmitted over the WLAN is generally easier, as it can be done from a considerable distance outside of the building perimeter without any physical network connection. The information intercepted can be read if transmitted in the clear, or easily deciphered if only WEP encryption is used.

Traffic Analysis

The attacker gains information by monitoring wireless transmissions for patterns of communication and data flow between parties, and deciphers encrypted traffic that has been captured. Traffic analysis can result in the compromise of sensitive information.

Data Tampering

The information transmitted over the WLAN can be deleted, replayed, or modified by the attacker via man-in-the-middle attack. This can result in a loss of data integrity and availability.

Masquerading

The attacker gains unauthorized access to the information and network resources within the WLAN or other interconnected network by impersonating an authorized user. The attacker can cause further problems by launching attacks or introducing malicious code that can disrupt operations.

Denial-of-Service (DoS)

The attacker can jam the entire frequency channel that is used for wireless data transmission using a powerful signal generator, microwave, or a massive amount of broadcasted network traffic from a rogue wireless device. With high-gain antennas and WLAN attack tools, the perpetrator can cause denial-of-service without being close to the targeted WLAN, and although it is not impossible to direction-find (DF) the perpetrator, it is difficult and requires tools that are only now becoming available.

Wireless Client Attacks

The attacker can potentially gain access to the information shared or stored in the wireless client when it is connected to an unprotected ad hoc WLAN or an untrustworthy third-party WLAN. Additionally, the compromised wireless client can potentially serve as a bridge to the internal network, thus allowing a perpetrator to gain access to or launch attacks against the internal corporate network and its resources.

Other Issues

Spread Spectrum Isn't Very Secure

Several of the 802.11 wireless LAN standards use spread spectrum, which is a modulation technique developed to prevent radio jamming. Spread spectrum, in general, is capable of changing the "spreading codes" in a way that makes decipherment impossible without knowing the correct codes. Wireless LAN vendors today still advertise the security that spread spectrum provides. This would be fine except that the 802.11 standard describes the spreading codes publicly so that companies can design interoperable 802.11 components. This means that a hacker or intruder would only need an 802.11-compliant radio NIC as the basis for connectivity, which nullifies the security benefits of spread spectrum.

SSIDs Are Not Designed as Passwords

The Service Set Identifier (SSID) is the name of a WLAN. All wireless devices on a particular WLAN must use the same SSID to communicate with each other. SSIDs were first introduced as a way to prevent people from connecting to the access point (AP) without foreknowledge of the SSID, which has now been incorporated into every AP as "Disabling broadcast SSID." So SSIDs serve a very useful function — identification of the AP or network; however, it should not be relied upon as a password.

WEP is Weak

The Wired Equivalent Privacy (WEP) protocol was designed to add security to WLANs. WEP was intended to give wireless networks the equivalent level of privacy of a comparable wired network. However, WEP occasionally produces cryptologically weak ciphers that are easily broken with modern tools. A step-by-step description of how the WEP protocol is cracked follows, to give you a better idea of the weakness of WEP and the speed with which it can be compromised:

1. A hacker runs Kismet, a wireless LAN discovery tool, to determine what wireless LANs are in the area. When the hacker discovers the SSID, the channel number it is operating on, and its BSSID (*Basic Service Set Identifier* — its Ethernet address), he has all the information needed to mount an attack to recover the WEP key.

2. If the SSID is unknown because the WLAN's owner has enabled a mode that hides it (known as *SSID Cloaking* or *SSID Broadcast Disable*), the hacker can discover the SSID by waiting for a client to connect, in which case both the client as well as the AP disclose the SSID. Or the hacker can obtain the SSID by forcing an already-connected client to disconnect and reconnect. This is done by sending a specially crafted packet pretending to be from the AP that tells the receiving client that it is no longer authenticated. The client has no way to tell that this is not actually coming from the AP, and so it attempts to rectify the problem by disconnecting from the AP and reconnecting, yielding the SSID in the process.

3. The hacker puts his wireless card into a "monitor mode" in which the WLAN card eavesdrops on a WLAN without having to connect to it. He commands the WLAN card to monitor the channel on which the target AP is located, and begins capturing and saving all of the traffic monitored from that AP to disk in a file called a *capture file*.

4. The software used to capture the data notes the reception of packets encrypted with a weak Initialization Vector (IV), which in cryptography is a value used to initialize a cryptographic process. WEP misuses these IVs in an exploitable way, and when a certain number of weak IVs have been captured, the WEP key can be determined. Roughly 125,000 packets are required to crack most 40-bit WEP keys, and 200,000–250,000 packets for a 128-bit WEP key.

5. On a slow WLAN, capturing the requisite number of weak IVs can take some time. To accelerate the attack, the hacker will next inject a captured WEP frame back into the network to generate more

traffic. This takes advantage of the fact that WEP has no "replay protection" mechanism to prevent this. An injection rate of 512 packets per second generally results in the required number of IVs being captured between 10 min for 40-bit and 30 min for 128-bit WEP. If no client is present on the WLAN to generate traffic that can be captured and reinjected, in most cases the attacker's own system can be made to do so.

6. After a sufficient number of IVs is captured, the hacker runs the AirCrack tool, which will attempt to crack and disclose the WEP key.

7. Once the WEP key is known, the hacker can connect to the AP just as a legitimate client would — and the WLAN owner would be none the wiser.

War-Driving

War-driving is derived from the *war-dialing* exploits of the teenage hacker character in the 1983 movie *War Games*, who has his computer randomly dial hundreds of numbers. He eventually winds up tapping into a nuclear command and control system!

With the growth of the Internet, scanning was the next version of this type of exploit. People often scan through large numbers of IP addresses looking for computers that are running certain types of servers.

The wireless age has introduced a new type of attack called *war-driving*. Originally, war-driving was when crackers drove around in a car equipped with wireless gear looking for unsecured wireless networks to gain illicit access to. Over time, the term has evolved to include harmless types like us simply checking on the radio frequency (RF) environment.

The Basic War-Driving Kit

The basic kit consists of the following:

■ Laptop computer
■ Wireless NIC
■ Antenna (optional)
■ Software
■ GPS unit (optional)

Table 2.1   War-Driving Software

Linux	Windows	Apple	PocketPC	Palm OS
Airsnort	Aerosol	KisMAC	Airscanner	NetChaser
Airtraf	ApSniff	Airport	Pocket Warrior	
AP-Status	Netstumbler	AP Scanner		
E-Wireless	Wlan	MacStumbler		
Gwireless	Pong	IStumbler		
Wirestat	APTools			
Wvlanmon	Link Ferret			
Prismdump				
Prismdstumbler				
Radiate				
THC-WarDrive				
Wavemon				
Wellenreiter				
Kismet				

Figure 2.1   Access points that have been discovered and overlaid onto a Google-Earth map.

Why Are People War-Driving?

There is no clear answer to this question, because the act of war-driving can have so many different motivations. Technology is not bound to ethics. It is the application and use of that technology that brings ethics into it.

If someone is simply driving around a city searching for the existence of wireless networks, with no ulterior motive, it cannot be deemed illegal. However, if you are searching for a place to steal Internet access, or commit computer crimes, then war-driving is considered malicious and could be treated as such in court. Also remember that in the United States, simply receiving radio transmissions on the cellular telephone frequencies (895–925 MHz) is illegal.

A key differentiator here is that cellular interception takes place with equipment exclusive to the normal process of service, i.e., you don't use a cell phone to intercept someone else's call, you use a scanner. War-driving (and wireless sniffing) uses the same equipment that you'd use to participate in a WLAN as a normal user. Further, because you have the right to monitor your own network, making monitoring tools illegal would certainly be questionable, especially in light of the current thinking that perhaps companies ought to be held liable for malicious activity occurring through their inadequately secured WLANs.

War-Chalking

War-chalking actually started out as something else. It was a secret sign language once used by hobos to alert fellow travelers of dangers or opportunities for food and work on the open road. Today, war-chalking is an extension of war-driving, in which people use chalk to place a special symbol on a sidewalk or other surface that indicates a nearby wireless network, especially one that offers Internet access. Figure 2.2 shows a few standard war-chalking symbols.

War Flying

In yet another flavor of war-driving that has emerged in recent years, hobbyists are now taking their skills to the air. The term is appropriately named *war flying* and those using this technique are detecting hundreds of wireless LAN APs during short trips in private planes cruising at altitudes between 1500 and 2500 ft.

On one war-flying tour over an area of San Diego County, a private plane detected 437 APs. Detection of so many APs is due to the increased range that wireless networks can broadcast upward because of lack of obstructions. However, the limit is currently around 2500 ft because most WLANs are vertically, not horizontally, polarized, and so most of the RF energy goes out parallel to the Earth's surface.

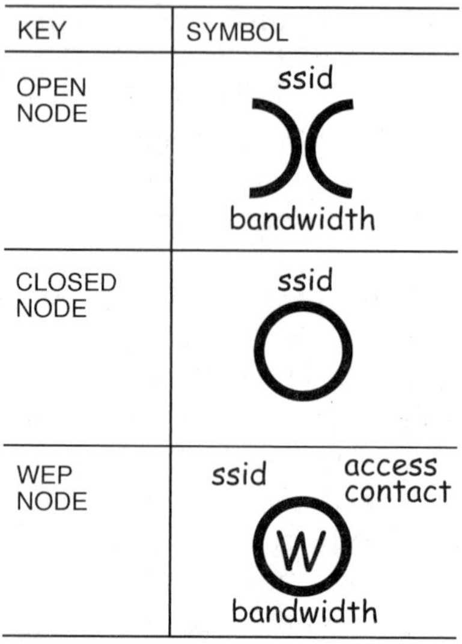

KEY	SYMBOL
OPEN NODE	ssid)(bandwidth
CLOSED NODE	ssid O
WEP NODE	ssid access contact (W) bandwidth

Figure 2.2   The basic war-chalking symbols.

War-Driving and War-Chalking Ethics

In the previous subsections we have covered war-driving, war flying, and war-chalking; however, when we look beyond the definitions and techniques, we get into the ethical issues of these activities. Three questions come to mind:

1. Is it theft?
2. Is it harmful?
3. Is it stoppable?

Is It Theft?

According to the standard definition, theft is defined as "the felonious taking and removing of personal property with intent to deprive the rightful owner of it." Although war-chalking and war-driving activities identify and mark wireless networks, they do not remove or deprive the owner of his or her wireless connectivity. However, if common sense prevails here, this would be considered theft.

Is It Harmful?

War-chalking is only a process of identifying networks. It would be similar to going around a neighborhood and somehow making marks on public property identifying houses with weak security.

Is It Stoppable?

Not really, unless you are planning on installing lead walls. Owners of wireless networks can modify or shield their equipment, but it is by no means foolproof.

Proactive Measures

Now that we've seen an example of what's possible, let's look at some steps that can be taken to help protect a wireless network. In this section and the one that follows, we will cover some tools and best practices that will allow you to be proactive with your security. By using the same tools that hackers use to penetrate your network, you can to find and plug security holes beforehand. This, combined with using established security practices and policies, can help deter or prevent intrusions.

Tools for wireless networks:

WLAN discovery tools
- Netstumbler — Versions for Windows and Linux
- Kismet — Linux
- MacStumbler — Mac OS
- MiniStumbler — Pocket PC
- Mognet — Java

Wireless network sniffers
- AiroPeek — Windows
- AirTraf — Linux
- Ethereal — All OSs
- Sniffer Wireless — Windows and Pocket PC
- BSD AirTools — BSD

WEP cracking tools
- WEPCrack — Linux
- AirSnort — Linux
- BSD-Tools dweputils — BSD
- AirCrack — Linux and Windows

Common Wi-Fi Security Recommendations: Actions versus Reality

In the previous section we looked at some tools that will help you find out more about your wireless network and the information traveling across it. In this section we will take a closer look at what is commonly recommended when securing wireless, and how effective those recommendations really are.

Recommended action: Turn SSID broadcasting off.
Reality: Several software tools (such as Kismet) exist that will discover the SSID when a client connects — and common hacker tools can force a user to reconnect to the AP at will — thus giving up the SSID. In reality, this measure stops only two commonly used WLAN discovery tools from finding a WLAN, namely, Netstumbler and Windows XP.

Recommended action: Utilize static IP addresses.
Reality: Static IP address pools can be found quickly through simple traffic analysis, much quicker than you can eliminate DHCP from your network.

Recommended action: Turn 128-bit WEP encryption on.
Reality: WEP can be cracked in tens of minutes in essentially every case.

Recommended action: Change WEP keys periodically.
Reality: New WEP keys can be cracked just as quickly as old ones.

Recommended action: Enable MAC address filtering.
Reality: Simple traffic analysis will yield the authorized MAC addresses (which, after all, are the only ones passing traffic over the network). Because MAC addresses can be specified by a hacker for his WLAN card, this has no real security benefit. In fact, this "security tip" offers essentially zero security while requiring great effort to implement.

Recommended action: Utilize shared key authentication.
Reality: Again, WEP can be cracked quite rapidly.

Recommended action: Use personal firewalls.
Reality: A good idea to prevent anyone who does manage to connect with the AP from communicating with your mobile device and potentially obtaining data or doing harm. However, because

attacks exist that fool the mobile device into believing that a hacker's system is a trusted one, this is not a panacea.

Recommended action: Administer wireless devices using secure protocols like SSH or HTTPS, instead of telnet or http. With the tunnel in place, anyone who tries to monitor the conversation between your laptop and the mail server will get something resembling line noise.
Reality: Unless the hacker is able to perpetrate a man-in-the-middle attack. SSH and HTTPS have been found vulnerable in the past to man-in-the-middle attacks in certain circumstances; wireless connections are easier to exploit in this regard than wired ones.

Personal Digital Assistants

PDA Threats and Vulnerabilities

Mobile Device Attacks

Although attacks on mobile devices are not as widely published or as prolific as the viruses and worms that infiltrate network security defenses, they do exist and can be equally dangerous. The open handheld operating systems are often left insecure, making the device highly susceptible to a variety of attacks. Some common attacks include: copying or stealing information from the device, loading malicious code onto the device, or destroying key files or applications on the device.

How a PDA Connects to Other Computers

A PDA connects to other computers by one or more of the following methods:

- Desktop synchronization
- Hardwired network interface card
- Wireless network interface card
    - Bluetooth
    - Wi-Fi

Viruses, Trojans, and Worms

As with desktop and laptop computers, PDAs and the programs they run can be vulnerable to malicious code, which include:

- Trojans: A program disguised as another program.

- Worms: Stand-alone programs that make full, running duplications of themselves, stealing system resources.
- Logic bombs: Programs within programs that perform destructive acts based on a trigger event.

One of the first reported wireless viruses was called Phage and was aimed at the Palm OS, back in 2000. Viruses depend on the type of PDA OS you are running. PDAs are also more likely to be a carrier of a virus than the actual target of an attack; however, this is probably of little comfort after a PDA has been synced with a workstation or worse, an enterprise.

Theft of the PDA Device

PDAs and BlackBerrys are clearly more at risk for theft because of their size and weight. It's much easier to lift a device designed to go into your pocket as opposed to one that's not. The devices are often the main interest of the thief as they are typically worth a higher price tag despite their small size. However, this will not always be the case because as the data capacity and battery life increase, the data that resides on the device will interest the average thief.

Data Theft

Again, thanks to the portability of these devices and their ability to hold, in some cases, a variety of memory expansion cards, it often doesn't take much time for someone to quietly download all of your information to a removable flash card.

Mobile Code Exploits

Mobile code is software that is transmitted across a network from a server or other remote source to a local system and is then executed on that local system. Often, this is done without direct action by the user. This code may have flaws that can allow an attacker to compromise a PDA.

Authentication Theft

The theft of the device can also result in the theft of authentication information, which can allow access into additional resources or a larger network.

DoS Attacks

A DoS attack is an incident in which a user or organization is deprived of the services of a resource they would normally expect to have. In the instance of a PDA, everything from a mobile code exploit to the theft of the actual device constitutes a DoS.

Session Hijacking

Session hijacking is when someone takes over a TCP session between two machines, or in this case, a PDA and another PDA or network. Most authentication only occurs at the start of a TCP session, allowing the hacker to gain access to the PDA or its host network.

PDA Security

Anti-Virus Software

As with workstations and servers, running an anti-virus program on your PDA will help reduce the risks of data loss or corruption, and help prevent your PDA from being a target of attack when it syncs to a computer or network. Norton, Symantec, F-Secure, and Kaspersky all produce PDA anti-virus products.

Other PDA Security Measures

The following are important PDA security measures:

- Database security and authentication
- Faraday bag (which blocks all wireless signals to the device)
- Encryption — Ccrypt, PDA Secure (TrustDigital)
- Firewalls — Mobile Firewall Plus
- Password enforcement — HotSync security, PDA Defense
- VPN — VPN 3000 (Cisco), MovianVPN

Combating Handheld Attacks

As we've seen, mobile device platforms have their own set of threats and vulnerabilities. These pose unique challenges to security administrators. Every mobile user and mobile enterprise needs to carefully evaluate its own device-side security needs.

The following best practices, from Bluefire Security Technologies, Baltimore, Maryland, provide a basic guide to begin the process:

1. Define handheld security policy
2. Centrally enforce and monitor handheld security
3. Enforce use of power-on passwords
4. Block unauthorized handheld network activity
5. Detect handheld intrusions
6. Protect handheld integrity
7. Encrypt sensitive data stored on handhelds
8. Protect traffic sent/received by handhelds
9. Maintain up-to-date anti-virus protection
10. Back up frequently

Cell Phones

Cell Phone Threats and Vulnerabilities

SMS Spoofing

It is a relatively trivial task to forge the originating address of an SMS and send flash messages to certain phones that don't display any information about the sender. SMS can even be spoofed to look like an internal message.

Camera Phones

A nontechnical vulnerability with cellular phones is the introduction of cameras on the phones themselves. Many phones sold today have cameras included, or attachable, to send images to other phone users, or to someone's e-mail. This poses a social engineering threat to an organization. Similar to small Cold War spy cameras, these phone cameras could be used to discreetly take pictures of documents, images, or physical security areas. Another downside to camera integration is the loss of personal privacy associated with not having an obvious camera. A traditional camera is big enough to notice, and therefore you are usually aware that your picture is being taken. Cellular cameras are smaller and more compact than most, allowing them access to private areas into which cameras would not have been allowed before.

Signal Interception and Interference

Much like a DoS on the Internet, the interception or interference of a cellular signal can create real problems. Factors such as ease of signal interception, the jamming of cellular frequencies, rerouting of traffic through hostile base stations, and attacks on the base stations themselves make this a very effective method of disrupting cellular communications.

Viruses

Cell phone viruses are relatively new, but as mobile phones become more sophisticated with added functionality, viruses and worms are inevitable.

Cabir.H and Cabir.I are two of the more well-known cell phone viruses that affect Symbian mobile phones. It was largely written as a proof-of-concept virus designed to show what could happen, and how quickly. Additionally, other viruses have been transmitted via SMS (short message service) targeting SIM cards and phones. Some other cell phone viruses are Skulls.A, Commwarrior.A, Locknut.B, and Fontal.A. Most anti-virus companies, including F-Secure, Trend Micro, and Symantec, offer anti-virus software for mobile phones.

Handset Theft

One of the biggest vulnerabilities associated with mobile phones is the theft of the actual device. Typically, a thief won't be interested in the information on your phone but in reselling the handset. Some mobile e-mail/calendar solution providers offer a way for an IT administrator to command the handset to purge sensitive company e-mails and information from a stolen device.

Exploiting Cellular Technology: Cell Phone Fraud

Viewing or Changing Phone Settings

Most cell phones have a test mode; this is where special functions can be accessed. These functions can be as simple as changing the setup for the telephone, modifying the Security Identifier (SID), the Mobile Identification Number (MIN), and listing the Electronic Serial Number (ESN). However, some phone functions allow one to use the cell phone as a scanner, scroll through the cellular frequencies, and eavesdrop on analog radio broadcasts.

Phone Network Sniffing/Scanning

The key to the cellular systems operation is that each phone is identified by the ESN and the MIN. Using these two numbers, the cell tower computer system cross-checks the pair with valid customers and will allow access or refuse access depending on the result of the verification. Because this all takes place in a wireless environment, anyone can simply listen in on the proper frequencies and record other people's ESN and MIN codes. The cellular network can easily be monitored to gather all kinds of information.

SIM Cloning

SIM cloning started out as phone cloning. SIM cloning has become a new form of identity theft, allowing someone's identity to be stolen through his or her phone. In typical GSM phones, the SIM card associated with these devices maintains all the data associated with network and user access within a system. Typically, minimal access of less than 5 min was required for a SIM to be removed and copied. The new SIM would then be used for, typically, a period of less than 30 days before it was discarded. In that time period all the services utilized by the thief would be billed to the victim. This type of cloning is not as popular as it used to be, but is still practiced today. It is possible to illegally obtain blank chips and an EPROM burner to program it.

Phone Tumbling

Phone tumbling is a term used to describe a weakness in the cellular telephone system. Tumbling is the use of a counterfeit chip that is installed into a phone, allowing a caller's first call to be completed before the billing status is verified.

However, depending on where you're roaming and how busy the cellular network across the country is, you can make a phone call before that procedure is completed. To exploit that weakness, underground engineers designed a counterfeit chip that generates a different, phony identification number on each call, tricking the cellular telephone exchange into thinking each call is the first. Unlike other cellular frauds, these phones aren't trying to copy valid ESN numbers; they simply generate a new random number for each call. Phone PIN numbers are also sent in the clear.

Subscription Fraud

Now that cellular carriers are finding new customers through the Internet and telemarketing, it is becoming more difficult to verify the identity of the purchaser of the phone service. In the 1990s, cell phone service was mostly purchased in person at a company-owned store, and clerks could verify identity. Today that is not the case. To help combat this, Title 18, Section 1028, of the U.S. Code, "Fraud and related activity in connection with identification documents and information," has now made it a federal crime to steal someone's identity information with intent to defraud.

How Does Cellular Fraud Occur?

Cellular fraud is defined as the unauthorized use, tampering, or manipulation of a cellular phone or service, and since 1993, has been a federal crime.

Detecting Fraud

There are certain signs that you, as a cellular subscriber, can watch for to detect fraudulent use of your mobile phone number even before the phone company does. AT&T Wireless has developed a list of common symptoms to watch for:

■ Frequent wrong-number phone calls to your phone, or hang-ups.
■ Difficulty in placing outgoing calls.
■ Difficulty in retrieving voice-mail messages.
■ Incoming calls constantly receiving busy signals or wrong numbers. Make a point of asking people who call you often if they are having any difficulty reaching you.
■ Unusual calls appearing in your phone bills.

What Is Being Done?

Task forces dedicated to combating fraud have been developed by many long-distance and local cellular carriers. In 1991, a Fraud Task Force (FTF) was formed by the Cellular Telecommunications Industry Association (CTIA). The FTF works to initiate and assist in investigations. It also conducts research and helps educate the public on cellular fraud and preventative technology.

What Can the User Do?

Unfortunately, the hard reality is the consumer is rather helpless against cellular fraud. Technically sophisticated thieves, referred to in the industry as *bandits*, have free access to anything being transmitted over the airwaves. However, all is not lost. Certain measures can be taken to make cellular fraud a bit more difficult and less likely to occur. This list, provided by Bell Atlantic NYNEX Mobile, outlines some steps you can take to protect yourself:

- Do not leave your *subscriber agreement* in your car or other easily accessible places.
- Have a fraud protection feature installed.
- If applicable, remove the handset and cellular antenna from the car to avoid drawing attention to it.
- Allow only authorized cellular service technicians to install, test, or repair the cellular phone.
- Eliminate international or long-distance dialing capabilities if you will not use them.
- Beware of purchasing clones, or *extension* phones, that promise free service; they are illegal.

New Security

To protect the privacy of cell phone (and PDA users), Lucent Technologies' Bell Labs has developed a set of software tools that constitute the Privacy-Conscious Personalization (PCP) framework. PCP is designed to give wireless users complete control over who can and can't track them.

The PCP framework promises to give mobile users the benefits of sharing location information without having to buy into a monolithic surveillance mechanism. This alone would go a long way in reducing one method by which identity thieves could gain information.

The PCP framework would enable consumer and business users to specify which individuals, groups, or businesses can see where they are, based on the users' preferences. For example, during working hours, field salespeople may opt to grant access to their bosses, no matter where they are, but come 5:30 p.m., location sharing with them can be disabled.

Cell Phone Hacking and Phreaking

Phreaking

Phreaking is a slang term for the action of manipulating a telephone system for access to functions not available to the general subscriber. Because phreaking constitutes theft of telephone service, it is an illegal activity. However, phreaking was formerly pursued by a large number of computer and electronics hobbyists out of curiosity.

Most phreaking techniques are no longer effective because of changes in the telephone system. Some were evolutionary, such as digital cellular, and others were designed specifically to disallow such access. Additionally, the cost of telephone calls has fallen to the point where few would find it worth the risk to engage in toll fraud. Also, there are numerous competing providers of telephone service.

Disassemblers

Disassemblers are programs that translate object code into native Assembler language. There are some disassemblers that reveal more than 90 secret commands for controlling mobile phones. Checking the part number on the CPU embedded in the phone will tell you which disassembler to use.

Hackers Tracking People

It is quite possible for a skilled hacker to set up a scanning system with a cell phone and a laptop that can draw a map of each cellular phone call currently being placed in a particular cell. When phones travel from one cell to the next — as they tend to do in a car — information is passed on in the form of hidden code that is tied to the phone transmission. A prepared hacker could, and would, know where each local cell is, and could display the approximate geographic locations of each phone that is currently active.

Vampire Phones

This method is another form of scanning that exploits a cellular phone's radio frequency leakage, the inevitable low-power radio emissions that a phone will generate. A phone that is set up as a scanner could take advantage of this frequency leakage and glean information such as the electronic serial number.

With this type of attack you'd have to be pretty close to the target phone to pick up the radio frequency. However, if successful, and an attacker is able to get the identity codes, a reprogrammed phone would become digitally indistinguishable from the original.

Who's Tracking You and Your Cell Phone?

Enhanced-911

In 1996, the FCC issued a report and order requiring all wireless carriers and cell phone manufacturers to provide the capability for automatically identifying to emergency dispatchers the location from which a wireless call is being made. The wireless Enhanced-911 (E911) was the result of that order.

The E911 program is divided into two phases, which are described in the following subsections.

Phase I

Requires cellular carriers, upon legitimate requests by a local public safety answering point (PSAP), to report the telephone number of a wireless 911 caller and the location of the antenna that received the call. Phase I also requires wireless carriers to deliver to the emergency dispatcher the telephone number of a wireless handset originating a 911 call, as well as the location of the cell site or base station receiving the 911 call, which provides a rough indication of the caller's location.

Phase II

Requires cellular carriers to provide precise location information, usually to within 50 to 100 m. Phase II requires carriers to deliver more specific latitude and longitude location information, known as Automatic Location Identification (ALI), to the dispatcher. The FCC established a 4-year rollout schedule for Phase II, beginning October 1, 2001, and to be completed by December 31, 2005.

"Find Friends"

Initially, location-tracking technologies were only meant to facilitate emergency services; however, cellular carriers are planning on squeezing some profit from these enforced upgrades. AT&T Wireless has already rolled out a premium service called "Find Friends," which lets you track friends and family — and lets them track you. Other carriers are considering services that allow companies to follow their employees, as well as allowing restaurants and retail stores to track potential customers.

PCP Framework

Similar in concept to Find Friends, the Privacy-Conscious Personalization (PCP) framework is designed to give wireless users complete control over who can and can't track them. PCP will give mobile users the benefits they want from sharing location information while maintaining some level of general privacy.

Cell Phone Security

In this next section I'll outline how to secure and defend against some specific vulnerabilities affecting cellular technology.

Combatting Sniffing and Cloning Phones

Fortunately, as time passed and advancements were made, newer digital technology has made it more difficult to sniff and scan for phone traffic. Additionally, Congress passed an amendment to Title 18, Section 1029, of the U.S. Code, making it a federal crime to own a scanning receiver or a cell phone programmer with intent to defraud. It also makes it a crime to knowingly, and with intent to defraud, use a counterfeit phone, to traffic in such phones, or to possess 15 or more of them.

These two factors in concert have helped deter this type of phone fraud.

PhonePrint

PhonePrint is a combination of hardware and software used by cellular operators in high-fraud areas. It is installed in base stations and characterizes all the handsets that ask it for service, and catalogs their radio frequency fingerprint. The database soon acquires entries for almost all the active users in the area. On future service requests, PhonePrint compares the stored signature with the live one. If they fail to match, the call is broken before it can be completed.

Cell Phone Jamming/Silencing

Cell phone jammers are electronic filters that fool cellular handsets into thinking there are no frequencies available to make or receive calls, or they actually broadcast bogus transmissions on cellular frequencies to cancel out real ones. The reason for these jammers is to prevent unwanted calls in public areas such as conference rooms, churches, and movie theaters.

Other security-related applications are to prevent a *bug* phone from being left in a room to eavesdrop on conversations, or for a traveling motorcade, to prevent phone use, which could assist an enemy in identifying the motorcade's location. In the United States, it is illegal to use these devices unless it is for government purposes. A few exceptions to this rule exist — churches, for example, employ these devices.

Precautions for Cellular Phones

Businesses concerned about the risks of insecure communication should consider using alternatives such as Terrestrial Trunked Radio (Tetra) or secondary voice encryption technologies like PGPPhone or SpeakFreely.

The following list is designed to help secure cellular voice systems:

- Never say anything over any wireless phone that you would not mind the whole world knowing.
- Never give a credit card or telephone credit card number over a cellular phone.
- Try to dial 800 numbers whenever possible when on the road, rather than making credit card calls. An astute hacker can capture your Touch-Tone digits when you make an automated credit card call, even if the number is not read to an operator.
- Monitor your cellular bill closely and report any unusual calling activity to your cellular provider immediately.
- Consider upgrading to digital cellular service. Although not foolproof, digital technologies require more sophisticated equipment to monitor and are thus more difficult to intercept by hackers.
- Ensure that phones don't use the autoanswer feature. This could allow a phone to be used as a bug to listen to private conversations when left in a room.

Other Threats and Vulnerabilities

Wireless Denial-of-Service Attacks

In May 2004, AusCERT announced the presence of a DoS vulnerability in IEEE 802.11 devices. The DoS attack takes advantage of a test mode of operation present in a range of 802.11b WLAN adapters to continuously transmit a DSSS signal on a target channel. This continuous transmission affects all stations, both clients and APs, within range of the attacker, resulting in the reporting of the media as *busy* for the duration of the attack. Simply put, no station within range of the attacker will be able to use the media for transmission, resulting in DoS.

Attack Significance

This attack is significant for a couple of reasons:

1. Requires off-the-shelf hardware and a low level of skill to carry out.
2. Requires only low power and no custom hardware.

Attack Mitigation

Presently there are no known strategies for mitigating the attack other than not to use 802.11b-based technology in environments where ongoing availability of communications is required.

GPS Jamming

Recently *Phrack Magazine* presented an article that provided a detailed guide on how to build a low-cost, portable GPS jammer from components that can be obtained from most electronic supply shops. These GPS jammers are designed to attack commercial signals, but have the potential to affect military signals as well. A GPS jammer targeted at civil GPS signals, known as the C/A code, could also threaten military systems, because most military GPS receivers must first acquire the C/A signal before locking onto the military signal, known as the P(Y) code.

GPS receivers are vulnerable to jamming. This is because GPS satellites are 12,000 mi up, and the signal diminishes as it travels through the intervening space and atmosphere to reach Earth. Because these signals are weak, a GPS receiver needs to be particularly sensitive and sensitivity implies vulnerability. For example, a relatively low-powered jammer transmitting static on the GPS frequency band can overpower legitimate GPS signals over a wide area, as much as a 75 mi circle using only 1 W of radiated power.

The current GPS constellation is old and in need of modernization. A new program is underway that will launch new satellites with greater signal power, thus making them harder to jam. The only trade-off is that the new modern satellites will have significantly reduced orbital lives.

Identity Theft

Identity theft has become a very serious issue in the United States in the last 10 years, because of which I've included this section. Although this topic may seem a bit out of place in a wireless forensics book, I think it will be valuable to cover the basics of identity theft, ways to protect yourself, and how wireless devices will affect identity theft in the future.

History and Overview of Identity Theft

America, simply put, is a trusting nation, and it is this fact, combined with the growth of the Internet, that has made identity theft such a serious problem. Virtually unknown a few years ago, identity theft is now something the majority of, if not all, Americans are aware of. It is estimated that 9 percent of Americans have been victimized, with annual losses totaling a staggering $53 billion!

In response to this problem, in 1998 the Senate Judiciary Committee approved a bill that proposed making identity theft a federal crime following an amendment that includes, in the definition of illegal acts, the fraudulent use of wireless and other telecommunications instruments to assume the identity of another person.

However, identity theft continues to be a growing problem.

Whatever form identity theft takes, it typically has two main characteristics:

1. It involves the unauthorized use of another person's identity for criminal purposes.
2. It is rarely an end in itself, but a means to make it easier to commit other crimes.

Identity thieves get false identities by either obtaining real documents or counterfeiting them. With the false identities they can change the addresses on existing accounts, and have new ATM cards, checks, and credit cards issued. They can also create new accounts, which is harder for the victim to detect.

"Virtual" Identity Theft

With the flood of new technologies that have, and continue to, hit the market, most users are only dimly aware of exactly how they work. It is this lack of knowledge that makes people much more vulnerable to hi-tech thieves.

This subsection is a quick overview on ways to protect yourself from identity thieves in the virtual world.

What Does the Virtual Thief Want?

Basically, a virtual thief wants the same things a real-world thief wants; your information. With this information, they can then create a new identity — your identity — and use it for his or her purposes and leave you with the bills and responsibility.

Where Does the Virtual Thief Find Information?

Here's where the differences between the real-world and virtual thief begin to show. Without proper safeguards, today's new technologies can create significant gaps in your personal information security. If you have a PC, think of the information that could be stored there, such as bank account information, tax return information, insurance information, spreadsheets and word processing documents, and so on. This line of thought can be extrapolated to modern PDAs and cell phones, which can hold similar information as a PC.

How You Can Defend Yourself?

Awareness is the first step. The next is education and implementation of the suggested security precautions. Remember, no one is going to protect your identity as well as you will. Naturally the best place to look for information on identity theft prevention is the Internet. The National Cyber Security Alliance (www.staysafeonline.info) is a good place to start.

Wireless Identity Theft

In the future, new cell phone handsets will be preloaded with encryption software and digital certificates that will make it much harder for others to impersonate the rightful owner. Unfortunately, this level of protection is not available yet and, currently, wireless companies are scrambling to plug these security gaps. Even with this new security, the bad news is that a determined hacker or criminal will always eventually succeed.

Today, corporate networks frequently carry and transmit:

■ Personal e-mail
■ Business plans
■ Company finances

In the wireless world, everything is up for grabs when the network is left unsecured.

Recently, the company Interhack conducted one such test for one of its clients. Personal data such as names, addresses, telephone numbers, dates of birth, and social security numbers were being broadcast in the clear. By sitting in a car several hundred yards away, Interhack's Red Team successfully intercepted this information and more. Imagine what an identity thief could do with such information!

The cost of wireless networking is very low. However, when considering using a wireless network, individuals and companies need to be sure to consider the cost of securing and maintaining those networks. A good comparison is the automobile, which is not just restricted to the purchase cost, but also the costs of fuel and insurance. A wireless network may be very cheap when you pick up all of the necessary pieces from your local computer store, but could turn out to be very expensive if your identity is stolen because your information was not properly secured.

Using Wireless Devices for Identity Theft

Criminals are using PDAs to load and transmit stolen credit card numbers. This is referred to as *skimming*. In many cases, an unsuspecting restaurant patron hands over his credit card to pay the bill. The waiter then swipes the number into a handheld device he has secreted in his pocket, capturing the number and selling it later.

New Technologies to Help Prevent Identity Theft

When it comes to identity theft, the consumer isn't, and shouldn't be, the first line of defense. Typically, identity theft doesn't start with an action taken by a consumer. In most cases, as I'll outline at the end of this section, the root of identity theft lies in the business community.

There is a new program available called Graph Theoretic Anomaly Detection (GTAD) that dynamically detects unusual patterns based on the identity data elements included on an application, such as name, address, phone, and social security number. The resulting graphic patterns are identified as high-probability frauds or likely legitimate applications. The fraudulent anomalies identified by GTAD are used by commercial companies and the Identity Theft Resource Center (ITRC) to create analytic scores that assess the risk of identity theft.

Identity Theft and Terrorism

As unsettling as it sounds, terrorism and identity theft go hand in hand. On page 393 of the 9/11 Commission Report, there are ten pages of discussion and suggestions for dealing with the connected problems of terrorism and identity theft. For terrorists, impersonation and viable travel documents are key tools for success.

Here are just a few of the disturbing facts associated with terrorism and identity theft:

- The al-Qaida training manual includes provisions for trainees to leave camp with five fake personas.
- Terrorists are regularly schooled in the art of subsisting off credit card fraud while living in the United States.

■ The fact that identity theft is so easy in the United States makes terrorist watch lists essentially useless.

Suddenly, fraud isn't the only problem with identity theft.

Breeder Documents

In the United States there are 240 valid forms of driver's licenses, and 10,000 different agencies can issue birth certificates. These documents are known as *breeder documents*, and are the cornerstones of identity theft.

Corporate America and Identity Theft

A couple of years ago I wrote a report for Congress on the threat of trusted insiders within government organizations and ways of reducing that threat. During the course of that project I got quite an education on what constitutes a threat from inside an organization, and the degrees of damage that can be caused. The most widely known type of insider is, of course, a spy. People such as Karl Hannsen and Aldrich Ames are notorious. Nevertheless, there are other types of insiders who can do almost as much damage, people who aren't necessarily malicious, but who through either carelessness or laziness can create huge vulnerabilities.

When discussing identity theft in the United States, a critical area of concern is corporate America, currently the main source of stolen identities. Roughly two-thirds of the time, identity theft begins with the theft of employee data. Those working to reduce identity theft in this country suggest that there must be federal legislation to force companies to guard personal data more carefully, decreasing the availability of identities that can be stolen by terrorists. Recently this has taken form as The Personal Data Privacy and Security Act. If passed, it will subject data brokers to much tighter regulations, rewrite computer crime laws to create new penalties for database intrusions, and so on. It is a necessary step to help bring identity theft under control.

Bibliography

Aftab, P., *The Parent's Guide to Protecting Your Children in Cyberspace*, McGraw-Hill, New York, December 1999.

Berry, J., Defence in Depth: Preventing Going Hairless Over Wireless, SANS Institute, April 2002.

Brewin, B., War Flying: Wireless LAN Sniffing Goes Airborne, *ComputerWorld*, August 2002.

Buck, K., Wireless Networking: Compromising Security for Convenience?, SANS Institute, September 2001.

CBS 11 Investigates Wireless Identity Theft, CBS Broadcasting, February 25, 2004.

Costa, D., What's War-Chalking?, *PC Magazine*, October 2002.

Couch, J., Wireless Is Not the Problem, SANS Institute 2002.

Dailey, L., Identity theft is on the rise, FBI agent warns, tbnweekly.com, April 2004.

Duntemann J., Jeff Duntemann's W.F. Guide, April 2003.

Ellison, C., This Time, Cell Phone Virus is for Real, eweek.com, June 2004.

Etter, A., A Guide to Wardriving and Detecting Wardrivers, SANS Institute, 2002.

Farshchi, J., Wireless Intrusion Detection Systems, SANS Institute, November 2003.

Federal Communications Commission, Enhanced 911 — Wireless Services, June 2005.

Fidler, B., Mobile Medicine, SANS Institute, 2001.

Flickenger, R., The FBI takes an interest in War Chalking and War Driving, O'Reilly Network, August 2002.

Fred, Wardriving HowTo (Un-official), April 2002.

Hodges, K., Is Your Wireless Network Secure?, SANS Institute, September 2001.

Hoe, K., Security Guidelines for Wireless LAN Implementation, SANS Institute, August 2003.

Jeffs, T., Wireless Application Protocol 2.0 Security, SANS Institute, November 2001.

Keeney, F., Vacation War Driving, Pasadena Networks, LLC, December 2006

Kurtz, N., Securing A Mobile Telecommunications Network From Internal Fraud, SANS Institute, 2002.

Mark, R., Internet Identity Theft Bill Introduced, Internet.com, January 2003.

Markoff, J., Hacking Chips on Cellular Phones, *Wired Magazine*, March 1993.

Mathieson, R., mTerrorism: real and present danger on the wireless web hijackings, *Cooltown Magazine*, December 2002.

McCullagh, D., Senators Propose Sweeping Data-Security Bill, *CNET News*, June 2005.

Metz, C., Who's Tracking You and Your Cell Phone?, *PC Magazine*, January 2004.

Miller, S., War Driving, *Information Security Magazine*, November 2001.

Montcalm, E., Identifying the Risk Involved in Allowing Wireless, Portable Devices into your Company, SANS Institute, 2003.

Owen, D., Wireless Networking Security: As Part of your Perimeter Defense Strategy, SANS Institute, January 2002.

Paro, D., Wireless Application Protocol: What Is It All About ... How Does It Work, SANS Institute, 2001.

Peterson, K., Identity Fraud Study by ID Analytics: Mobile Carriers an Entry to Crime Spree, 10meters.com, May 2003.

Poulsen K., War Driving by the Bay, SANS Institute, 2001.

Reed, T., Learn War Driving, Airshare.org, November 2003.

Reed T., War Chalking, Airshare.org, November 2003.

Reed T., War Driving, Airshare.org, November 2003.

Reed T., War Flying, Airshare.org, November 2003.

Renderman, Stumbler Code of Ethics, www.worldwidewardrive.org, November 2005.

Roshaimi, W. and Abdullah W., Wireless LAN Security — Defense In Depth, SANS Institute, 2003.

Rubenking, J., Identity Theft: What, Me Worry?, *PC Magazine*, March 2, 2004

Shim, R., As Security Concerns Ease, Businesses Warm to Wi-Fi, *CNET News*, November 2003.

Strom, D., "Phishing" Identity Theft Is Gaining Popularity, InternetWeek.com, November 2003.

Taylor, C., Tales From The Hood: I've Been Warchalked!, *Time Magazine*, November 2003.

Tyrrell, K., An Overview of Wireless Security Issues, SANS Institute, 2003.

Warchalking, www.warchalking.org, April 2004.

Ward, M., Hacking with a Pringles Tube, *BBC News*, March 2002.

Wireless Added to Identity-Theft Bill, *Mobile Phone News*, July 20, 1998.

Wireless: PhonePrint to Protect Cellular Users in GTE Wireless, Gulf Coast Cambridge Telecom Report, June 30, 1997.

Wrobel, L., *Protecting Against Dial-In Hazards: Voice Systems*, CRC Press, Boca Raton, FL, 2002.

Chapter 3

Wireless Crime Fighting

Wireless Crime Prevention Techniques

Introduction

In this new century we are entering a new age of policing. An age in which wireless technology will play a key role. Traditionally, police work has involved interviewing the public, searching the houses of suspects, and putting them under surveillance to discover whom the suspect was in touch with, where they traveled, etc. Today, in many cases, these techniques would reveal very little.

In the future it will be far more useful to look at surveillance videos, review the suspect's e-mail and computer hard drive, and most importantly, gain access to cellular records as they will show where the suspect was and whom they were in contact with.

E911

As we discussed in Chapter 2, E911, short for Enhanced 911, is a location technology promoted by the FCC that will enable mobile, or cellular, phones to process 911 emergency calls and enable emergency services to locate the geographic position of the caller.

When a person makes a 911 call using a land line, the call is routed to the nearest public safety answering point (PSAP), which sends the emergency call to the proper service, such as the police, the fire department, etc. The PSAP receives the caller's phone number and the exact location of the phone call. This is how things would work if you were calling from a landline.

But what about mobile phones?

Before 1996, all 911 calls made using a mobile phone would have to access their carriers first. The carrier would then have to verify subscription of service. Once verified, the call would be routed to a PSAP. The FCC refined this process, and ruled that all 911 calls must go directly to the PSAP without receiving subscription verification from the cellular carrier.

Intrado of Longmont, Colorado, is a company that provides 911 solutions for wireless cellular carriers. Intrado has so far deployed Phase 1 of the E911 directive, which identifies the cell site from which a cellular call originates. More than 190 million 911 calls are placed annually, and almost 50 million of those are made from wireless phones.

Police Use of Wireless Devices

The police and law enforcement forces have used the radio for decades. The maxim "You can't outrun a radio" when referring to a car chase with the police is just one small example. Today, police and law enforcement officials are using some newer programs that surpass the traditional radio.

PacketCluster

PacketCluster Patrol software allows patrol cars direct access to crime-fighting information from a car-based laptop. This technology is in practical use in Salinas and Monterey County in California. Using a wireless network, more than 400 patrol officers can access records from county, state, and federal databases.

TotalRoam

TotalRoam is another in-vehicle platform that is designed to manage data routing for wireless network communications. TotalRoam allows highway patrol officers to use the wireless system to instantly and directly access critical information from databases covering vehicle registration, outstanding warrants, and much more.

TotalRoam will also enable the wireless transmission of information gathered by other onboard equipment, such as breathalyzers and GPS. Another significant quality of TotalRoam is its redundancy. Its multiple networking design guarantees continual communication, ensuring that during emergency situations officers will always have backup.

Hi-Tech Patrol Cars

In the Sacramento Police Department, all 190 police cars are being fitted with wireless IP networking equipment and onboard computers, allowing each officer to access any database the department would normally have access to. SACPD cars will also be fitted with equipment to allow them to view live video feed from police helicopters. This will help officers make much better decisions during a chase, as well as aid superior officers in making more informed decisions in, for example, hostage situations.

SACPD is also working toward moving to a paperless, or paper-reduced, system by giving officers wireless PDAs to streamline the paper-work process. Additionally, these systems will eventually be integrated with the electronic tagging systems used by the judicial and prison services.

Personal Security and RFID

How Does RFID Work?

The radio frequency identification (RFID) technology process starts with a tag, which is made up of a microchip with an antenna and a reader with an antenna. The reader sends out radio frequency waves that form a magnetic field when they join with the antenna on the RFID tag. Passive RFID tags generate power from this magnetic field and use it to energize the circuits of the RFID chip. The chip in the RIFD tag sends information back to the reader in the form of radio frequency waves. The RFID reader converts the new waves back into digital information. Semipassive RFID tags use a battery to run the circuits of the chip, but communicate by drawing power from the RFID reader.

Personal Security

Applied Digital Solutions, Palm Beach, Florida, provides an RFID tag called VeriChip. Currently they charge a $9 monthly subscription fee for anyone who wants to be *tagged*. Typically, the people who use this service are those who are afraid their loved ones will get lost or kidnapped.

Virtual Prisons

An English philosopher by the name of Jeremy Bentham devised what he called a *panopticon*, a circular prison with glass walls in which all inmates could be constantly watched from a single location in the middle

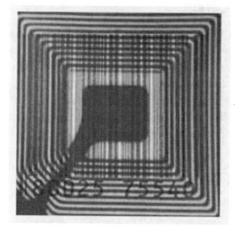

Figure 3.1   RFID chip.

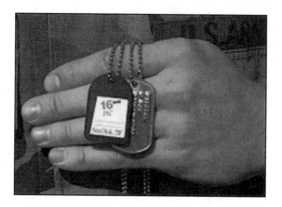

Figure 3.2   RFID tag.

of the chamber. While Bentham's idea was never realized, the wireless world seems to have created a close equivalent. In the United Kingdom a former cabinet minister, Jonathan Aitken, was released after serving 7 months of an 18-month sentence for perjury and conspiracy. His release was made possible by a tag he wears that ensures he stays at home from 7 p.m. to 7 a.m. In 1999, as many as 14,464 prisoners were released in the United Kingdom with these new tags and a detention curfew. This new method had a 95% success rate.

In the United States, the criminal justice system also uses RFID tags to keep track of convicts, parolees, and to place nonviolent offenders under

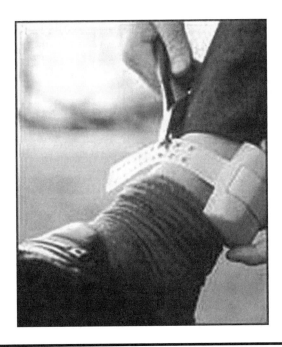

Figure 3.3   Tagging device.

house arrest. This type of technology was recently used to enforce Martha Stewart's house arrest.

Tagging Stalkers and Sex Offenders

Taking this idea a step further, stalkers and sex offenders could be tagged to monitor their movements. Under this plan, the authorities would be automatically alerted when violent or obsessive persons enter an area from which they have been banned.

Wireless Honeypots

To quote Lance Spitzner, the leader of the Honeynet Project, the definition of a honeypot is:

> A honeypot is an information system resource whose value lies in unauthorized or illicit use of that resource.

A wireless honeypot, used properly, could reveal pertinent and accurate statistics about attacks on your infrastructure, including:

■ The frequency of attacks
■ The attacker's skill level
■ Goals and methods

Wireless honeypots, similar to their wired counterparts, can help protect your networks by diverting the attacker's time and resources on fake targets. In the black hat community, hackers enjoy penetrating wireless networks for the following reasons:

■ They are somewhat safe, because the attacker isn't directly connected to the network.
■ They are easy to hack, because there are a huge number of open or unsecured access points (APs) around.
■ They are fun to attack, because the wireless network is still considered relatively new.
■ They allow for a great deal of anonymity.

There are a couple of wireless honeypots openly available. These are considered in the following subsections.

Honeyd

This honeypot can be configured to simulate a large network in a wireless environment. With such an architecture, an intruder will be led to believe that he has stumbled onto a big network and could lose hours of time before realization dawns.

Another interesting feature of Honeyd is the ability to simulate an AP. By creating fake TCP/IP stacks to fool remote fingerprinting tools, you can easily create your own fake services. For example, by copying well-chosen Web pages used to manage an AP, you could simulate an AP. This technique could then be used to monitor attackers who would try to connect to the management interface using well-known default passwords, or who would try other opened services, such as attacks over SNMP, DNS, DHCP, TFTP, etc.

FakeAP

FakeAP can send specific wireless network traffic to fool basic attackers. This tool is specifically for dealing with war drivers and is designed to create multiple targets for your wireless network to hide among. The theory is that targeting one network is an easy task, whereas dealing with a cloud of targets could be more difficult.

As a war-driving countermeasure, FakeAP generates 802.11b beacon frames as fast as possible, by playing with fields like MAC, ESSID, channel assignments, and so on. To quote from the Web site of the authors: "If one access point is good, 53,000 must be better." FakeAP was a good idea when it was first released, but now most updated tools can advise the attacker that the detected APs are unusual; for example, no traffic may be generated on the discovered networks.

How and Where It's Used

If you are going to deploy a wireless honeypot, remember that it will have to perfectly simulate reality. Wireless honeypots are affected by the same problems as wired ones, as well as other problems specific to the wireless environment. Also, a skilled attacker may be afraid of a network that appears too open.

So when deploying a wireless honeypot:

- The better you simulate reality, the better the chances that you'll catch skilled attackers — but expect fewer intrusions.
- The less you deal with stealth, the more you'll see successful attacks — but expect script kiddies rather than skilled attackers.

Bibliography

Barnes, P., Database of "Potential" Criminals Stirs Controversy, TechTV, September 2002.

BBC News, Stalkers Could Be Tagged, Says Blair, January 16, 2000.

Blair, K., Wireless Crime-Fighting will Put Cameras throughout Gulf Breeze, PersonalNewsJournal.com, October 2003.

California Communities Tap Wireless Crime-Fighting Data, FCW.com, June 1999.

Caterinicchia, D., Wireless Crime-Fighting, CNN, August 1999.

Cell Phones In The New Security Paradigm, *mPulse Magazine*, December 2003.

Ed, Cops Fight Crime with Wireless Palm Handhelds, PalmInfocenter.com, November 2001.

HP news release, Massachusetts State Police Teams with HP to Roll Out High-Tech Patrol Cars, Hewlett-Packard Corporation, June 2003.

McKay, N., Wireless Crime Fighting, The Feature, February 2003.

Padcom, California Highway Patrol Selects Maximum Flexibility, Instant Access to Crime-Fighting Info with Padcom's® TotalRoam™ Mobile Data Solution, October 2000.

Prendergast, J., Citizens on Cyber Patrol, The Cincinnati Enquirer, June 2003.
Staff, V-One Extends Software for Crime Fighting Network, dc.internet.com, October 2002.
The Honeynet Project, www.honeynet.org, 2005.

Chapter 4

Digital Forensic Principles and Wireless Forensics

CyberCrime and Forensic Principles

What Is Cybercrime?

Cybercrime is broadly defined as criminal activity committed on computers or the Internet. The term also includes crimes that are committed offline, but facilitated by a computer. Cybercrime is also referred to as Internet crime, E-crime, hi-tech crime, and computer crime.

Types of Cybercrime

Although cybercrime is as old as computers, the ability to carry out serious crimes was enhanced by computer networks, the Internet, and now wireless computing. Here are some of the most common crimes committed using computers and computer networks:

1. Cracking
2. Harassment or cyberstalking
3. Corporate or economic espionage
4. Fraud

5. Child pornography
6. Identity theft
7. Copyright piracy
8. Extortion

These crimes are described in the following subsections.

Cracking

Cracking, which is the term used for the darker side of hacking, in simple terms means an illegal intrusion into a computer system or network. Crackers do what they do for a variety of reasons; typically, a hacker's motives fall into one or more of these categories:

- Greed
- Power
- Publicity
- Revenge
- Adventure
- Desire to access restricted information
- Destructive mindset
- As a marketing tool to sell security services

Harassment or Cyberstalking

Cyberstalking is defined as repeated acts of harassment or threatening behavior of the cybercriminal toward the victim through the use of Internet services. Cyberstalking is an existing crime committed using new technology. Cyberstalking may only be a prelude to something worse, such as violence or physical harm to the victim. Thus, cyberstalking should be viewed and treated seriously.

The Nature and Extent of Cyberstalking

Although online harassment and threats can take many forms, cyberstalking shares important characteristics with offline stalking. Many stalkers, online or offline, wish to exert control over their victims and engage in similar types of behavior to accomplish this end. In many cases, the cyberstalker and the victim will have had a prior relationship, and cyberstalking begins when the victim attempts to end the relationship. However, there also have been many instances of cyberstalking by strangers.

Also, the fact that cyberstalking is not physical in nature may create the misperception that it is less of a threat than physical stalking. This is not necessarily true. As the Internet becomes an increasingly integral part of our personal and professional lives, stalkers can take advantage of this ease of communication, as well as improved ability to access personal information.

Corporate/Economic Espionage

Economic or corporate espionage is encountered daily by law enforcement agencies. Usually, corporations acquire information about their competitors by legal means, typically, by surfing their Web sites and viewing online brochures and patent filings to gather intelligence. However, to maintain a competitive edge, companies will sometimes dig deeper, employing hackers to do some technological surveillance or buying trade secrets from insiders. Some companies will even go as far as to hack into government sites to find out the terms of a tender for a government contract to underbid the competition. With the end of the Cold War and the rise of Information Warfare, attacks from a number of foreign countries are becoming commonplace, meaning you could be going up against a well-funded adversary.

Child Pornography

Child pornography remains the most high-profile type of cybercrime. The Internet usually played a crucial role in child pornography. Pedophiles often contact children by posing as their peers in chat rooms. Additionally, peer-to-peer software programs make it easy for pedophiles to share pornographic images. And while difficult to detect, steganography is also something else to watch for, as it is also being used by this group to communicate and exchange images covertly.

Fraud and Spam

Here's a startling statistic: 40 percent of all e-mail sent throughout the world is spam. That's over 12 billion messages! Although most spam usually promotes a legitimate product, nearly 10 percent of them are scams. Some of these messages are designed to appear legitimate, looking as though they have come from a reputable company. Others are blatantly direct. One of the best-known Internet scams is where a stranger in Nigeria offers millions in exchange for a few thousand dollars to unfreeze assets.

Credit Card Fraud

Some hackers break into computers for the sole purpose of locating credit card numbers; once obtained they use them to purchase items over the

Internet or the numbers are sold to illicit organizations. Every year, credit card companies lose an average of $4 billion to this type of fraud. Additionally, calling card numbers are also a sought-after target by hackers.

Identity Theft

Identity theft has been, and continues to be, a rapidly growing problem in the United States. With your social security or driver's license number, criminals can access your credit line or potentially frame you for some other crime they're involved in. Identity theft is also a useful tool for people involved in terrorism, but I'll discuss that in greater detail in Chapter 5.

Copyright Piracy

The easiest and most well-known example of this is Napster, the file-sharing program that allowed people to exchange MP3's on an unprecedented scale. Since Napster other types of programs have appeared that allow for the sharing of virtually any type of pirated file, full-length movies being one of the most common since the explosive growth of broadband services.

There's also a black market on the Internet for passwords. Many shareware programs require passwords and some shameless people sell them to people who don't want to pay the nominal fees.

Extortion

Most criminal hackers today are carrying out their acts with a clear purpose: they're doing it for the money. Denial-of-service (DoS) attacks can be used to demand money from organizations in return for restoring normality to their online operation. In Russia, cybercriminals have sent ransom notes to companies demanding money to unlock files they have locked with a virus on a victim's computer. One step beyond this is the demanding of money for not wreaking havoc on a particular machine or network.

Investigating Cybercrime

Principles of Computer-Based Electronic Evidence

> *Principle 1:* No action taken should change data held on a computer or storage media that may subsequently be relied upon in court. Simply put, ensure that you have a forensically sound copy of your evidence to perform analysis on.

Principle 2: In extraordinary circumstances in which it is necessary to access original data held on a computer or on storage media, the forensic investigator must be competent to do so and be able to give evidence explaining the relevance and the implications of his or her actions.

Principle 3: An audit trail or other record of all processes applied to computer-based electronic evidence should be created and preserved. An independent third party should be able to examine those processes and arrive at the same conclusions.

Principle 4: The person in charge of the investigation, usually the case officer, is responsible for ensuring that the law and these principles are adhered to.

Roles and Responsibilities

Independent of the type of incident investigated, there will always be similar roles and responsibilities common to each case. When planning for incidents, the roles and responsibilities of people conducting an investigation should be outlined. There is a generic set of roles and responsibilities that can be identified; keep in mind that sometimes one person may perform more than one duty.

First Responders

First responders are trained personnel who, as the name suggests, arrive first on the scene and provide an assessment and appropriate response. First responders secure the scene, bring in the necessary support, and assist with collecting evidence.

Investigators

Investigators handle the nuts and bolts of the digital evidence by managing the preservation, acquisition, examination, analysis, and reporting. There may be more than one investigator. The lead investigator ensures that all the activities at the scene are done correctly and in the right sequence. The lead investigator's responsibilities also include developing evidence and writing the case report.

Technicians

Technicians handle additional details under the direction of the lead investigator. Technicians are trained to seize electronic equipment properly and acquire digital images. Typically, there is more than one technician on scene because different skills and knowledge are often needed.

Evidence Custodians

Evidence custodians protect all the evidence that is gathered and store it in a secure, central location. Evidence custodians are responsible for ensuring all evidence is properly tagged, checked in and out of custody, as well as for maintaining a strict chain of custody.

Forensic Examiners

Forensic examiners reproduce images and recover digital data from seized equipment. Examiners find data that is hidden, deleted, or damaged and recover it to be used as evidence. Forensic examiners move beyond the abilities of forensic technicians by using highly specialized software and other equipment to recover digital data.

Forensic Analysts

Forensic analysts evaluate the final products of the forensic examiner for significance to the case. In short, they turn data into relevant information.

Network Forensics in a Wireless Environment

Points of Evidence: Where Forensic Fingerprints Can Be Gathered

The following zones, or areas, were originally described in Casey's *The Handbook of Computer Crime Investigation* and because of the concise and accurate description, I've included a summarized version here:

> **Zone 1:** Includes almost anything that can be connected to a wireless device that would allow for the movement of data. It could be a laptop, a network storage device, Ethernet card, 802.11, Bluetooth, and IR.
>
> **Zone 2:** Includes the mobile device itself, as well as any removable or interchangeable pieces that can store data. Cell phones have two areas of evidence with the device and some have subscriber identity module (SIM) cards. Personal digital assistants (PDAs) have the data on the device and can have a variety of expandable memory cards.

Zone 3: Includes the wireless network. The mobile switching center, or MSC, which is the central nervous system of a mobile network, can contain important evidentiary information. Other devices connected to it can be rich sources of information as well:

- VLR: Visitor Location Register contains subscriber information on all users in a particular network.
- HLR: Home Location Register contains user information such as billing address and phone number.
- SM-SC: The Short Message Service Center processes SMS messages.
- OMC: Operational and Maintenance Center can provide a view of network activity, including finding a particular mobile call in progress (called a mobile trace).

Zone 4: The surrounding networks, or the subsequent networks (if any) that the caller accesses. Forensic evidence can be collected by accessing other networks that have roaming agreements with the target's primary carrier. This also works in other countries, and although it may not yield hard forensic data, it can be used to determine whether the subject was in the area.

I included this section to illustrate what is possible by way of evidence. However, beyond this quick overview I won't be going into the specific details of acquiring forensic data from these sources. That alone would take another book. This book, and the remainder of this chapter, is designed to show you how to do wireless forensics on Zone-2 devices in a localized lab.

802.11 Forensics

Introduction

Although the main focus of this book is on wireless devices such as cell phones and PDAs, I did want to touch on the 802.11 wireless environments (WLANs). Before beginning forensics in a WLAN environment, I always keep a particular point in mind: A secure wireless network does not necessarily mean a forensically viable one. Conducting forensics in a WLAN environment isn't as volatile a process as wireless device forensics, so I will not go into it as extensively. In an 802.11 environment, the data and evidence appear and behave in much the same way as a traditional wired network, which is a huge advantage considering how volatile cell phone and PDA technologies can be in comparison. Even with these advantages there are special points of evidence and detection methodologies for discovering them.

Looking into a WLAN for Forensic Evidence

To discover evidence on a wireless network, the first step is to discover what equipment comprises the wireless network, and whether that equipment is authorized or not. There are a myriad of wireless devices today that can comprise a wireless network. No longer are devices limited to be part of the network for connectivity purposes alone; now they are storage, video, and connection. Naturally, as an investigator you look for traditional access points (APs), network adapters and repeaters, but this is the wireless setup of the past. The new wireless investigator now has a much larger task, searching for wireless hard drives, cameras, as well as cell phones and PDAs. Each component plays a different role in your examination process and can give you a good idea of the breadth of the WLAN you are dealing with.

In discovering and documenting all the components of a wireless network, it is important to be looking for rogue APs as well, keeping in mind that they may be carefully disguised to look like something else. Also, it is useful to understand the radiation patterns of the different types of antennas, both directional and omnidirectional, as this will aid you in homing in on a specific target, which could be valuable in an investigation.

Where to Find the Hardware?

Wireless hardware could be housed just about anywhere. It just needs to have a power source and, if meant to be concealed, it needs to fit in the space provided. And that's about the end of it. Walls, ceilings, shelves, storage closets, and so on, are all good places to conceal wireless devices. When looking for wireless hardware, it is important to look for associated documentation, install disks, and so on, prior to removing the items. This will give you a better idea of what you are dealing with and what it could potentially be connecting to.

Identifying Digital Artifacts

As you progress in looking for wireless devices and equipment, there are artifacts that are also left behind on host systems both as applications and within the operating system that are associated with the WLAN. In the case of applications, look for wireless setup programs and drivers as well as specific utilities for wireless capture and monitoring, as well as known hacker tools. Within the operation system, aside from the aforementioned device drivers, you should also be looking for links or shortcuts to network shares, and also examine the registry for indications of wireless devices or connections.

Once you find these types of items, you know that your examination has just hit the next level and you need to be aware that you are dealing with a live wireless network that no longer has the traditional boundaries of a LAN. It is important to remember that each device in the WLAN will contain a different point of evidence and should be treated separately for acquisition of the data; then compare the data cumulatively in the analysis stage.

Capturing Wireless Traffic

Kismet, Netstumbler, Airsnort, and a host of other tools mentioned in Chapter 2 are useful in capturing wireless traffic. Once the traffic is collected and verified, analysis can be done with traditional network forensics tools.

PDA Forensics

Performing forensics on a PDA is an emerging discipline that follows some different rules from those normally associated with traditional computer forensics. In this section we'll discuss the basics of PDAs, what tools are available to capture and view an image, and best practice procedures to ensure that evidence is not corrupted during the investigation process.

The Term "PDA" in Forensics

PDA is a term for any small, mobile, handheld device that provides computing and information storage and retrieval capabilities for personal or business use, often for keeping calendars and address book information handy. In forensics a PDA is any small, mobile, handheld device that has active memory as the main method of storage for data. PDAs typically connect through a proprietary interface, which serves as a primary function contact and task management.

Standard Features of a PDA

- Microprocessor
- Operating system

- Memory
- Batteries
- LCD display
- Input options (keyboard, touch screen)
- Input/output ports
- Desktop software

Physical Device Structure

Figure 4.1 gives the schematic of a typical PDA.

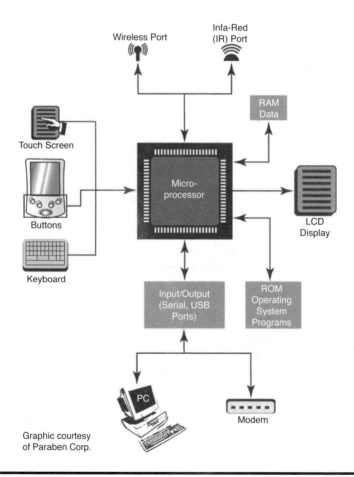

Figure 4.1   PDA Structure.

PDA Operating Systems

- Palm OS
- Pocket PC/Windows CE/Mobile (Microsoft)
- RIM BlackBerry
- Embedded Linux
- Symbian/EPOC

PDA Memory and Storage

In PDAs 1 MB of memory can store over 4000 addresses and over 100 e-mail messages, a potential gold mine of evidence. However, one of the unique issues associated with PDA devices is the use of active memory for data storage.

Read-Only Memory (ROM)

Typically, "read only" is associated with intact memory and data that is unchangeable, with or without power. However, with PDAs this is not always the case. With most PDA devices, there are segments of ROM that the user can write to. The average consumer will not have the skill to write to these areas, but a power user could potentially store data in this area.

The evidentiary significance is that the suspect can store data completely in an area hidden from the naked eye. This area is typically unaffected even by a power failure, on account of a residual backup battery designed to retain just this area of storage.

Random-Access Memory (RAM)

RAM is used as the main storage for all files and applications. It's in this area that the majority of evidence files are stored. The data structure of the Palm device is done in associated databases. Some types of data that are located in this area are: Preferences, New Applications, and User Data.

PDA Power Sources

PDAs typically use Lithium, AA, or AAA batteries.

Some features and applications on a PDA that create a significant drain on the batteries are:

- Pocket PC operating system
- More memory
- Color LCD display
- Voice recording
- MP3 player

Determining the power requirements of a Palm device is a big issue because the power lifespan and the lifespan of the evidentiary data associated with the device depend on it.

Summary of Available Software and Tools

Palm pdd

Palm dd (pdd), developed by Joe Grand, is a Windows-based command line tool that performs a physical acquisition of information from Palm OS devices. pdd was designed to work with the majority of Palm-OS-based PDA devices. Development on pdd is no longer progressing now that the technology has merged. As of January 2003, pdd is no longer supported as it has been incorporated into Paraben's PDA Seizure.

Paraben's PDA Seizure

Paraben's PDA Seizure is currently the widest used PDA forensic tool available. It covers a variety of operating systems to include Palm OS, Windows CE/Pocket PC, RIM BlackBerry, and will be releasing support for Symbian devices this year. PDA Seizure is a Windows-based tool that allows for the acquisition and analysis of PDA devices. The graphical user interface that is used with PDA Seizure makes the acquisition of the variety of the devices very easy for an investigator who is new to the field of wireless and handheld forensics.

Pilot-Link

First, let me say that Pilot-link was not intended to be used for forensics. Pilot-link is an open source software suite originally developed for Linux to allow information to be transferred between Linux and Palm devices. It runs on a number of desktop operating systems besides Linux, including Windows and Mac OS. About 30 command line programs comprise the software suite, and Pilot-link uses the HotSync protocol. The two programs of interest to forensic investigators are pi-getram and pi-getrom, which retrieve the contents of RAM and ROM from a device, similar to the physical acquisition done by pdd and PDA Seizure.

Guidance Software's EnCase

Mostly used for examining PCs, EnCase does support Palm OS devices. EnCase allows for the creation of a complete physical bit-stream image of a Palm device. The resulting bit-stream image can be mounted as a read-only file or "virtual drive," from which EnCase proceeds to reconstruct the file structure utilizing the logical data in the bit-stream image.

POSE — Palm Operating System Emulator

POSE is a software program that runs on a desktop computer under a variety of operating systems, and behaves exactly as a Palm OS hardware device, once an appropriate ROM is loaded into it. The emulator program was originally designed for use with development of Palm applications. However, it has some excellent forensic applications because of its ability to act as a file viewer for the data associated with the examination. Built-in PIM applications (e.g., Datebook, Address Book, To Do, etc.) run properly and the hardware buttons and display react accurately. One of the unique aspects of the forensic tools is their ability to generate a ROM image that is compatible with POSE.

POSE is an excellent tool for examiners to use in their validation process of the data that is processed as it is produced directly from the manufacturer. The other advantage of this type of technology is that it allows for the snapshot that is generated through a forensic acquisition to be recreated so that both parties can view precisely the same instance of that snapshot.

Conducting PDA Forensics

Looking back at our discussion on the different aspects of forensics, it is clear that determining basic rules or regulations that can be followed when dealing with this type of evidence is crucial. The first rules or procedures that are discussed are designed for most typical PDA devices, including devices running the Palm OS and Windows CE/Pocket PC operating system.

These rules apply to PDA devices that are considered *active* memory devices. There is a change occurring with new devices, however, which are no longer designed around using active memory for storage. Fortunately, this simplifies the forensic process because the information they hold is not as volatile. However, it is still advised to follow these simple rules because there is no physical characteristic to help determine whether the PDA is an active memory device or not.

Forensic Rules for PDAs

The following forensic rules for PDAs are discussed in the following subsections:

1. Unit must have power.
2. Unit must have cables.
3. Data is always changing.
4. Understand the fundamentals.

Unit Must Have Power

A loss of power will result in a loss of data. The volatile nature of the PDA device makes working with it in a forensic environment difficult because of issues such as power. The device must be able to maintain a charge to its main battery supply. Battery times vary on the devices from 2 h to 2 months. When the device is seized on scene, it is recommended that the device receive fresh batteries, or be supplied with a remote power source on scene, to ensure continued data integrity. Therefore, after seizure always be sure to set the device in the appropriate power-charging device, and continue to monitor to ensure it has power.

Unit Must Have Cables

Cradle units are crucial to the seizure of a PDA because the device communicates with a PC through them. If a cradle is not seized, then one will need to be purchased through the many PDA vendors. As mentioned previously, some of the forensic tool providers also provide appropriate cable options.

Data Is Always Changing

With active memory as the main storage, nothing remains the same. Hash values have a high probability of changing. Based on this fact, the data that is acquired is where the main validation occurs with the use of traditional forensic hash values on the process post acquisition. Snapshot forensics requires that instead of looking at the original device for validation, we need to look to the data after acquisition and ensure no changes occur in the valuation process. Examiners need to be aware of this change with snapshot forensics so that they make proper and valid statements and testify to the nature of the changing data.

Understand the Fundamentals

To quote Amber Schroader, CEO of Paraben Corporation, "PDA forensics is a lifestyle choice." This is simply and accurately put. With each new device comes a change to the techniques and procedures that need to be followed. Therefore, to understand the fundamentals, you must be trained and stay current.

Palm OS Modes of Operation

Doze
- Runs on only a small amount of power to ROM and RAM
- Can activate in less than a minute after last input by a user
- Encryption methods can be activated in Doze mode

Sleep
- Runs on a medium amount of power to ROM and RAM
- Can activate in 1 to 3 minutes after last input by a user

Running: The processor is actively functioning. There is some forensic significance to the different modes of operation. *Doze*, *Sleep*, and *Running* all revolve around the user's last contact with the device and thus allow you to estimate the time of last contact based on the current mode of operation.

Palm OS Reset Options

Soft reset
- Refreshes the operating system
- Clears dynamic RAM, leaves storage RAM intact

Hard reset
- Reverts to the factory settings
- Data in ROM remains intact
- Data in RAM lost!

The different reset options can affect the data integrity of the device, and the device should be removed from suspect's control as soon as possible to avoid reset issues.

Structure of the Palm OS

Cards

Theoretically, a Palm OS can support 256 cards, although most devices only support one. Cards share the same physical address space, and the Palm OS automatically maps to the largest available size. Cards are the equivalent of hard drives in a typical computer. Each drive can support the storage of data, and the default card for the device is typically mapped to be card 0. Data for both ROM and RAM can exist on the same card.

ROM

The ROM contains:

- Manufacturer, name, signature, and OS version
- The operating system (Palm OS)
- Default databases
- Default applications

Palm OS devices contain specific information about the user of the device that is typically stored in the ROM header of the device. This header information can contain baseline information on the device, user, and allocation of memory. A screen capture from Paraben's PDA Seizure of a fictitious user is shown in Figure 4.2.

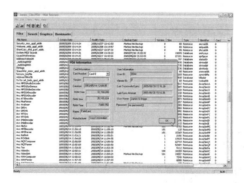

Figure 4.2   Paraben's PDA Seizure.

RAM

The RAM contains:

- Storage
- Preferences
- New applications
- User data

Data that is added to devices through typical application interaction is typically stored in the RAM area of the device. RAM is the area of the device that will typically hold the main potential evidence stores for the device.

The HotSync Process

The HotSync process is a method of transferring data from the handheld device to a desktop computer.

Some of the forensic applications use the HotSync process that has been built into the device for the transfer of data. This process is typically not forensically sound because of the writing of data to the device. However, with some implementations similar to that found in PDA Seizure, the data transfer is done in a forensically sound read-only manner.

Figure 4.3   The HotSync symbol.

The HotSync Manager

- Runs on the desktop in the background
- Allows synchronizing of multiple users
- Is an interface for conduit tweaking
- Reinstalls data in case of hard reset

Most of the desktop systems that have had a Palm device synchronize data back and forth will have the HotSync application running on the system. The examination of data synchronized with the desktop system is an important part of the forensic process. Some of the forensic applications available can also work as a file viewer for some of the proprietary data associated with the synchronization.

The HotSync Process: The Steps

The following are the steps of the HotSync process (Figure 4.4):

1. Validate and locate
2. Synchronization type
3. Desktop application notification
4. Backup conduits checked
5. Installation
6. Conduits executed
7. Second installation (3.0.1 or later)
8. Database backup
9. Sync update
10. Close communication with desktop
11. Handheld modification

Palm Communication Methods

Bluetooth

It is a short-range, low-cost wireless networking technology that uses the 2.4 GHz radio band and allows for Web surfing, exchange of data without a user interface, and multiplayer gaming.

Web Clipping

The clipping of Web page data into a format that can be displayed on a Palm.

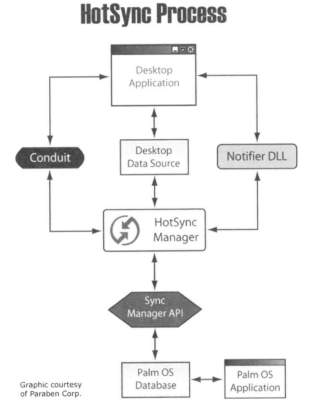

Figure 4.4   The HotSync process.

Telephony

Works with embedded phones as well as phones connected through a cable and allows for auto dialing, phone configuration, and Short Message Service (SMS).

IrDA

Industry-standard Infrared Data Association allows for communication with cell phones, pagers, and desktop and laptop computers.

Examination Essentials: Palm OS

When conducting an examination on a Palm OS, there are a variety of places data can be stored. Below is a list of areas that will usually yield the most evidence:

- Address Book (AddressDB.PDB)
- Task/To Do Lists (ToDo.PDB)
- Memos (MemoDB.PDB)
- Appointments (DatebookDB.PDB)
- Unique software
- Expense-tracking software
- Graphics associated with the device or the attached camera

There are a lot of different data stores associated with the Palm OS device; typically, most of the data will be stored in some type of database. However, as a general rule you should evaluate at least the data associated in the areas listed earlier as they are typically the largest potential stores for evidentiary data.

Security Issues with Palm OS Version 5.0

When conducting an examination on a v5.0 OS, it is important to be aware of, and prepared for, the security features you may encounter. They are the cryptographic provider manager and the authorization manager.

The Cryptographic Provider Manager

- Allows encryption of any item that can use CPM
- Provides systemwide strong 128-bit encryption
- Uses RC4, SHA-1, and signature verify with RSA-verify
- Incorporates Secure Socket Layer for communications
- Supports unique device identification
- Mobile Access Number (MAN), Flash ID, Electronic Serial Number (ESN)
- Is capable of installing plug-in cryptography program allowing for Advanced Encryption Standard (AES)

The Authorization Manager

- Uses rule-oriented authorization options including user of passwords, PINS, and pass-phrases, all stored with Authorization Manager.
- Allows for authorization growth to include biometrics, handwriting, voice recognition, and smart cards.

Protection Inherent in the Palm OS

The protection that is inherent in the Palm OS is associated with the protection of access to the device itself. Otherwise, there are many other options that can be implemented on the device that allow for protection of any of the following items:

- Encryption of private records
- Encryption of entire memo pad
- Organization/encryption of user's passwords
- Encryption of databases

Frequently Used Encryption Standards

- Blowfish
- IDEA
- SAFER-SK
- Triple DES

Password Protection Options

- Button combinations
- Unique character
- Unique ID (ATM style)
- Signature restriction

Now that you have got a solid introduction to the workings of the Palm OS and some of the snags you could run into during a first response, let's move into the acquisition process. As I mentioned earlier in the chapter, there are a number of tools available; however, the most comprehensive and extensively used tool is Paraben's PDA Seizure, which is what we will cover in the remainder of this section.

PDA Forensics on a Palm

Treatment of PDAs

Because they have no hard drives, the goal is to change the evidence in main memory as little as possible. Also, it is best to try to keep the PDA in the same state as it was when it was seized. You should also gather all power cords, spare batteries, and external memory cards as well.

There are two methods for acquiring PDAs, one for standard devices and the other for encrypted ones. Although the methods are similar, there are differences. We consider both in turn in the following subsections.

The Palm OS Flowchart Processes Using Paraben's PDA Seizure

Figure 4.5 to Figure 4.7 depict flowcharts designed to guide you through the processes of seizure, acquisition, and analysis.

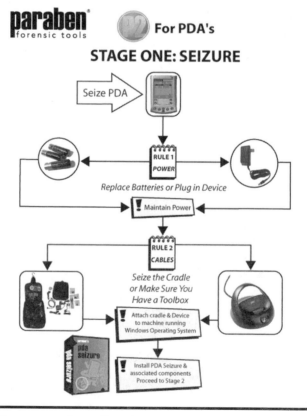

Figure 4.5 Stage one: seizure flowchart.

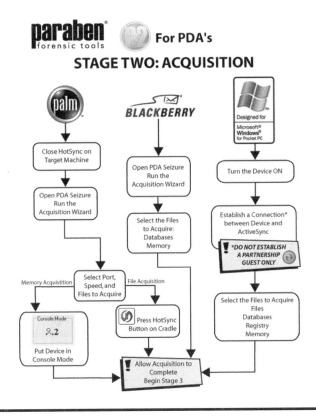

Figure 4.6   Stage two: acquisition flowchart.

Step 1: Close the HotSync Program on the Target Machine

Typically, the icon resides in the system tray on a Windows machine. This must be disabled to prevent an automatic HotSync from occurring, and thus a change or loss of evidence data. With your main forensic system, make sure that you do not have HotSync running when connecting any evidence. Port protocols and potential synchronization can risk the integrity of your evidence. *Note:* Debug mode is the mode of communication that was designed to provide an interface between a target and host.

In Reference to PDA Seizure

PDA Seizure uses the Palm Debug mode to gain low-level access to the device to acquire a physical image of the RAM and ROM areas. Debug or Console Mode allows for an interface between the PDA device and the forensic acquisition process for memory images.

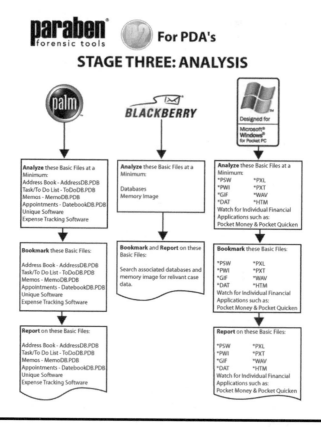

Figure 4.7   Stage three: analysis flowchart.

Debug Mode constitutes the sending of packets back and forth between the target and host.

There are three packets:

■ Command Request
■ Command Response
■ Message Packet

Step 2: Open PDA Seizure and Run the Acquisition Wizard

PDA Seizure was designed to acquire both the logical and physical data associated with PDA devices. Figure 4.8 to Figure 4.14 illustrate the process.

Step 3: Examine the Evidence

Search and validate text (Figure 4.15).

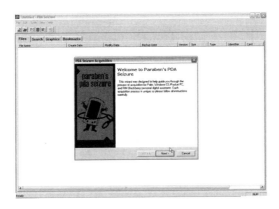

Figure 4.8 PDA Seizure wizard welcome screen. The welcome screen is the starting point of the acquisition process.

Figure 4.9 PDA Seizure file output. The file output that is generated through PDA Seizure is a *.PDA file. This is a file type proprietary to PDA Seizure and cannot be viewed by other applications.

Evidence-Handling Procedures for Encrypted Devices

Encrypted devices require different evidence-handling procedures and processing. The encryption that is associated with the device is dependent on the version of the operating system and any third-party applications that may have been used. The general seizure procedures for encrypted PDA devices are similar to that of traditional forensics:

- Ask the suspect for passwords.
- Search the area associated with the suspect for passwords that may have been written down.

Figure 4.10 Available device types to acquire (Palm OS device). The device types that are covered by PDA Seizure are broken down by operating system. One must know the operating system of the device to be able to acquire it. PDA Seizure has a built-in control that will protect a device if the wrong operating system selection is made.

Figure 4.11 Connection settings and acquisition type (Palm OS device). There are multiple connection settlings that are available in PDA Seizure to be able to communicate to the different devices. All the settings are done through read-only access to enable forensic integrity. The acquisition options are also selected here based on the type of unit selected, a Palm device in this case. Typically, an investigator will want to select either logical and physical acquisitions or all of the options that are displayed to them.

■ If the device is powered on, make sure that it stays in active mode; this mode means that the device password has already been entered.

Figure 4.12 Palm Console Mode. This option will only appear when a Palm OS device is selected and marked for physical acquisition. Console Mode must be activated on the device for physical acquisition to occur.

Figure 4.13 Card selection (Palm OS device). The card selection is based on what data you would like to acquire. This screen only appears once the device has been placed in Console Mode. The card selection is Card 0 for the default card on the device and Card 1 or more for expansion cards on the device.

■ To keep the device in active mode, tap the screen at regular intervals to simulate data input into the device; this tapping will keep the device in active mode.

■ Tapping will be required during the complete acquisition process to ensure that it does not change the status of the device.

■ Ensure the device remains powered at all times and follow traditional acquisition procedures.

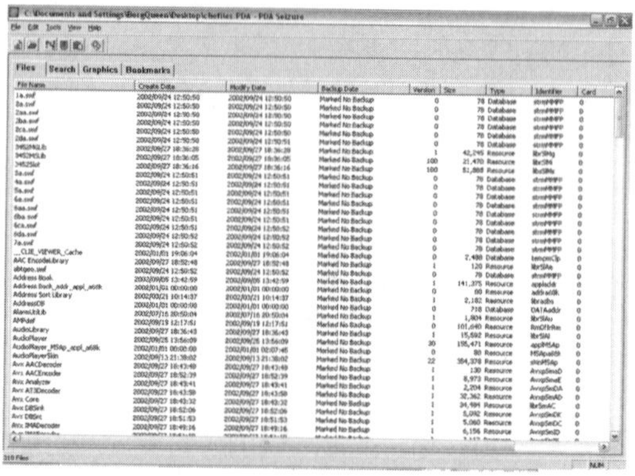

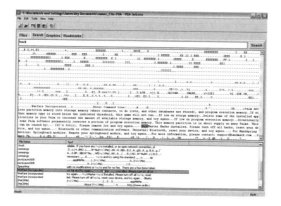

Figure 4.14 Completed acquisition (Palm OS device). Typically, if both logical and physical acquisition are selected, this is how the completed acquisition will be displayed.

Figure 4.15 Text string search. The text string searching option in PDA Seizure will search either the entire acquisition (as shown) or just an individual file.

There are many different encryption methods available for the different PDAs, so procedures might change depending on what has been implemented on the device. With certain encryption options, you can bypass the issues with some of the available forensic tools.

Password Override

Password override for use in PDA Seizure will only work on devices below version 4.0 of the Palm OS (Figure 4.16 and Figure 4.17).

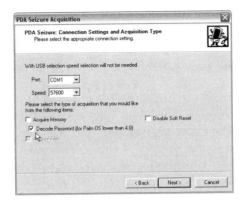

Figure 4.16 Password override (Palm OS device). The password override function in PDA Seizure will display what the user's password was on the device.

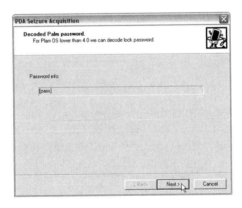

Figure 4.17 Password decoded (Palm OS device). The password will be displayed. The investigator can enter it into the device for acquisition.

PDA Forensics on a Windows CE/Pocket PC

There are some major differences with the operating systems that are used on PDA devices. These differences are immediately seen in the various types of devices available that run the different operating systems.

Devices That Use Windows CE/Pocket PC

> *The Handheld PC*: Handhelds with displays 640 × 240 touch screen with a small keyboard and Compact Flash or PCMCIA slot.

The Palm PC: Palm-sized devices with displays of 240 × 320 that have no keyboard or mouse, and support a Compact Flash slot. *The Auto PC*: In a car system supporting voice activation, wireless communication, and built-in navigation system.

Each of these systems still relies on the baseline file system of Windows CE. Although Microsoft has changed the name of their PDA operating system numerous times, it is still based on the core file system of Windows CE. This file system is the basis of doing forensics on these devices. The procedures associated with the forensic process are dramatically different from those of the Palm operating system.

What Is Windows CE?

Windows CE was designed to be an open, scalable, 32-bit operating system. The operating system was designed to be embedded for use in cameras, Internet appliances, interactive televisions, etc. This is the basis of all the spin-offs of the operating system.

The Difference between Pocket PC and Mobile PC

There are two main divisions that are currently available with the Windows CE file system. The Pocket PC, which is based on the more traditional PDA device and uses active memory as its main method of storage, and Mobile PC, which is typically based on a cellular device that has other available storage such as a SIM card.

Pocket PC

Typical characteristics of Pocket PC devices are the use of active memory, and some of the more typical baselines of a PDA. There is a large range of applications on a Pocket PC device, such as the Pocket Office suite and other personal information managers that are provided as part of the default ROM install for the devices.

Mobile PC

The Mobile PC device is where the areas of PDA forensics and cellular forensics begin to intersect. These devices have a lot of the traditional applications associated with the PDA, but with some enhancements that are available to cellular devices with chat, Internet, and integrated applications. With any type of device in which the functions start to overlap, there are different forensic procedures that need to be followed to be able to maintain the proper evidence standards.

Windows CE Desktop Software

With any of the flavors of the Windows CE file system, there is one aspect that remains consistent, and that is the use of the desktop for offline data storage. With the Windows CE desktop, you are typically using an application that allows the desktop to communicate back and forth with the device. The most common application is ActiveSync.

ActiveSync is a Microsoft application that acts as a translation and conversion tool between the handheld devices, the desktop system, and the applications. With each of the applications, a synchronization of the data has to occur so that they are compatible with the desktop application equivalent. For example, a document that is made on a PDA device is created with Pocket Word and the desktop application that matches this file is Office Word. A conversion is required to be able to make this file compatible. This conversion process is handled by the ActiveSync application.

Differences between the devices will change the process that is used to gather the evidence associated with them. With each type of device, adaptation is important for being able to deal with the slight variations that will exist even within one operating system, let alone two. Typical differences between Palm OS and Windows CE devices are shown in the following table.

Palm	Windows CE
Smaller operating system	System rooted in NTFS
Graffiti	Character recognition
Single-level password option	Multilevel password option
Macintosh-compatible	No Macintosh compatibility
Less expensive	More expensive

Reset Options with Windows CE Devices

With the Palm OS, there are very limited reset options that are typically very standard despite changes in device manufacturers. However, with Windows CE devices, there are large differences between soft and hard reset results.

As an example, a Toshiba PDA that runs Windows CE does not have the typical soft reset option. Instead, most of the Toshiba devices have an integrated hard reset option so that the device will erase the data if any reset is done. This becomes an issue in forensics as it allows suspects to remove their data very easily.

Before resetting any PDA device that is Windows CE based, refer to the device manufacturer's documentation to determine if there is a soft and a hard reset option and what resulting effect it could have on the potential evidence. You can use the following general rules:

Soft reset:
- Loses all unsaved information
- Loses all active open information

Hard reset:
- Completely purges RAM
- Returns the device to typical factory settings

Windows CE Structure: ROM

Windows CE has multiple elements that make the forensic process different. One of those elements is rooted in the Flash ROM of the device. Typically, most PDA devices have a ROM that was not intended to be written to; that is not the case with Windows CE devices. There are many reasons for this type of structure, the most important being that it makes the device much easier to upgrade. However, the forensic impact of this type of structure is that evidence can be hidden easily by a less skilled user, or the device operating system can be changed completely.

Windows CE Structure: RAM

- Main storage
- Preferences
- New applications
- User data

RAM is still the main location for evidence on the device. Any of the default applications for the device will typically write the data into the RAM of the device. RAM is as volatile with a Windows CE device as with a Palm OS device, so if the power is lost the data in RAM will also be lost. The issue with Windows CE devices is that the battery power is typically not as robust as Palm devices and dies somewhat faster.

There are two sections of RAM storage that are typically available on a Windows CE PDA: the program memory and the storage memory (or object store). These areas will both contain evidence in some form; however, you will not, in most cases, be able to do full recovery, depending on the area of RAM.

Program Memory

Program memory is the actively changing section of RAM on a device. Data is loaded into this area of memory, allowing a program to execute. Usually, you will not find large amounts of evidence in this area of the device.

Storage Memory: Object Store

Storage memory is the RAM on the device that provides persistent storage for the majority of an application and its associated data. This is where the majority of evidence will be found.

What Is the Windows CE Registry?

Windows CE is a registry-based file system. This means there are many registry keys and associated information that can contribute to your forensic examination. There are different conditions associated with the registry based on the version of the operating system and the manufacturer who implemented it. The registry stores data about applications, drivers, user preferences, and other configuration settings.

The Windows CE Acquisition Process Using Paraben's PDA Seizure

The acquisition process is shown in Figure 4.18 to Figure 4.21.

BlackBerry Forensics

BlackBerry devices are one of the newest PDAs, which are rapidly growing in popularity. They are very unique PDA devices because they have elements that make them very desirable to consumers, and also very undesirable from the forensic point of view.

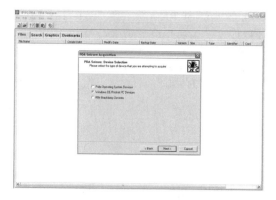

Figure 4.18 Available device types to acquire (Windows CE device). Devices are divided into categories based on which operating system version they are using.

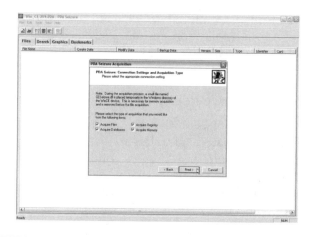

Figure 4.19 Connection settings and acquisition type. The connection settings for a Windows CE device are determined through the use of ActiveSync. The data associated with the acquisition is also selected on this screen. Typically, you will want to select all the items available to get as much data as possible from the device.

What Is RIM BlackBerry?

A BlackBerry, by Research in Motion (RIM), Waterloo, Ontario, is a small mobile handheld device designed to allow wireless e-mail access as well as basic PDA functions such as address book, calendar, tasks, etc.

The wireless aspect of these devices has a bearing on the forensic process. The phrase *snapshot forensics* comes into play even more with

Figure 4.20   ActiveSync initialization. ActiveSync is what allows PDA Seizure to communicate with a Windows CE device. When using ActiveSync it is imperative to establish a GUEST connection with the device.

Figure 4.21   Completed acquisition (Windows CE device). Once the device has completed acquisition, a display showing all of the data acquired from the device will appear. There are more files on a Windows CE device than on any of the other PDA devices, so acquisition time is longest with this type of device.

BlackBerry devices because of their wireless capabilities. There are two editions of the BlackBerry device: Enterprise and Internet.

Enterprise Edition

This edition is typically implemented in corporate environments because of the available functionality that is associated with network e-mail systems.

The primary e-mail systems that are used with BlackBerry devices are Microsoft Exchange and Lotus Domino. With all BlackBerry devices, encryption is also a standard addition to the design of the PDA; typically, Triple DES encryption is available on the device.

Internet Edition

The Internet edition was designed to be available for a consumer application where integration into large mail server applications is not required. These devices are usually sold through general service providers. Interaction between the device and service provider still occurs with respect to the mail associated with the handheld device.

Devices That Use RIM BlackBerry

The two editions of the devices can come in many different forms and sizes and can be classified into two categories: palm size and pager size. Some of the device types, such as the pager-style device, are no longer available. However, many of these devices are still in circulation and should be accounted for in the forensic examination.

Overviews of various devices follow:

> The Palm PC/Phone: Palm-sized BlackBerry devices are typically integrated GSM devices that have multiple storage areas, where evidence can potentially exist. The GSM phone system allows the device to have a SIM card storage area that can house evidence. With these types of devices, it is a multistep process to be able to acquire the data by combining the rules of PDA forensics with those of cellular forensics.
>
> The pager: Pager-style devices are no longer available for purchase from providers. However, because of their size and excellent use of battery power, these devices remain popular with consumers. The same functionality exists in the pager-sized device as in the larger palm-sized device.
>
> RIM BlackBerry (950 and 850)
> - 950 runs on 900 MHz Mobitex network.
> - Cingular in the United States or Rogers AT&T Wireless in Canada.
> - 850 runs on 800 MHz DataTAC network.
> - Motient in the United States or Bell Mobility in Canada.
> - Both have built-in wireless modems.

- Optimized keyboard and track wheel.
- Built-in applications.
- E-mail, calendar, address book, task list, and memo pad.

RIM BlackBerry (957 and 857)
- 957 runs on 900 MHz Mobitex network.
- Cingular in the United States or Rogers AT&T Wireless in Canada.
- 857 runs on 800 MHz DataTAC network.
- Motient in the United States or Bell Mobility in Canada.
- Both have built-in wireless modems.
- Optimized keyboard and track wheel.
- Built-in applications.
- E-mail, calendar, address book, task list, and memo pad.

RIM BlackBerry 5810
- Java 2 Micro Edition (J2ME).
- Built-in wireless modem.
- Optimized keyboard and track wheel.
- Built-in applications.
- E-mail, calendar, address book, task list, and memo pad.

RIM BlackBerry 6720/6710
- Java 2 Micro Edition (J2ME).
- SMS and browser support.
- Built-in wireless modem.
- Optimized keyboard and track wheel.
- Built-in applications.
- E-mail, calendar, address book, task list, and memo pad.
- 6720-Dual-band GSM/GPRS 900/1800 MHz.
- Europe and Asia-Pacific region coverage.
- 6710-World-band GSM/GPRS 900/1800 MHz.
- North America, Europe, and Asia-Pacific region coverage.

RIM BlackBerry 6510
- Java 2 Micro Edition (J2ME).
- Digital cellular and digital two-way radio.
- Text and numeric paging and browser.
- Integrated speaker/microphone, removable rechargeable battery, and external antenna.
- Built-in wireless modem.
- Optimized keyboard and track wheel.

- Built-in applications.
- E-mail, calendar, address book, task list, and memo pad.

BlackBerry devices are primarily used in corporate environments to allow constant connection to the office. Some of the common functions of the devices or applications that are used are the following:

- Instant messaging
- Games
- Telnet/SSH
- Secure e-mail
- Streaming financial information
- System management
- Point of sale — payment system

BlackBerry has over 1 million subscribers. Some of the countries in which BlackBerry devices are common are:

- Canada
- United States
- Australia
- Hong Kong
- Philippines
- Singapore
- Austria
- Germany
- Switzerland
- Ireland
- Netherlands
- United Kingdom
- France
- Spain
- Italy
- Mexico

Fundamental Differences between PDA OS and BlackBerry

The forensic evidence and procedure are dramatically different for these devices.

Palm OS	Win CE	RIM BlackBerry
128-Bit encryption	Proprietary encryption	Triple DES encryption
Smallest OS	Rooted NTFS	Proprietary
Graffiti	Handwriting	Thumb board
Wireless optional	Wireless optional	Wireless integrated
Numerous third-party applications	Growing number of third-party applications	Limited third-party applications

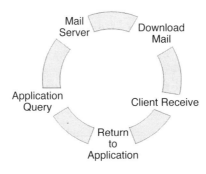

Figure 4.22   The "pull" method of wireless e-mail.

Standard Wireless Connect

Typically, as we have discussed previously, most wireless communication works in a pull fashion, in which a query must be sent to be able to establish a connection to the server (Figure 4.22).

How Does a BlackBerry Connect?

BlackBerry devices do not communicate wirelessly in the typical fashion. They do not query the wireless server prior to gaining wireless access. With these types of devices, *push* wireless functionality is employed so that the device is constantly sent an active wireless signal (Figure 4.23). This also means that BlackBerry devices require a different set of forensic procedures to be able to secure evidence.

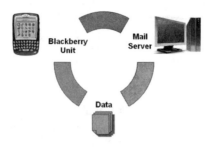

Figure 4.23 The BlackBerry method of wireless e-mail.

Forensic Rules for RIM BlackBerry Operating System

BlackBerry devices, as well as other devices that are considered *live* devices, have different evidence-handling procedures. These procedures take into account the fact that these devices can receive data at any time, after seizure through live data transfers.

Rule 1: Radio Control/Faraday Control

With BlackBerry devices, there are two ways to control the wireless signal and still maintain the evidentiary value of the device. First, the device has the ability to turn off the wireless signal through the main menu. There are icons that the investigator can scroll to and select "turn off wireless." The second option, if interaction with the device is not desired, is to place the device in a faraday cage of some type. This will prevent the device from receiving any wireless data that could potentially contaminate the evidence.

Faraday Technologies

The term *Faraday* comes from Michael Faraday, who was a bookbinder with a passing interest in electricity. Michael Faraday conducted many experiments that resulted in advancements in physics; however, his name is most associated with a device to contain electromagnetic waves. The principle of a Faraday device is that the signals or waves from the device are restricted to a cage; the signals will bounce off the cage back onto the device. The first Faraday cage was made in 1836.

There are a couple of ways to achieve Faraday protection for a device. One of the less expensive options is to use a metal paint can. There are some rules that need to be followed. It is vital to ensure that all the

General Operating Procedures for StrongHold Bag

Before you place the wireless device in the bag make sure the device has a complete charge or is attached to a Paraben Battery Supply.

To place a device in the bag properly, open the bag and put the device in the inside opening as shown here: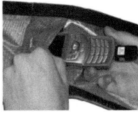

Seal the Velcro opening securely. If you have a cable connected, seal the Velcro snugly around the cable.

Fold the bag and tightly seal the Velcro around the entire bag as shown below. Be sure there is a complete seal around the bag.

If you have a data cable connected to your device, do not allow more than ¼" of an inch of the end of the cable to show as some cables can act as an antenna in certain devices.*

When connecting a device to a computer for forensic acquisitions, please keep as much of the cable inside the bag as possible.

*Please note, certain cell phone cables have such a strong antenna effect with connected data cables that Paraben cannot guarantee complete wireless protection when data cables are used. Paraben strongly suggests the use of wireless protection for forensic acquisitions such as Paraben's StrongHold Tent when doing forensic data acquisitions.

(C) Copyright Paraben Corporation 2005.

Figure 4.24   Proper use of a StrongHold bag.

connections with the lid of the can are direct metal-to-metal connections, meaning that all coatings on and in the can have to be removed. There are also some excellent commercial options, such as a bag to place wireless devices in. The bag, namely Paraben's Wireless Stronghold Bag (Figure 4.24), was designed with copper, silver, and nickel interwoven and designed to block incoming signals. Paraben also has a battery that can be attached to the device allowing the device to remain powered inside the shielded bag.

Any device that needs to maintain power from any type of external power supply will also need to be shielded to make sure the Faraday cage is not broken.

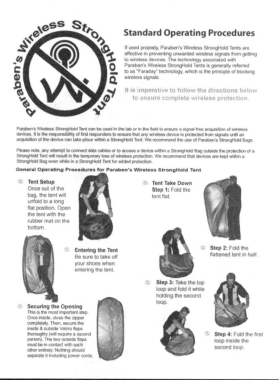

Figure 4.25 Proper use of a StrongHold tent.

Other options for Faraday protection include a variety of tents (Figure 4.25) that can be used to shield the device, as well as the investigator, from the wireless signal.

Rule 2: Power Control

Power is an issue with BlackBerry devices because they are still considered to be active memory devices. This active memory is still volatile and is dependent on a steady stream of power to maintain the data storage. Typically, the more modern BlackBerry devices use rechargeable batteries and simply need to maintain power connectivity when the device is Faraday-protected. If you opt to Faraday-protect the device and maintain power to it, shielding the power supply is also required. Older devices such as the pager-style devices typically use standard AA batteries that can be changed on scene as long as the device is not without power for more than 50 s.

Rule 3: Cables and Accessories

Data connection to the device is required to acquire the data associated with it. If you do not have access to the suspect's data cables, you can purchase the cables from various vendors. One of the unique items that usually come with BlackBerry devices is a belt clip, which is often how users carry the device. Using the belt clip once the seizure has occurred is an excellent way to conserve battery power. Once the device goes into the belt clip, it goes into a sleep mode that uses less power than when it is active. However, be careful, because sleep mode will also activate any encryption on the device.

Rule 4: Data Always Changing

As with all active memory devices, the data on the devices constantly changes and affects the typical validation methods used in forensics. With all *snapshot-forensic*-type devices, a point in time is identified during acquisition. It is that point in time which is the basis for the evidence and is maintained throughout the rest of the analysis process. Statements or testimony on the state of these devices should follow the rules previously discussed with snapshot forensics.

Rule 5: Understand Fundamentals

BlackBerry devices are not as well documented as the other PDA devices, so finding information on new devices and understanding their internal functionality can be somewhat difficult. However, RIM does have a resource bank of basic information in the form of an e-mail newsletter.

Additional resources are available at www.blackberry.net, www.rim-road.com, and www.rim.net.

How BlackBerry Uses RAM

Static Random-Access Memory (SRAM)

Memory that retains data bits in its memory as long as power is being supplied.

Flash Random-Access Memory RAM (FRAM)

Nonvolatile memory that is constantly powered and that can be erased and reprogrammed in units. This area stores OS PAGER.EXE. *Note:* Check the charts in manual for exact numbers of allocation.

BlackBerry Security

One of the reasons the BlackBerry device has become so popular is the use of secure encryption on the device. Typically, the devices implement Triple DES encryption.

Triple DES encryption is the implementation of a combined key from DES. It is possible, but unrealistic, to crack this level of encryption because the time and resources required would be too impractical for a forensic investigation. However, the real issues pertain to how encryption has been implemented on the device. BlackBerry devices have been designed to limit the number of times a user can attempt to enter the proper password; the device overwrites the data in RAM after the limit is exceeded. This implementation precludes the use of conventional brute force methods to gain access to the device.

BlackBerry Examination Essentials

The data capacity of the BlackBerry device is substantially less than that of other PDAs. However, there are some key areas that should be evaluated for forensic evidence. The databases in the device act as the main areas of storage for enterable data associated with the device. One of the other main areas of acquisition for the device is the memory dump. This area represents the physical device and can contain a representation of allocated — active data or unallocated — inactive data. This area should be searched for remnants of data that has been deleted by the suspect.

BlackBerry Flowchart Processes Using Paraben's PDA Seizure

These are illustrated in Figure 4.26 to Figure 4.28.

Cell Phone Forensics

Cell phone forensics is a very new field in the United States. Only recently has it started being incorporated into the mainstream digital forensic laboratories. The main reason that kept cell phone forensics in the background was limitations based on available technologies. As time passed, new tools entered the arena and now this new discipline is emerging in full force.

The basis of cell phone forensics is to acquire the data that has been received on the phone in a manner that maintains the evidence quality of that data. The data that is acquired is not live talk associated with the

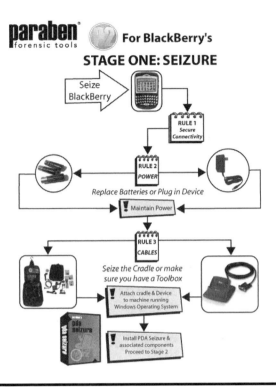

Figure 4.26 BlackBerry seizure process.

phone; rather, it is the residual data stored on the device. This is an important distinction because very different legal guidelines are required for live wire, or wireless, interception of data.

There are some basic rules that can be used in the handling of data associated with cellular devices. These rules are guidelines, and will help to ensure that the integrity of the evidence is maintained.

Summary of Available Software and Tools

BitPIM

BitPIM is a phone management program that allows the viewing and manipulation of data on cell phones. This data includes the phone book, calendar, wallpapers, ring tones, and the embedded file system. BitPIM is distributed as open source software under the GNU General Public License and runs on Windows, Linux, and Mac OS.

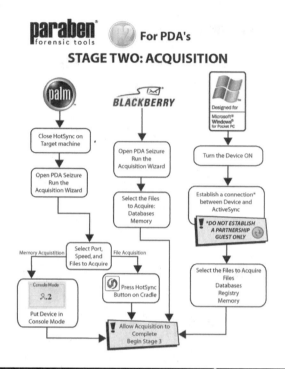

Figure 4.27   PDA Seizure acquisition processes.

GSM.XRY

GSM.XRY, from Micro Systemation, is a forensic software toolkit for acquiring data from GSM, CDMA, 3G phones, and SIM/USIM cards. Data acquired from cellular devices are stored in the .XRY format and cannot be altered, but can be exported into external formats and viewed with third-party applications. Depending on the phone's functionality, the following fields may contain data: Summary screen, Case data, General Information, Contacts, Calls, Calendar, SMS, Pictures, Audio, Files, Notes, Tasks, MMS, Network Information, Video, etc.

Oxygen Phone Manager

Oxygen Phone Manager, the forensic version, is available for police departments, law enforcement units, and all government services for investigation purposes. Oxygen Phone Manager allows examiners to acquire data from the device and export it into multiple supported formats.

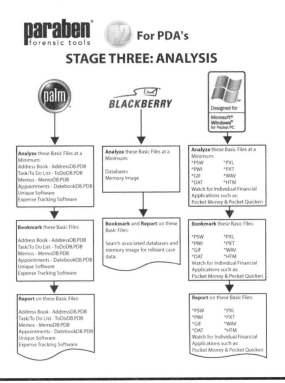

Figure 4.28 **PDA Seizure analysis recommendations.**

MOBILedit!

MOBILedit! Forensic can acquire data logically as well as search, examine, and report data from GSM, CDMA, and PCS cell phones. Data acquired from cell phone devices is stored in the .med file format. The following fields are populated: Subscriber Information, Device Specifics, Phonebook, SIM Phone-book, Missed Calls, Last Numbers Dialed, Received Calls, Inbox, Sent Items, etc. One additional feature is access to the myPhoneSafe.com service, which provides access to the IMEI database to check for stolen phones.

Cell Seizure

Cell Seizure, from Paraben, is a forensic software toolkit that allows exam-iners to acquire, search, examine, and report data associated with cell phones on CDMA, TDMA, and GSM networks. Cell Seizure features include bookmarking of information to be filtered and organized in a format report, searching for case-sensitive whole-word text and hexadecimal values, and automatic assembly of found images under a single facility.

TULP 2G

TULP2G (2nd Generation) is an open source forensic tool that allows for the extraction and reading of data from mobile cell phones and SIMs. TULP2G acquires data from mobile phones using a data cable, Bluetooth, or IrDA connection and a compatible protocol plug-in.

SIMIS

SIMIS, by Crownhill in Conneticut USA, is a tool that allows examiners the ability to extract data from a SIM securely and protect the integrity with cryptographic hashes. The SIMIS desktop is capable of decoding Unicode data found on the SIM Card, including active and deleted text messages and phone book information. Crownhill also offers the SIMIS Mobile Handheld Reader.

ForensicSIM

ForensicSIM Toolkit, by Radio Tactic, consists of the following components: acquisition terminal, control card, data storage cards, analysis application, and the card reader. The ForensicSIM toolkit deals with two processes: acquisition of data and analysis of data. Data acquisition is carried out using the acquisition terminal. The toolkit allows examiners read-only access to SIMs and generates textual reports based on the contents acquired.

Forensic Card Reader

Forensic Card Reader is a combination of a smart card reader with USB connection and software that gives examiners the ability to acquire data from SIM cards without modification. The usual data elements are acquired: phone directory, abbreviated dialing numbers, fixed dialing numbers and SMS messages as well as the identifiers of the SIM and the subscriber. Deleted SMS messages can also be acquired.

SIMCon

SIMCon works with any standard smart card reader. Besides standard SIM file content, SIMCon also has an option to do a comprehensive scan of all directories and files that may be present on the SIM and to acquire nonstandardized directories and files.

Forensic Rules for Cellular Phones

Rule 1: Stop Wireless Receiving

With live wireless data being sent to the device at all times, it is critical that the device maintain its evidentiary integrity. For this, the use of Faraday equipment is a must.

Most examiners will attempt to employ the same techniques that have been used in the past with digital evidence, where it is quite common for the device to be turned off. With cellular devices this technique is not recommended because of the use of a Personal Identification Number (PIN) with the device. If the device is powered off, this encryption is activated on the device, and it would prohibit the investigator from being able to acquire the associated data on the device.

Rule 2: Charge Device

As we've discussed previously, power still remains an issue with most of the handheld wireless devices when it comes to maintaining the viability of the evidence. With cellular devices, it is recommended that the device at least have a 50% charge before the acquisition process begins so that the connection to the device through the data transfer cable can be maintained without a need for power as well. Typically, they are both plugged into the same area of the device. Power is also an issue because acquisition times can vary greatly from device to device. A 50% charge for the device is a good rule of thumb for being able to do a complete device acquisition.

Rule 3: Cabling and Accessories

Cabling for cellular devices is very unique because cables are usually designed for a specific model. Unfortunately, the same cabling needs to be used to create the proper connection and conduct a forensic acquisition of the device. There are a variety of cables available from the different manufacturers. Some of the forensic software providers have put together a collection of cables for some of the common phones in different toolbox kits.

There is a vast array of accessories available for the modern cell phone, ranging from charms and trinkets to the more advanced cameras and recorders. With any of these types of accessories, it is necessary that they also be examined in the context of attachment to the phone as well as an independent storage device.

Rule 4: Acquire in Laboratory

The recommendation is that acquisition be performed in a laboratory, where you can have controlled conditions. If Faraday tents are used, you can maintain that same level of wireless signal control in the field, but with either option, you should test and ensure that the evidentiary quality of the device is maintained.

Laboratories do not have to be redesigned to be able to accept cellular evidence, but they should employ proper handling with the use of some type of Faraday enclosure for the devices in a bag, and acquisitions in a controlled area such as a complete Faraday room or tent system.

Cell Phone Flowchart Processes Using Paraben's Cell Seizure

The flowcharts of cell phone seizure, acquisition, and analysis processes are shown Figure 4.29 and Figure 4.30.

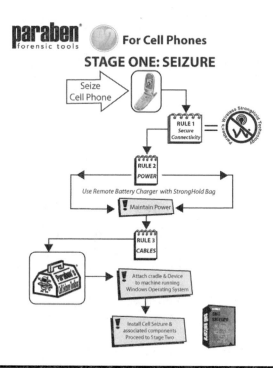

Figure 4.29   Cell phone seizure process.

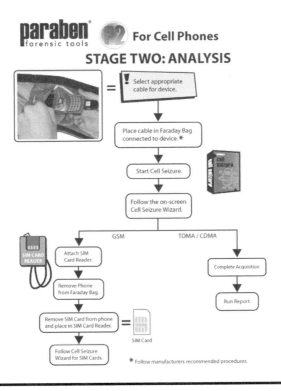

Figure 4.30   Cell phone acquisition and analysis process.

Cell Phone Data Storage

In 1997, a wireless phone cost, on average, about $132. In 2003, the average cost was down to $88. Today, most plans offer basic cell phones for free with purchase of service. The accessibility of this type of device continues to increase, with the cost of the equipment and the services decreasing with each passing day. Currently, cell phone usage has increased to 2 billion subscribers and is growing daily.

The amount of data that is evidentiary in nature from cell phone devices is as vast as the number of cellular devices that are available. The information available from phone calls and text messages only increases as the potential storage capacity of the devices increases. One of the best ways to look at a cellular device from an evidence standpoint is that it is a complete imprint of your suspect's activities for a period of time. With that in mind, here are some of the fundamentals of the different cellular devices.

Device Storage Areas

There are many storage areas for data on cellular devices. The following are the different types of data that can be gathered as evidence:

Calls

- Phone calls
- Received calls
- Dialed calls
- Missed calls

Graphics

- Downloaded
- Camera Images

SMS

- Sent SMS
- Received SMS
- Templates
- Unsent SMS
- Deleted SMS (SIM)

Sounds

- Downloaded
- Ring tones
- Voice memos
- Music (MP3)

Phonebook Data

With cellular evidence, some of the most common areas that can be used as evidence can contain a lot more details than would originally be expected. For an investigator, being able to gather and understand the specific areas and issues can be critical.

One of the items to note with a majority of the data in a cellular device is the date and time stamp associated with the data. Remember that GMT

(Greenwich Mean Time) will need to be adjusted to the suspect's time zone. This type of data could include:

- Phone numbers: general, mobile, work, fax, home, pager, other
- Address information: postal address, email1, email2, URL, street address, city, state, zip, country
- Date: date, text date, and time zone (GMT offset)
- Personal information: name, last name, first name, company, job title, caller group
- Custom fields: custom1, custom2, custom3, custom4
- Binary data IDs: ringtone ID, picture ID

Other items can exist in the phonebook allocation of memory, such as Notes data entry.

Calendar Data

Calendar note types:

- Reminder or date
- Call
- Meeting
- Birthday or anniversary or special occasion
- Memo or miscellaneous
- Travel
- Vacation
- Training remainders
- Alarm
- Alarm repeating each day

SMS

Size:
- 160 Character Latin alphabet
- 70 Character non-Latin
- Broadcast mode
- Point to point
- SIM storable
- Binary data transfer (ringtones, logos)

Formats:
- Pager
- Fax
- Email
- Text

Status:
- Sent
- Unsent
- Read
- Unread

Encoding:
- Unicode
- Default GSM alphabet
- 8-bit encoding

With all the SMS, traffic typically will travel on a different channel from cellular calls.

How SMS Is Sent

The path SMS traffic goes through has multiple points the forensic investigator can gather evidence from, as it can exist on both the provider side as well as on the device side (Figure 4.31).

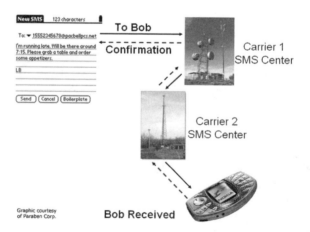

Figure 4.31 The SMS process.

A Unique Feature of SMS

SMS has a few unique features because of which the data can again leave multiple forensic fingerprints:

- Multi-Send: SMS concatenation; stringing of multiple messages together
- SMS compression: allows the user to access the SMS dictionary to abbreviate an SMS message.

Both these options are currently available with existing GSM technology.

What People Do with SMS

SMS is what is commonly referred to as text messaging. It is the ideal quick communication method between parties, as it is less intrusive and easily receivable in more situations than a phone call. During Christmas in the United Kingdom there were over 20 million messages sent in one day. This method of communication is growing in popularity by leaps and bounds. The cost-effective nature of text messaging (on the order of a few cents) also makes this an ideal form of communication. SMS is used for various purposes:

Everyday people
- Person to person
- Informational
- Advertising
- Hobby — sports

Corporations
- E-mail notification
- Mobile commerce
- Customer service details

Other uses
- Vehicle positioning
- Remote monitoring

The Future: Multimedia Message Service (MMS)

The next level of text messaging is MMS. This new MMS is able to embed pictures, sounds, and video with messaging. The potential evidence obtainable with this type of communication has increased in conjunction with the camera phones that have come into the market over the last year.

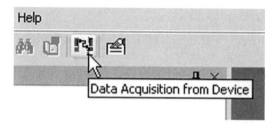

Figure 4.32 Data acquisition toolbar. The data acquisition options for cell phones can be accessed through either the menu or toolbar.

Figure 4.33 Data acquisition menu.

Cell Phone Acquisition Process Using Paraben's Cell Seizure

The cell phone acquisition process is illustrated in Figure 4.32 to Figure 4.45.

SIM Card Forensics

There is another level of forensics that needs to be covered with cellular devices. That is the SIM card. In some cases the device itself is not always the only potential source of evidence. The SIM card associated with GSM devices is also a potential area of evidence for suspect data, and should be examined using the following guidelines.

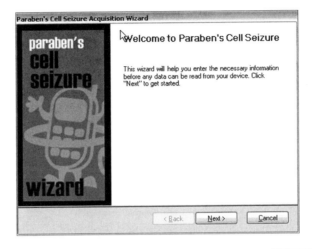

Figure 4.34   Acquisition wizard. The acquisition wizard was designed to guide you through the process required to gather data from a cellular device.

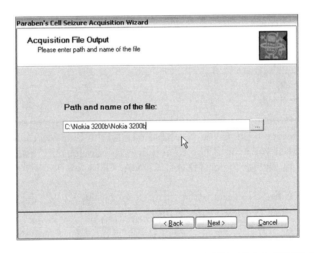

Figure 4.35   Filename. The output associated with Cell Seizure is a *.CSZ file that is proprietary to the Cell Seizure application. All of the data associated with the acquisition will be contained in this file.

SIM Card Seizure Rules

1. Acquire the complete device with SIM card intact before removing the card from the device. This can apply to traditional cellular devices as well as some of the unique blends of the PDA and cellular device that you would see with BlackBerry devices.

Figure 4.36 Confirmation of filename. To protect the user from any errors, Cell Seizure will confirm the filename for the *.CSZ file prior to writing it.

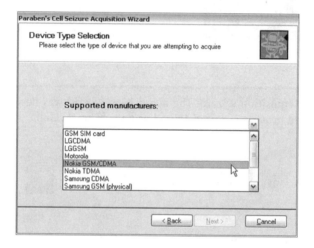

Figure 4.37 Device type. Once you have named the file, you need to select the type of device that you would like to acquire. The devices are listed by manufacturer and then by device type (TDMA, CDMA, GSM, etc.).

2. Remove the SIM card from the device. Typically, the SIM card will be located beneath the battery, so it must be removed to gain access to the SIM card. Once removed there is a risk that the next time the device is turned on the encryption associated with the PIN or a third-party tool could be activated.

3. Place the SIM card in an appropriate reader with forensic software for SIM card acquisition. The majority of the SIM-card-reading tools out there have the ability to write to the SIM card, so it is critical that you select a software package that only allows reading of data through the SIM card reader. The majority of write protection for SIM card acquisition is done through the software interface to the SIM card.

4. Acquire the associated data.

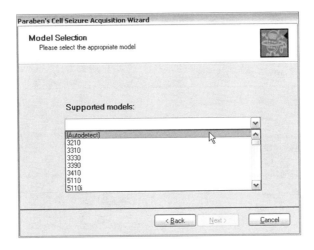

Figure 4.38   Model selection. The model selection will list all the models that are currently supported through Cell Seizure. It is recommended to select the AutoDetect option in the majority of cases.

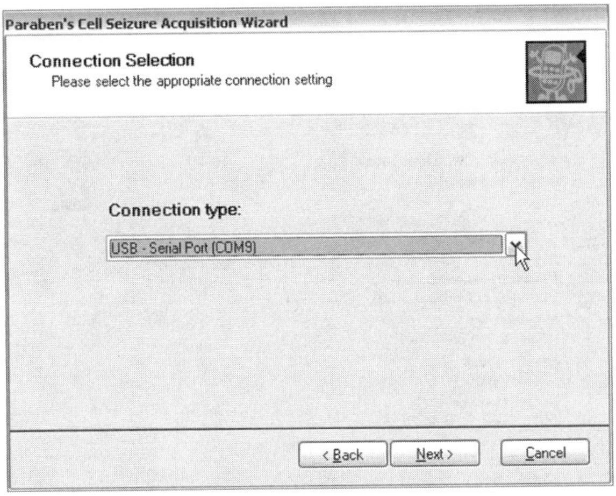

Figure 4.39   Connection type. The connection type for the device is based on the connection associated with the cable attached from the device to the PC.

An example of SIM card done using Paraben's SIM Card Seizure is shown in Figure 4.46 to Figure 4.55. The same technology for SIM card seizure is also available in Paraben's Cell Seizure software.

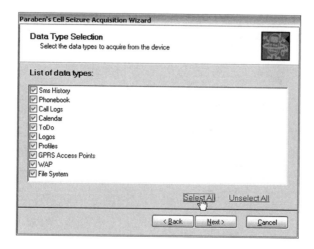

Figure 4.40 Data type selection. The data associated with the cell device will display. This is all the data that Cell Seizure can currently acquire. You should always check with the manufacturer of the software for updates to make sure you have the latest version of the software.

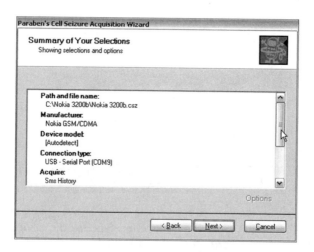

Figure 4.41 Summary of acquisition. Once your selections are complete, you will have one last chance to review those selections to ensure that no errors have been made.

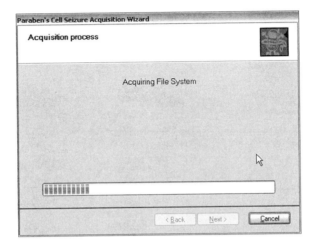

Figure 4.42 Acquisition. Once acquisition has begun, you will be shown a progress dialog that will process each section of the device.

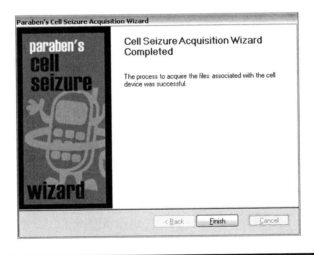

Figure 4.43 Completed acquisition. Once the acquisition process has been completed, the Finish button will need to be selected. This will allow the data to be saved to a file.

Forensic Data Associated with SIM Cards

There is a lot of data that can be acquired from the SIM card that could be valuable in a forensic examination. The SIM card is a static evidence store. Typically, there are two main states of a SIM card:

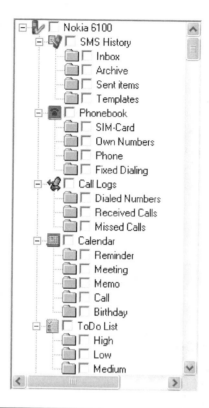

Figure 4.44   Tree view of acquisition. The completed device acquisition will be displayed with a tree view as well as a contents view to the right. This allows for easy navigation through the data.

1. Operating state: Execution of a command or transmission
2. Idle state: Not in active use, but retains all pertinent data

There are a variety of areas that are available with the SIM card which allow for the system information for the provider as well as the device:

- Identifier: IMSI number (International Mobile Subscriber Identity)
- 15-Character Number (Shows Country and Network)
- Handset identifier
- Able to block or bar from network
- Security key

SIM cards act as secure storage devices and authentication keys. This causes forensic acquisition of the complete data to be more difficult, as some aspects of the devices are not designed to communicate once they

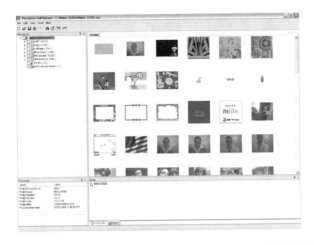

Figure 4.45 Contents view. The contents view allows for the display of the detailed data associated with the acquisition. Above is a listing of all of the graphics associated with a device.

Figure 4.46 SIM card acquisition. The acquisition wizard for SIM cards will guide you through the stages to complete a physical acquisition of the SIM card.

are locked into the device. In the following subsection we give charts of the SIM card data structure, and what data will be typically acquired in the acquisition process.

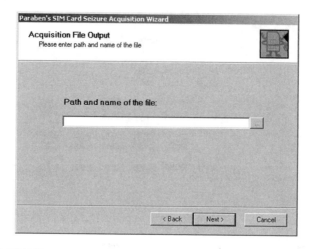

Figure 4.47 Filename. The SIM Card Seizure file format is *.CSE. This is a proprietary format associated with SIM Card Seizure. It acts as a container for all data associated with the acquisition process.

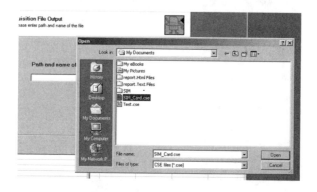

Figure 4.48 Supported manufacturers. SIM Card Seizure currently supports basic GSM SIM cards. There are a variety of different types of SIM cards available, and it is always good to cross-verify your acquisition using more than one tool.

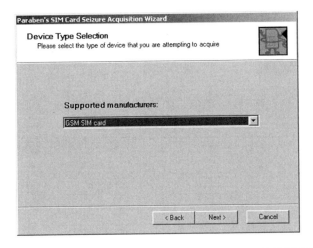

Figure 4.49 Device type selection will prompt you to choose the type of SIM card you are acquiring.

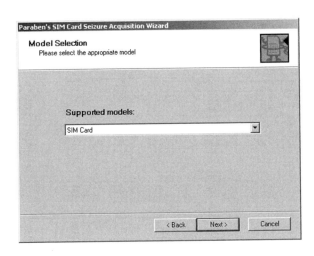

Figure 4.50 Connection type. There are limited SIM card readers that are compatible with SIM Card Seizure. However, there are both USB and serial devices that are supported. To ensure the integrity of the SIM card, special drivers are built into the software to guarantee the read-only process associated with the acquisition.

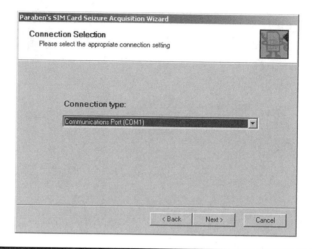

Figure 4.51 Data type selection. All of the data associated with the SIM card that is currently acquired through SIM Card Seizure will be listed. It is always recommended to check with the manufacturer of the software you are using to make sure you are current with the latest versions.

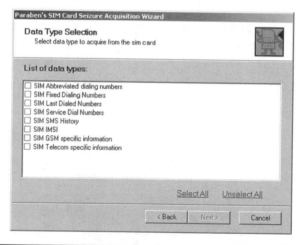

Figure 4.52 Summary. Once you have completed your selections, you will be shown a summary. This is to verify that no changes need to be made prior to acquisition.

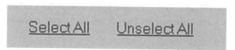

Figure 4.53 Acquisition process. As the acquisition processes through the different areas of the card, you will be shown a progress dialog for each area.

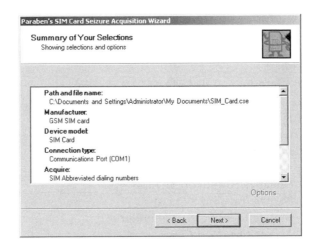

Figure 4.54 Acquisition completed. Once the acquisition is complete, you will receive a success screen. Once you select Finish, the data associated with the acquisition will be saved.

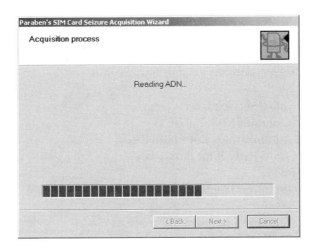

Figure 4.55 Completed acquisition. The data associated with the SIM card will be displayed in a tree view with a contents view to the right. You can also easily sort through the data by using the Bookmark function.

SIM Data Acquired

GSM Folder:
EIA/TIA 553 NAM Information (EIA/TIA-553)

SID	System ID
GPI	Group ID
IPC	Initial Paging Channel
COUNT	s-p Call Count
NSID	Negative/Forbidden SID List
PSID	Positive/Favored SID List
MIN	Mobile Identification Number
ACCOLC	Access Overload Class
S-ESN	SIM Electronic Serial Number
REG-THRESH	Registration Threshold
AMPS-UI	AMPS Usage Indicators

SoLSA Subscribed Local Service Areas

SAI	SoLSA Access Indicator
SLL	SoLSA LSA List

MExE Execution Environment Related Information

MExE-ST	MExE Service table
ORPK	Operator Root Public Key
ARPK	Administrator Root Public Key
TPRPK	Third-Party Root Public key

LP	Preferred languages variable
IMSI	IMSI
Kc	Ciphering Key
PLMNsel	PLMN Selector
HPLMN	HPLMN search period
ACMmax	ACM maximum value
SST	SIM Service Table
ACM	Accumulated call meter
GID1	Group Identifier Level 1
GID2	Group Identifier Level 2
PUCT	Price per unit and currency table
CBMI	Cell broadcast message identifier selection
SPN	Service Provider Name

CBMID	Cell Broadcast Message Identifier for Data Download
CBMIR	Cell Broadcast Message Identifier Range Selection
NIA	Network's Indication of Alerting
KcGPRS	GPRS Ciphering key
LOCIGPRS	GPRS location information
SUME	SetUpMenu Elements
PLMNwAcT	User-controlled PLMN Selector with Access Technology
OPLMNwAct	Operator-controlled PLMN Selector with Access Technology
HPLMNAcT	HPLMN Selector with Access Technology
CPBCCH	CPBCCH Information
INVScan	Investigation Scan
RPLMNAT	RPLMN last used Access Technology
BCCH	Broadcast control channels
ACC	Access control class
FPLMN	Forbidden PLMNs
LOCI	Location information
AD	Administrative data
Phase	Phase Identification
VGCS	Voice Group Call Service
VGCSS	Voice Group Call Service Status
VBS	Voice Broadcast Service
VBSS	Voice Broadcast Service Status
eMLPP	Enhanced Multi Level Pre-emption and Priority
AAeM	Automatic Answer for eMLPP Service
ECC	Emergency Call Codes

Telecom Folder:

GRAPHICS	Graphical Information
IMG	Image
ADN	Abbreviated Dialing Numbers
FDN	Fixed Dialing Numbers
SMS	Short Messages
CPP	Capability Configuration Parameters
MSISDN	MSISDN
SMSP	SMS Parameters
SMSS	SMS status
LND	Last Number Dialed
SMSR	Short Message Status Reports
SDN	Service Dialing Numbers
EXT1	Extension1
EXT2	Extension2

EXT3	Extension3
BDN	Barred Dialing Numbers
EXT4	Extension4

Note: This list changes frequently, and more data can be acquired as new tools are released.

Data Acquisition Options

The available data acquisition options with the different types of cellular devices are very broad. Depending on the device, you will not be able to do a traditional forensic acquisition using a data transfer cable.

What Data Is Available from Mobile Phones?

Below is a list of data that is typically acquired through a forensic data transfer method based on types of device.

TDMA	Phonebook
CDMA	Phonebook
	Calendar
	SMS
	Call history
	Gallery
	Voice recordings
GSM	Phonebook
	Calendar
	SMS
	Call history
	Pictures
	Voice recordings
	SIM card

With each of the preceding devices, the examination of the data will have to be adjusted to account for some of the acquisition limitations based on the type of phone. For example, with a TDMA device, it is recommended that the acquisition be done initially with a data cable and software. The remaining data can then be acquired through the use of a digital camera and scrolling through the device.

What Do the Providers Keep?

With cellular forensics, there is another level of fingerprint available for the investigator. This fingerprint is the records for the device at the provider level. Special legal considerations also come into play in getting this data, if it is available:

- IMSI of caller
- IMEI of caller
- Call duration (transmitting and receiving)
- Customer name and address
- Billing name and address
- Username and address
- Billing account details
- Telephone number
- IMSI
- PIN/PUK for SIM
- Service allowed

The data will vary depending on the service provider.

How to Analyze Cell Phone Data

The data acquired from a cell phone is not as extensive as that available on a hard drive; also, the type of data is very different. This is important to remember during the analysis phase because the data on a cell phone can be considered *accessory* evidence. Accessory evidence may not be as obvious as e-mail information, for example; however, it is still worthy of investigation. Here are a couple of simple examples of the data that can be gathered from a cell phone:

- Obvious: SMS = Drugs arrived
- Subtle: Phonebook = Victim knew suspect
- Interesting: WAV = Found on dead body

SIM Card Security

The A3 is used to authenticate the mobile station (MS) to the network; A8 is designed to generate the encryption key in the SIM, and random number (RAND) 128 bits across the SIM–ME (mobile equipment) interface. The output of this combined function is the signed response (SRES) — done by SIM (32 bits) and cryptographic key (Kc) (64 bits).

PIN versus PUK

Personal Identification Number (PIN) has the following features:
- Stored on SIM
- Three mistypes and you are locked out
- PUK required after lockout

PIN unlock key (PUK) has the following features:
- Found only through network provider
- An 8-digit code
- Ten mistypes and the SIM is permanently locked

Handling Instructions for Mobile Phones

Any interaction with the handset on a mobile phone could result in loss of evidence, and it is important not to interrogate the handset or SIM.

Before handling, decide if any other evidence is required from the phone (such as DNA, fingerprints, drugs, and accelerants). If evidence in addition to electronic data is required, follow the general handling procedures for that evidence type or contact the crime officer on the scene.

General advice is to switch the handset off because of the potential for loss of data if the battery fails or new network traffic overwrites call logs or recoverable deleted areas (e.g., SMS); there is also potential for sabotage. However, investigating officers (OIC) may require the phone to remain on for monitoring purposes while live enquiries continue. If this is the case, ensure the unit is kept charged and not tampered with. In all events, power down the unit prior to transport.

Recovery and Packaging

1. Package and secure the phone in a rigid box (e.g., FSS box) with plastic ties. This will prevent accidental operation in transit.
2. Insert the box into a tamperproof bag and seal. Fully complete exhibit and production labels.
3. Submit the phone with detailed examination requirements (i.e., DNA, fingerprint. electronic data recovery). It should be noted that not all fingerprint enhancement methods will be used, because of the potential for damaging the electronic memory.
4. The phone will then be examined for security measures such as PIN. If a PIN is in place, the OIC will be informed and will need to apply for a PUK from the service provider. To obtain the PUK, the OIC must contact his or her force's single point of contract

(SPOC), who will require certain information from the phone and from the SIM card.

Legal Issues

Title III and the Electronic Communications Privacy Act (ECPA)

Under Title III and the ECPA, there appear to be two main legal points that relate to cellular phone analysis:

1. The Federal Wire Tapping Act: Because a cell phone is a device capable of receiving aural, or voice, communications and because part of that communication travels along a wire, it falls under Title III.
2. Stored data: Because a cellular device can hold e-mail, SMS, MMS, graphics, etc., it also falls under the ECPA.

Issue 1: Federal Wire Tapping Act

The Federal Omnibus Crime Control and Safe Streets Act of 1968, also known as the Federal Wire Tapping Act, prohibits interception of wire, oral and electronic communications (see 18 U.S.C. §§ 2510-2520). This act also creates criminal liability for any person who "intentionally intercepts, endeavors to intercept, or procures any other person to intercept or endeavor to intercept, any wire, oral, or electronic communication." See 18 U.S.C. § 2511(1).

Exceptions

There is one exception to the wiretapping rule, and it is designed for corporate environments. The act provides that there is no violation where one of the parties (i.e., the employee) has given prior consent to have a communication intercepted. See 18 U.S.C. § 2511 (2) (d).

Issue 2: Stored Data

The ECPA regulates how the government can obtain stored account information from network service providers, such as ISPs. Data acquired through providers in reference to cell phone data traffic falls under ECPA. The Patriot Act created some exemptions within the ECPA which are listed in the next section.

Exceptions

The following exceptions apply:

- Interception pursuant to a § 2518 court order.
- The "consent" exception, § 2511(2)(c)-(d).
- The "provider" exception, § 2511(2)(a)(i).
- The "computer trespasser" exception, § 2511(2)(i).
- The "extension telephone" exception, § 2510(5)(a).
- The "inadvertently obtained criminal evidence" exception, § 2511(3)(b)(iv).
- The "accessible to the public" exception, § 2511(2) (g) (i)

Law Enforcement Questions

If you seize a cell phone pursuant to a court order that has e-mail or other data stored on it, can you legally search or retrieve the data? *Answer:* Check with your local DA/ASUA, but according to Title III, it should be okay. Consider Title III. Consider ECPA.

Private Sector Questions

As a private practitioner, can you seize and search an employee's cell phone?

Answer: Essentially, this depends on the company policies that are in place. The courts do not have a definitive answer on this topic. It is all based on whether the handset information or the information the provider stores is allowed to be accessed by the company, based on its policies.

Do you need a warrant?

Answer: Yes, as it is better to be safe; however, it is still based on the individual company policy.

Bibliography

Beach, N., Handheld Security: A Layered Approach, SANS Institute, June 2001.
Casey, E., *Handbook of Computer Crime Investigation: Forensic Tools and Technology*, Academic Press, San Diego, CA, October 2001.
Gray, P., Mobile Phone Hacking Expected to Spread, ZDNet, February 2003.
Kistner, T., HomePlug Poised to Ride WiFi's Coattails, *Network World*, January 2003.
Lau, D., A Whole New World for the 21st Century, SANS Institute, March 2001.

Lettice, J., Al-Qaeda Boss Confused Phone SIM with Cloaking Device, The Register, May 2005.

McCue, A., Cyber Cops Get Forensic Code, Silicon.com, September 2003.

Montcalm, E., How to Avoid Ethical and Legal Issues In Wireless Network Discovery, SANS Institute, 2003.

National Institute of Standards and Technology, Cell Phone Forensic Tools, http://www.nist.gov/.

National Institute of Standards and Technology, Computer Forensics Tool Testing (CFTT) Project, http://www.cftt.nist.gov/.

Oudot, L., Wireless Honeypot Trickery, SecurityFocus, February 2004.

PDAStreet.com, PDA Security 101, Jupitermedia Corporation, 2003.

Poulsen, K., Wi-Fi Honeypots a New Hacker Trap, SecurityFocus, July 2002.

Sundgot, J., Palm OS Forensics, infoSync World, January 2002.

U.S. Department of Justice, Computer Crime and Intellectual Property Section (CCIPS) of the Criminal Division of the DOJ: http://www.cybercrime.gov/.

U.S. Secret Service, Best Practices For Seizing Electronic Evidence http://www.ustreas.gov/usss/electronic_evidence.html.

Van Natta Jr., D. and Butler, D., Terror Network Was Tracked by Cellphone Chips, *International Herald Tribune*, Thursday, March 4, 2004.

Chapter 5

The Wireless Future

Any sufficiently advanced technology is indistinguishable from magic.

Arthur C. Clarke

Nothing changes so quickly as yesterday's vision of the future.

Richar d Corliss

Each generation has a defining technology — the baby boomers were defined by the television ... We will have a cohort of people around the world who have mobile devices giving them togetherness. And we can expect this identification to have certain consequences for how we constitute and carry ourselves politically.

Howar d Rheingold, Futur ologist

Introduction

One of the fundamental rules of any investigation is that nothing happens in a vacuum, and wireless forensics is no different. Technology is progressing so fast that it tests even the most talented of investigators. This chapter will hopefully help prepare you for what you can expect to see in the future, and therefore will have to know or understand later. It's not enough to forensically know the technology; you also have to know where it's being used and why. So, some parts of this chapter deal with specific technologies, and others deal with emerging trends.

As all of this mobile technology develops, changes, and integrates itself into our everyday lives, remember that what we use for tools, criminals will use as weapons. Forensic investigators constantly have to keep in mind the smartest potential suspect. This chapter will provide you with some interesting new information and ideas that will help you stay ahead of the game, in the field and in the laboratory.

Some of this technology is only listed to create awareness of some of the new ways in which wireless technology is being used. I came across an interesting line in a novel I was reading the other day that described technology as being one small step behind imagination. I stopped reading for a moment to ponder the profound truth of that simple statement. As I describe these technologies, I will do my best, where possible, to illustrate where new sources of evidence may appear as a result of their adoption by the marketplace and society.

New Twists

Wearable Computers

Most of us have been hearing about wearable computers in *Wired Magazine* for years, and thanks to the wireless revolution it seems some are emerging in the marketplace. One item that caught my attention was the Motorola-Burton wireless sportswear (Figure 5.1), which is a new line of outerwear that uses interactive cell phone and music technology in snowboarding jackets and helmets.

These coats will have a control unit with caller ID, an on–off power button, voice dial, battery meter, and MP3 player operation. Stereo speakers are built into the jacket's hood and a microphone is embedded near the collar. The control unit, speakers, and microphone will be removable for washing and can be reattached afterward. The helmet and hat will have a Bluetooth-enabled MP3 player and Bluetooth connection to a wireless cell phone.

The potential for this type of integration is already going beyond sportswear. Levi's is currently creating jeans designed to carry an iPod. This shift is a big indicator of what is yet to come. Digital devices are becoming fashion items. It will be interesting to see all the permutations and combinations just this type of integration will create.

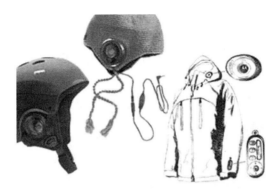

Figure 5.1   Motorola-Burton wireless sportswear.

Radio Frequency Identification (RFID)

As I outlined in Chapter 3, RFID technology employs a tag that is made up of a microchip with an antenna, and a reader with an antenna. The reader sends out radio frequency (RF) waves that form a magnetic field when they join with the antenna on the RFID tag. The chip in the RFID tag sends information back to the reader in the form of RF waves. The RFID reader converts the new waves into digital information. The year 2005 is being viewed as RFID's year; this year we will see this technology break out in whole new ways. A couple that are under development and being used now are discussed in the following subsections.

Grocery Shopping

In the supermarket of the future, shopping carts will be fitted with a personal shopping assistant (PSA) — a pen-and-tablet computer that allows customers to scan products and pay via an automated checkout, removing the need to pack and then unpack from the cart at a checkout counter. The PSA will also automatically tally your grocery total and debit the amount from your bank account as you leave the supermarket.

This process will not only benefit the shopper, but the store as well. When products fitted with RFID tags are moved from the shelves to the customer's shopping cart, staff will be alerted to restock items. This can help ensure that a store is never out of stock of a particular item because it can be replenished almost immediately. RFID will also reduce theft of products and allow for more precise tracking of expiration dates on fresh foods.

Figure 5.2   ShotCode object.

Nightclubs

Currently in a couple of nightclubs in Miami, VIP patrons have RFID tags surgically implanted in their arms. This allows for easier tracking, servicing, and billing of these clients while they are in the club. Although clearly a lifestyle choice, this also allows for unmatched convenience with respect to timeliness of service and payment of tabs or bills as no ID, cash, or credit cards are required.

ShotCode

Using the ShotCode Platform (Figure 5.2) from OP3, you can use your mobile phone to easily interact with computers of all shapes and sizes no matter what you're doing or where you are. Your phone becomes your own all-in-one mouse, keyboard, storage device, and authentication system.

How Does The ShotCode Platform Work?

The ShotCode reader runs on a mobile phone and performs real-time image processing to detect the ShotCode. Next, once the ShotCode image is found it is shown in the phone display where the data encoded in the tag, including relative orientation, position, and size, is transmitted via Bluetooth to a nearby computer. The ShotCode temporarily turns a mobile phone into a universal pointing device, personal display, and keyboard.

Features of the ShotCode Platform

■ Cost: Content providers won't need to run the risk of installing expensive touch screens, which could be vandalized or broken. Instead, the display can be protected, and the consumers use their own technology (their phones) to interact with them.

■ Personalization: ShotCode allows for applications that automatically personalize themselves as different users interact with them.

■ Billing: Mobile phone providers are starting to provide integrated billing services on mobile phones, which make for easy online transactions. ShotCode technology can also integrate billing into mobile applications.

■ Privacy: ShotCodes allow user interface elements to be pushed to the user's phone, allowing for extra privacy. Sensitive data can be entered on the phone, which is not possible with a public screen.

■ Paper interfaces: ShotCode can be printed onto a card, piece of paper, poster, etc., and the phone will translate the information.

Figure 5.3 shows how concert tickets can be purchased using ShotCode objects.

Grafedia

Grafedia, created by John Geraci, is a hyperlinked word, written on a physical surface that is linked to a file online. In essence, it is a tangible hyperlink; text is even written in blue and underlined. The interesting thing about Grafedia is that it can be written anywhere — on walls, streets, sidewalks, Coke bottles, people, etc. It works in much the same way as ShotCode (see previous subsection) in that viewers "click" on Grafedia hyperlinks with their cell phones, then use that word/hyperlink with @grafedia.net added on to get access to the digital content behind the link. This digital content can be a picture, a video, a sound clip, and so on (Figure 5.4).

A great deal can be done with Grafedia because every surface could be a potential Web page. For the casual user it can be used for leaving messages for friends, or creating dialogs in public places. I found Grafedia particularly interesting because it is also a form of steganography. Steganography is the art of hidden communication whereby a message is quite literally "hiding in plain sight." And Grafedia is very much meant to be in plain sight.

The aspect that concerns me as an investigator is, What file is the Grafedia link attached to? As investigators this may be something we

Figure 5.3 An illustration of purchasing concert tickets using ShotCode objects.

encounter in the future, perhaps a great deal. If a phone is seized during an investigation and a Grafedia link is discovered on it, the file that the link points to could be of great significance to a case. Or else, it could just as easily be a greeting or a joke. The use of Grafedia is neither good nor bad; my goal is to make you aware of its existence and the potentials of this new variant of communication.

Pervasive Computing and Cultural Shifts

The term *pervasive computing* describes connected computing devices in an environment. Pervasive or ubiquitous computing is a new trend in technology brought about by the convergence of advanced electronic technology, particularly wireless, and the Internet. Pervasive computing

Figure 5.4   Examples of Grafedia.

services for which there was never a market before will begin to appear. These new services will eventually be incorporated into society in such a way that life without them will be unimaginable.

A great example of this is e-mail. What started out as something novel has turned into a critical and indispensable application. The growing abundance of wireless devices, if implemented properly, will in effect act almost as pseudotelepathy. Information that is needed will be updated in real-time or near-real-time. This creates tremendous efficiency; however, the downside is when it stops working, the effects are instant and dramatic.

Pervasive computing will also bring about huge cultural shifts. Think about some of the social etiquette that didn't exist a few years back, but which do today. Etiquette with respect to cell phones is probably the biggest change. To say nothing of how mobile phones have changed how people live, work, and play.

Wireless Shifts and Trends

Tomorrow's use of technology has begun today with our youth. As the children and teens of today grow with the new wireless technology of today, we will begin to see shifts that will have an effect on how we look at and investigate wireless crimes. In its September 2001 report titled "The Wireless Future: A Look at Youth Unplugged," Cheskin Research has identified eight trends that will define current and future wireless innovation in the United States. I found these points to be very telling and insightful and have included a summary of them in the following subsections.

Social Connectivity and Entertainment

These two things will be defining characteristics of wireless devices in the youth market, and will in all probability spill over into the rest of the consumer market. Constant access to friends and entertainment (games, music, and images) are the main things that young people are using mobile devices for. Over time the larger consumer market will follow the behaviors of the younger market.

Young People Will Build Relationships via Wireless Devices

Typically, adults use digital and wireless communications to maintain existing relationships that have been established by other means, typically a face-to-face meeting at some point in time, whether at school, in church, at a party, etc. Although today's youth still meet face to face, the use of digital communications is playing a bigger and bigger role in maintaining these relationships. So much so that virtual relationships, in some instances, are the foundation rather than a supplement. This also results in a venue for teens to use this communication method as a form of exploration, evolving into something more practical, say business uses, as they grow to adulthood.

Multitasking Capabilities Will Flourish

Teens, and even preteens, today have fuller schedules and less time than past generations. As a result of this, they gravitate toward technologies that fit in with this new, busier lifestyle. Whether this multitasking ability is enhanced by technology or it is technology that encourages multitasking, today's youth appreciate the ability to do many things simultaneously. In the future, wireless technologies that support this behavior will certainly have market appeal.

Personal Security and Convenience

Typically, these two factors will be the biggest motivators for first-time mobile phone customers. The first time I gave in and bought a cell phone was for similar reasons, and over time it became invaluable for daily communication, not just for emergencies. Initially, many people acquired a mobile phone for emergency or safety reasons — young adults wanted to feel secure driving in remote locations, and parents wanted to keep track of their kids. Teens, on the other hand, don't view their mobile phones in this way at all. But as E911 mandates take effect and location-based tracking is incorporated into mobile phones, the perception of safety will be reinforced as a part of the device.

Personalization

Just as mass production was one of the calling cards of the Industrial Revolution, personalization is one of the calling cards of the information revolution. Today one size does not fit all, and the personalization of design, function, and interface will be a common expectation. Along with the ability to change mobile phone faceplates and ring tones, consumers will expect their wireless devices to be a personal accessory that reflects their individual tastes and identity.

Gap Fillers

While waiting in a restaurant one day not too long ago, a friend I was with pulled out a new cell phone and began playing a game of some sort. I mentioned that the new phone was a nice one. He thanked me, dismissed the importance of most of the features, and stated that he had bought it for the games it had. I remember thinking that preloaded games were an interesting first choice for features of a cell phone. But it points to the next trend that wireless entertainment and information applications will become favored gap fillers. Short-session gaming, quick-loading applications, and other mobile entertainment and quick-hit information sources will become new electronic pacifiers, freeing people from boredom. This is especially true of teens, who have the innate need for continual stimulation. They will be able to easily satisfy this desire via wireless mobile technology, and this expectation will be maintained as consumers mature.

Convergence

Strategic convergence will define the most successful wireless devices. Applications that complement each other will result in more appealing devices to users. Rather than creating monolithic devices that merge PDAs and mobile phones, successful devices will embody mutually enhancing functions, such as games, which encourage communication in combination with mobile phone and text-messaging capabilities, as mentioned in the previous subsection. Another example will be mobile phones and PDAs with location-sensing technologies for serving up location-specific content.

Entertainment will also drive the development of wireless cross-platform content. Wireless technology will drive the development of particular entertainment experiences that people can access throughout their day and from nearly any device. Although true wireless cross-platform experiences have not yet been realized, they are coming; and entertainment content that takes advantage of limited attention spans and anytime, anywhere mobility will become increasingly popular.

Text Will Rival Voice Communications

Even with the pervasive availability of landline and wireless phones that enable instant, two-way voice communications, young people still frequently communicate with each other via text. There are multiple reasons that make text messaging so compelling to young people:

1. With text messaging and buddy lists, they can immediately broadcast information to a large group of friends simultaneously.

2. Text messaging does not disrupt their current interactions the same way that pausing to make a phone call does. Teens are also protective of their privacy and may enjoy the low-key nature of text-based communications.
3. Text messaging allows for anonymity and convenience of message delivery.
4. Text allows individuals to assume multiple personalities with different groups of friends. Anonymous communication allows for greater personal exploration. "Finding one's self" is a normal aspect of being a teen. Teens and young adults try on new personalities all the time, looking for the right fit.

New Functionalities for Wireless Devices

As wireless devices continue to proliferate and grow in functionality and processing power, we will begin to see new ideas and services that would never have occurred to us before. This is a list of the more interesting ideas that I've seen in the past year; some are purely for entertainment and others could save a life. Some examples include:

- E-books that can be downloaded and read on the screen of a cell phone.
- Jiggle phones, which basically allow you to jiggle the phone in a certain way to dial a particular number rather than having to use the keypad.
- Biodegradable cell phones that grow into sunflowers when planted in the ground.
- GPS functionality — a cell phone that gives you directions.
- Substitutes for lighters during a concert (I actually did this recently at the band's suggestion).
- Amber Alert text messages that are transmitted to all cell phones within a certain geographic area.
- Newer cell phones have MP3-playing capabilities. Apple's iTunes-capable phone is a recent example of this.

The Home Element

Mobile devices — let's use Smartphones as an example — in the future will continue to integrate into your life much in this way. Some of you may be using these technologies already. Consider the following hypothetical scenario:

It's your morning wake-up time and your Smartphone alarm wakes you up. At the same time the Smartphone turns on the lights to your room. You proceed to get showered and dressed; all the while, the Smartphone is updating your calendar and schedule for the day, checking the weather, looking at current traffic conditions, etc.

By the time you've had your first cup of coffee, you are in the mood for news or perhaps some music. The Smartphone now acts as a remote and menu, allowing you to navigate through your choices on satellite TV, radio, or your personal library. You select a favorite playlist and enjoy some music while you get ready to leave. As you move from room to room, the music is transferred to the nearest speakers and lights are dimmed behind you and illuminated in the rooms you enter. As you walk from your house to the car, the phone activates the security system and transfers the playlist you were listening to in your house to your car and resumes the song you were halfway through listening to.

While en route to the office or a meeting, the Smartphone is constantly checking the traffic conditions and the GPS map is rerouting you to your specific destination as efficiently as possible.

While at lunch with a client, you transmit business card information and notes and documents between your phones. And the autopay sensor of the table allows you to transfer the amount for the meal to the restaurant from either a personal bank account or credit card, all through your phone. You take a moment before leaving to watch the latest headlines from CNN, which are being streamed to your Smartphone.

By the end of the day you head home, again with traffic and weather conditions factored into your directions. While en route home, you run a preset program that turns the heat up in the house, starts the sprinkler system in the front yard, and begins filling the bathtub. As you approach your house, the GPS senses your proximity and a signal is sent that automatically opens the garage door. Once out of your car, the alarm senses you are near the door and deactivates the alarm system.

And don't forget, you'll still use the Smartphone to talk to people.

Relationships, Virtual Communities, and Beyond

Dating: How Things Are Changing

I'd like to step back in time approximately 80 years for a moment and discuss a different piece of technology that brought about a huge social and cultural change, namely, the automobile.

Thanks to Henry Ford, car ownership became something of the norm for most middle- and working-class families of the 1920s; this one change had a massive impact on how young men and women met and socialized. It was very different before cars. Before the automobile, dating as people know it now did not exist. Rather, meetings took place at the girl's house under the supervision of a chaperone. With the automobile, a new level of mobility and privacy was introduced into the equation, changing everything. Now boys and girls could meet without parental supervision and the rest is history.

Today, the cell phone is playing a similar role in transforming scoiety.

Text Messages and Social Familiarity

Wireless devices, specifically cell phones with text-messaging capability, have given rise to completely new forms of courting. A recent survey showed that almost 70 percent of text messages are passed between romantic intimates. Whether it be a shy teenager too afraid to approach the object of his or her affection or lusty club patrons straining to type "R U up 4 it?," text messaging has changed the game.

Mobile phones have also become a new way of showing trust and displaying friendship. Teenagers who trust each other enough to borrow their phones, especially when they are not in the same place and unable to see what their phone is being used for, show tremendous trust by today's standards because you don't let just anyone use your phone.

Mobile Phones and Friendships

Mobile phones also help alleviate the feelings of alienation in modem urban life. By providing a means of connection that is anytime, anyplace, anywhere, a spontaneous connection is recreated similar to that enjoyed by a close-knit group in a small rural community. Also, the spontaneity and ease of mobile communications make it much easier to maintain existing friendships. Thanks to buddy lists, it's much easier to keep track of people you want to keep in touch with but might not remember to call as frequently as you'd like to because of the frantic pace of modern life. Mobile phones have also created a much more time-flexible society now that people can phone or text to say they are running late or just leaving.

One point of interest in this category: While I was working with one of the companies in the field of computer forensics, they mentioned that a lot of the devices that they had in-house for testing purposes were purchased from some of the online auction sites. They told me that many of these devices contained the data that was entered by the original owner. That data included phonebooks, text message breakups, and simple shopping lists, additional proof that wireless technology is spreading to every aspect of life.

Positive Effects

You can maintain a near-constant connection with your friends, allowing for much more interaction that would have otherwise not have taken place. Simply put, it is an aid to spontaneity. As 3G and 4G technologies emerge over time and location positioning is included, this feeling of connectedness will only be enhanced.

Negative Effects

Having this type of connectivity will definitely result in a loss of privacy. Especially if a part of the group culture is to stay online all the time. Someone shutting down their phone may be seen as breaking a social rule in some circles. Social prohibitions are breaking down with the use of more and more technology.

Virtual Communities

As we've seen so far, technology facilitates community growth. Before the World Wide Web exploded, communities were already using the Internet for social communication for 20 years, including:

- E-mail
- Automated mailing lists
- BBSs
- Usenet newsgroups
- Chatrooms
- Internet Relay Chat
- Instant messaging
- MUDs (multiuser environments for socializing and game playing)

In 1990 the Web's visual interface made it useful to the nontechnical masses, similar to the way the graphic user interface made the PC useful in the 1980s. Wireless communication from now through the end of this decade will bring everyday users to virtual communities, people who may never use a PC, but are texters or mobile game players.

Mobile communications and virtual communities will each have their own uniquely powerful characteristics. When combined, powerful hybrids are likely to emerge, just as the PC combined with the telephone system to create the Internet. However, before speculating too much about the characteristics of yet-to-be mobile communities, let us look at the individual characteristics of mobile communications and virtual communities; then we'll look at the hybrid, namely, *mobile virtual communities.*

Characteristics of Mobile Communications

■ Organized around existing social networks, meaning people you already know. People call and message people who are already in their address books.

■ Accessible anytime, anywhere, and are always on. The Internet is no longer tied to the PC and wired network, but has spread to a variety of wireless devices.

■ Evolving from text-based communications to text, sound, and graphics-based communications. Custom ringtones and basic graphics for SMS are only the tip of the iceberg.

■ Similar to how people behave in the physical world as well as having a strong impact on how social groups coordinate activities.

Characteristics of Virtual Communities

■ Organized around shared interests: They bring people together who most likely did not know each other before meeting online. Examples of virtual communities are almost limitless; people can communicate about anything, from a shared passion for *Star Trek* to a concern about a disease.

■ Many-to-many media: Virtual communities enable groups of people to communicate with many others. Whether a desktop or wireless device, it is also becoming a printing press, broadcasting station, and place of assembly.

■ Evolution of older text-based methods of communication to text-plus-graphics communications: Web-based media bring online graphics, animations, video, sounds, formatted text, and links into the conversation.

- Worldwide communication: Virtual communities are uncoupled from face-to-face social life in a traditional geographic community. People in virtual communities most often do not live close enough to meet face to face regularly.

Characteristics of Mobile Virtual Communities

- Many-to-many, desktop and mobile, and always on: Mobile virtual community resources are instantly available to people or their software agents wherever they are located, whether they are at their desks, in transit, or at home.
- Used to coordinate actions of group in a geographic area: These actions can be anything from teenagers meeting at the mall, to college students meeting at a club, or activists mobilizing in the street. A good example of this was the 2004 Republican National Convention.
- Feasible in almost any type of environment: Whether it is a gaming world, a social arena, artistic media, business collaboration tools, or political weapons, mobile virtual communities have unique advantages. Mobile virtual communities will start with young people as a form of entertainment and social interaction, and then move to other groups.

Currently in the United States one of the most popular virtual communities is "MySpace"; however, it still has a way to go before becoming a true mobile virtual community. Because cell phone use in Europe is much greater than that in the United States, mobile virtual communities have had a head start there. This head start also provides some interesting insights as to the shape of things to come. An example of a mobile virtual community follows.

Aula

In Helsinki there is a physical and cyber meeting place called Aula. Its creators are seeking to build a social-technical crossroads by linking groups of people together through on-site media in a physical location and through mobile communications to the community members who are not physically present. It's a new form of cyberplace that links the virtual and physical parts of the community.

The community started with around 150 members, who meet both in person and online. They plan to grow by invitation and word of mouth (or word of SMS) and are reserving space at the physical meeting place for future community members to help design the communication area.

Each member uses a RFID tag kept in his or her pocket, purse, or shoe, which makes information accessible to the mobile devices of others in the physical nightclub. Projections and monitors will mix virtual communication with the conversation in the club.

Other similar types of mobile virtual communities exist as well, and more are sure to be created as time goes on.

Hints of Tomorrow

The virtual communities of tomorrow will, first and foremost, generate a tremendous amount of traffic and revenue around the world. Currently, billions of SMS messages are being transmitted every day, and we're just at the beginning of the growth curve.

Second, participants in online communities will remain in continuous contact while crossing multiple platforms, be it desktops or mobile devices. This continuous contact will be used to coordinate group activities in the geographic world. Expect the first communities to be built by 12- to 25-year-olds.

Third, vendors and operators will still create tools and platforms, but the killer apps of the future are going to be more social than technical and will be invented by the users on the street, not engineers.

Vivienne: The Virtual Girlfriend

The software maker Artificial Life of Hong Kong has created a girlfriend for 3G cell phone users. Vivienne is composed of computerized voice synthesis, streaming video, and text messages. For a monthly fee of $6.00 plus cost of airtime, cell phone users can talk to Vivienne any time as well as, buy her virtual gifts, marry her in a virtual ceremony, and even get a virtual mother in law. Vivienne can converse on 35,000 topics and can translate six languages. It will be interesting to see if this subculture takes off. If it does, I also can't help but wonder if Artificial Life will eventually have to introduce a patch to allow for a virtual divorce?

City-Sized HotSpots

Today, Spokane Washington boasts one of the largest deployment of wireless Internet coverage in a U.S. urban area. As I've mentioned previously in this book, Wi-Fi hotspots are popping up everywhere, and this is just the next logical step. What is novel now will be common and indispensable in the next few years. The city of Spokane is designing this network for both public and private access. Private access will be for official business, meter maids writing tickets from a PDA and syncing up with main network, and police officers running license plates or looking up any other necessary information they might need. Public access will be for users to connect anywhere they choose. Currently, users are allowed to connect for 2 hr a day at no charge; the city has a billing plan in the works. Other cities that have created similar wireless environments include Chaska, Minnesota, Corpus Christi, Texas, and Cleveland, Ohio.

Another variant of this theme is called WAG, the Wireless Athens Group, from the University of Georgia. While their hotspot doesn't cover as large an area as Spokane, it does offer some innovative and interesting wireless applications.

Sports

WAG uses wireless to transmit instant replays to PDAs from current or recent baseball games. The stadium will be equipped with a series of cameras each of which a user can access to watch the whole game from a number of vantage points. Another WAG prototype will allow a devoted fan to beam a beer and snack order to a concession stand computer where your food can be prepared and delivered to you.

Music

Most college towns are known for having a large number of bands playing at local bars and coffeehouses. For someone interested in finding a band to suit his or her taste, and not wanting to pay the cover at every bar to find out, music samples could be made available, as well as links to band Web sites or even live stage broadcasts.

Dining

In this wireless environment, people rushing to pick up lunch could key in their order and transmit it to the restaurant or deli of their choice, pay via an online account, and have their food ready to go by the time they walked the three blocks to get to the café.

Commerce

These innovative uses of wireless technology are certainly exciting and bring a whole new level of interaction in a local environment, but similar ideas can be applied on a much bigger scale. There is an interesting book by Thomas Friedman called *The Lexus and the Olive Tree* that describes globalization and the business changes resulting from it. Wireless technology will play a huge part in that. Rather than limiting a user's choices to instant replay shots or ordering lunch, wireless networks could, and will, be set up to allow anyone, anywhere in by getting their product or service online and to the world.

RFID

RFID has the potential to be used in almost any product, anywhere, and it's changing the way businesses serve their customers. RFID enables consumers to pay for gas, food, and other items at the checkout counter with a wave of their hand. Now, customers do not even need a wallet; they will be able to use their phones or an RFID keychain to pay for their purchases.

This benefit not only allows for quick purchases but is also enabling businesses to learn more about their customers' buying patterns. Companies can use this information to individualize services for each customer, which will create customer loyalty, lower costs, and increase profits. Along with many other applications, this technology can also be used to allow personnel access, ticketing, pay-TV, gaming, and payphone applications.

New Types of Wireless Information and Trade

Ericsson has a new device out called the *Blip*, which is a tiny gadget that allows anyone to broadcast information to Bluetooth devices such as mobile phones and PDAs within a 10 m radius. Ericsson hopes it will kickstart the world of wireless information and trade. Some examples of where and how the Blip will be used are listed in the following text:

- A Blip in a clothes shop could let window-shoppers find out whether the clothes they liked were in stock, even when the shop was closed. A shopper could reserve the item they liked and come back and collect it later.
- A Blip at a bus stop could tell passengers how much longer they needed to wait for a particular bus.
- And a Blip in a town hall could tell residents about plans for a new bypass and address with their responses to the plan.

The Universal Wireless Payment Standard

Today the Infrared Financial Messaging (IrFM) *Point and Pay* profile is a wireless, proximity payment standard now available to the public. IR technology is well suited to transmitting wireless payment information confidentially utilizing cell phones and PDAs. The technology can be used to conduct transactions between card readers, ATMs, gas pumps, toll booths, etc.

Security and Privacy: RFID Passports

The Concept

Since 9/11, the Bush administration and the Department of Homeland Security have wanted the world to standardize on machine-readable passports. Future, and some current, U.S. passports will include an embedded computer chip. Not surprisingly, the chip will give the passport the ability to contain much more information than a simple machine-readable string of code and will allow passport officials to quickly and easily read that information. That's the good part. However, the Bush administration is advocating RFID chips for both U.S. and foreign passports, and that's a very bad thing because RFID chips can be read from a distance, meaning a receiving device can "talk" to the chip remotely, without any need for physical contact, and get whatever information is on it.

The Concerns and Consequences

Passport officials see this as a way to download all the information on the chip simply by bringing it near the reader; the problem is that RFID chips can be read by any reader, not just the ones at passport control. To put it another way, anyone carrying an RFID passport is broadcasting his or her identity.

This means that the person with an RFID passport is continuously broadcasting his name, nationality, age, address, and any other information on the chip. It also means that anyone with a reader can grab that information right out of the air without the passport holder's knowledge or consent. Potentially, a kidnapper or a terrorist will be able to easily and covertly select Americans out of a crowd. Suddenly, the RFID passport has become a very clear threat to both privacy and personal safety.

Latest Developments

In spite of criticism by civil libertarians and computer security professionals, in 2006 the U.S. government began issuing these passports to a group of diplomats with a scheduled national rollout of October 2006. Unfortunately, the encryption on these passports was broken in only a couple of hours, allowing access to the holder's digitized fingerprint, photograph, and all other data on the passport. Work is being done to strengthen the encryption, which unfortunately will only be a temporary fix at best.

Entertainment and Travel

Television

Texas Instruments recently unveiled a new chip that will allow cell phones to receive digital television broadcasts over a wireless network. The new chip will combine the functions of a TV tuner, signal demodulator, and channel decoder in a single device to bring television feed to mobile phones. The chip is designed to display 30 frames per second, twice what some of the best phones are capable of displaying today.

24 Conspiracy

Not wasting a moment before putting this new technology to use, Twentieth Century Fox studio is producing a unique series of 1-min dramas based on its hit show *24* exclusively for a new high-speed wireless service being offered by Vodafone PLC. The cellular version of the *24* series, titled *24 Conspiracy*, will be based on characters from the television show. Vodafone began airing the 1-min *mobisodes* in January 2005, in the United Kingdom, coinciding with the start of the fourth season of the show.

The Adult Market

According to a report by the Yankee Group, if these new mobile video services take off, the television industry may be offering adult content on mobile devices. The report went on to predict that by 2008, wireless adult content will be a $1 billion market. Considering that pornography has had a tremendous impact on technology in the past — the VCR, pay-per-view, and video over the Internet — it is quite possible that it may jump-start mobile video as well.

Music

Verizon has a service called V-Cast that allows for some remarkable flexibility with music and video through the cell phone. V-Cast essentially turns a mobile phone into a music player by synchronizing music that the user already owns and allows the user to purchase music from the online store either using the phone or PC.

Sports

Walt Disney Co. and ESPN are working in collaboration to launch a new brand of sports cast over mobile phones. The goal of this venture would be to stream audio and video media as well as graphics and news to sports fans, wireless devices.

Gambling

In July 2005 Nevada was the first state to approve the use of wireless, handheld gambling devices at its hotel casinos. Under this new law, the devices can only be used in public areas of casinos that have 100 or more slot machines and that offer at least one other gambling game. The devices would be barred from hotel rooms and other private areas, and they won't be available overnight.

Travel

Wireless technologies will eventually be combined with location-based technologies, creating a revolutionary new relationship between physical places and zones of information. Essentially, this will allow all available information about a place to be assembled and integrated at that place, at which point it can be accessed by wireless devices by locals and travelers alike. Eventually, the impact of these technologies will help dictate how urban architecture and public places are designed and created.

A variant of this service that Japan is piloting consists of lending foreign tourists PDAs with travel information and translation services as part of a tourism promotion scheme. The government plan is designed to find ways of making Japan more attractive to foreign tourists, who are often put off by the country's language barrier.

Agriculture

GPS technology and Wi-Fi networks are helping make agriculture and farming more efficient and productive. GPS receivers placed on the top of tractors communicate with a computer inside the tractor that memorizes the coordinates of the field and guides the tractor over the same path — for tilling, planting, spraying and harvesting. This allows farms to operate on a 24/7 basis if they so desire.

HealthCare

Wireless devices will help create a billion dollar market for the medical services that allow doctors to monitor patients remotely — services that depend on the ability of network operators to offer a fast and reliable unbroken connection. The solution uses a mobile handset combined with an always-on connection to monitor the patients' condition more effectively and detect early signs of, for example, an asthmatic attack. Whereas current asthma treatments usually rely on after-the-fact information, the mobile device can provide real-time information on patient health, allowing the asthma to be treated more proactively and, ultimately saving time and resources. An example is given in the following text:

> In countries such as China, where information is strictly controlled, the mobile phone will probably pose the biggest threat to that control. A great example of this happened in 2002. At that time there were over 200 million mobile phone users; right at the same time a media and political blackout was in effect about the existence of an outbreak of sudden acute respiratory syndrome (SARS). The first information that the Chinese people got about the virus was through their mobile phones. On 8 February, a text-message, "There is a fatal flu in Guangzhou," was resent 40 million times, 41 million times the following day, and 45 million times the day after that. As a direct result of this

rampant texting, the media, and ultimately, the Chinese government were forced to admit the existence of the virus. A footnote to this story: the mayor of Beijing and the country's health minister were promptly fired for their part in the cover-up. (Harkin, J., Mobilisation: The Growing Public Interest in Mobile Technology, *Demos*, June 2003)

Noppa

Another way that wireless technology will benefit the health industry is when it is used in concert with other technologies to create a whole new product. The Finnish government is researching a project that combines cell phones, wireless Internet, global positioning, and voice technology to help the blind move freely in cities. The project is called Noppa.

The Noppa guidance system will work with 3G phones and will be coupled with GPS receivers. The device will be able to tell the users where they are, how to get to where they want to go, and will give directions and explain obstacles by voice. Noppa will also be hooked up to municipal databases to warn users about construction areas when giving directions, as well as inform about train, streetcar, and bus timetables, and possible delays.

The core system contains speech recognition and speech synthesis software that relays requests and replies. These functions will be performed by a much more powerful central server, not the mobile device itself.

VeriChip

Currently approved by the Food and Drug Administration, Applied Digital Solutions is marketing an implantable RFID chip that is used for storing medical information. The VeriChip itself contains no medical records, just codes that can be scanned and downloaded in a doctor's office or hospital. With that code, doctors can unlock part of a centrally located, and hopefully secure, database that holds the patient's medical information. The electronic database, not the chip, would be updated with each medical visit.

Camera Phones

Researchers in Switzerland have discovered that camera phones are quite effective when used to help diagnose patients in remote locations. The University Hospital of Geneva looked at leg ulcers from 52 different patients; some were seen in person, and others were examined only from photos taken with a camera phone. What they discovered was a remarkably high agreement between the doctors who had seen the patient in person and those who saw the image. This system could work wonders for both the hospital and the patient, saving time and money on transportation when it perhaps isn't necessary.

Disaster Recovery

After Hurricane Katrina wreaked such extensive damage in the Gulf Coast in August 2005, ad hoc wireless networks were being created and used to allow survivors to make VoIP (Voice-over-IP) phone calls to speak to or track down loved ones. Almost immediately thereafter companies began donating wireless equipment and technical talent to allow for more extensive and stable wireless networks to aid in the relief effort. In disaster recovery efforts, communication is always one of the biggest challenges. With wireless, a communications infrastructure can be set up very quickly.

Education

Another huge benefit of wireless technology, specifically wireless LAN technology, is that it now provides ubiquitous computing for students ranging from first-graders to graduate students. Another possibly bigger benefit is illustrated by a joint venture between the South African government and Motorola. The Ulwazi E-learning project consists of using wireless broadband to allow students and teachers in five schools across the country to talk using whiteboards, microphones, and the Web. In South Africa, one or two teachers are typically responsible for 50 to 100 students. This new technology allows schools to share teachers and resources so more students have access to more material.

Military

The U.S.–U.K. assault on Iraq can be called the first wirelessly enabled war. Tanks and personnel carriers equipped with GPS allowed U.S. Army officers to watch the real-time pictures of the unfolding war. A device called Warlock was used to jam signals from mobile phones, garage door openers, and other remote-control devices that were being used to detonate car bombs. The officers on the front say that without these technologies, casualties would have been much higher. Thanks to this technology, the Pentagon estimates that some 40 percent of improvised explosive devices are now discovered before rebels set them off.

Conclusion

I hope this chapter has given you some insights and food for thought on what is here, and what is yet to come. Some of these ideas and technologies may only be fads and pass quickly into history; others may evolve and become driving forces in commerce, society, and in the commission and prevention of crimes. My goal was to give you something new to think about; to create an awareness that will cause you to look in places you might not have otherwise considered, because whether we like it or not these changes are coming.

Bibliography

Botelho, G., The Next Information Age, CNN, October 2003.

Cheskin, The Wireless Future: A Look At Youth Unplugged, 2001.

Commission for Communication Regulation, Future Mobile Applications, June 2003.

Erfanian, J., Future of Wireless Communications: Trends, Technologies, Services, and Landscape for Innovations, IEEE Communication Society, November 2003.

Friedman, T., *The Lexus and The Olive Tree*, Anchor Publishing, May 2000.

Geary, J., Brain Power, *Time*, June 2001.

George, L., Homing In on a Wireless Future, CNN, 2001.

Harkin, J., Mobilisation: The Growing Public Interest in Mobile Technology, *Demos*, June 2003.

Infrared Data Association, IrFM Point and Pay, www.irda.org, January, 2003.

Johansson, O. and Blennow, M., A Wireless Future — At What Cost?, Göteborgs-Posten, December 2000.

Lemon, S., WiMax Promises Broadband Breakthrough, *PCWorld*, October 2003.

Mpulse, Identification in a Mobile Landscape, December 2003.

Palen, L. Going Wireless: Behavior and Practice of New Mobile Phone Users, Department of Computer Science, University of Colorado, Boulder, December 2000.

Rheingold, H., Mobile Virtual Communities, *The Feature*, July 2003.

Salzman, M. and Youngs, E., Going Wireless: Behavior and Practice of New Mobile Phone Users, U.S. West Advanced Technologies, Design, and Usability Group, Boulder, CO, December 2000.

Terdiman, D., Hold the Phone on Mobile Gambling, *Wired News*, April 2004.

Wireless Watch, WiMax Trials Speed Up, *The Register*, September 2003.

Glossary

1G Refers to the first generation of mobile telephony systems. These were analog, circuit-switched, and only carried voice traffic. The 1G phones were less secure and prone to interference where the signal was weak. Analog systems include Advanced Mobile Phone System (AMPS), Nordic Mobile Telephone (NMT), and Extended TACS (ETACS).

1xEV-DO (1x Evolution Data Only) 1xEV-DO, also referred to as CDMA2000, is a 3G mobile standard that delivers a peak data rate of 2.4 Mbps using just 1.25 MHz of spectrum. It is intended to provide powerful data transmission capabilities for mobile phones. This upgrade to CDMA2000 requires a second 1.25 MHz channel that is used exclusively for data. Most CDMA2000 network operators are expected to combine 1x and 1xEV-DO channels in their systems to provide varying voice and data capacities as required by customer demand.

1xEV-DV (1X Evolution Data and V oice) 1xEV-DV (CDMA2000) is a 3G mobile standard that promises to provide data-rate speeds of 1.2 Mbps for mobile users, with peak data speeds up to 5.2 Mbps for stationary users. This standard will integrate voice and simultaneous high-speed packet data multimedia services.

1xR TT 1xRTT (CDMA2000), the next generation of standard CDMA, offers between 1.5 and 2 times the number of voice channels as a standard CDMA system, peak data rates of 153 kbps, and backward compatibility with cdmaOne networks. 1x stands for one times 1.25 MHz carrier, as used in 2G CDMA. RTT stands for radio transmission technology. CDMA2000 1x is 21 times more efficient than analog cellular and 4 times more efficient than TDMA networks.

2G Refers to the second generation of mobile telephony systems that use digital encoding. 2G networks support high-bit-rate voice, limited data communications, and different levels of encryption. 2G networks include Global System for Mobile Telecommunications (GSM), Time Division Multiple Access (TDMA), and Code Division Multiple Access (CDMA).

2.5G 2.5G is the interim improvement to 2G. 2.5G adds features such as packet-switched connections and improved data rates. 2.5G networks include Enhanced Data Rates for GSM (EDGE) and Generalized Packet Radio System (GPRS). These networks support Wireless Access Protocol (WAP), Multimedia Messaging Service (MMS), Short Message Service (SMS), mobile games, and search and directory.

2-in-1 Handset A subscriber handset acting as a remote handset to a base unit, which provides a network connection.

3G Refers to the third generation of mobile systems. 3G provides high-speed data transmissions of 144 kbps and higher. 3G will support multimedia applications such as full-motion video, videoconferencing, and Internet access.

3GPP The 3rd Generation Partnership Project, a grouping of international standards bodies, operators, and vendors with the responsibility of standardizing the Wideband Code Division Multiple Access (WCDMA)-based members of the IMT-2000 family.

3GPP2 The counterpart of 3GPP with responsibility for standardizing the CDMA2000-based members of the IMT-2000 family. 3GPP2 is headed by the American National Standards Institute (ANSI).

3GSM 3GSM is another name for the W-CDMA 3G standard.

3GSP (3G Service Pr ovider) A mobile operator that has a 3G license to provide 3G services to customers.

3xEV-DO/DV (3X Evolution Data Only/Data and V oice) Enhanced versions of 1XEV-DO or 1xEV-DV with three channels of data/voice. The details of 3xEV are unclear, and this service is likely to become operational only several years later.

8PSK Stands for "Octantal Phase Shift Keying," which is an air interface enhancement that makes more user bandwidth available by using a higher-level modulation scheme.

802.1X The Institute of Electrical and Electronics Engineers (IEEE) standard for access control for wireless and wired LANs. 802.1x provides a means of authenticating and authorizing devices to attach to a LAN port.

802.11 802.11, known as Wi-Fi, defines standards for wireless LANs (WLANs). WLANs provide half-duplex (not simultaneous bidirectional) connections that are shared, not switched. IEEE 802.11a and 802.11b and 802.11g define different physical layer standards for WLANs, and the 802.11 standard offers no provisions for interoperability between these physical layers. The Wi-Fi Alliance (www.wi-fi.org), previously known as WECA, promotes the standard, tests products for interoperability, and awards the "Wi-Fi" mark to those that pass. Security is one of the Wi-Fi Alliance's biggest issues with wireless LANs.

802.11a   802.11a operates at 5 GHz and provides data rates up to 54 Mbps using Orthogonal Frequency Division Multiplexing (OFDM) modulation, like European digital TV. 802.11a has four, eight, or more channels, depending on the country, and supports a maximum of 24 unique connections per access point, far more than the three connections supported by 802.11b and 802.11g. Compared to 802.11b, 802.11a offers higher theoretical throughput, more available frequencies, avoiding multipath echoes, but shorter range. Actual throughput at typical operating distances is often only 1 to 2 Mbps.

802.11b   802.11b operates in the 2.4 GHz band and supports a maximum theoretical data rate of 11 Mbps, with average throughput falling in the 4 to 6 Mbps range. 802.11b uses Direct Sequence Spread Spectrum (DSMM) modulation. Most WLANs deployed today use 802.11b technology. 802.11b supports a maximum of three unique connections per access point, and 802.11b-compatible products were the first ones to become available in the United States. Bluetooth devices, 2.4 GHz cordless phones, and even microwave ovens are sources of interference for 802.11b networks. Minimizing interference can be difficult because 802.11b uses only three nonoverlapping channels.

802.11e   Provides quality of service (QoS) that will be important for voice and multimedia transmission by describing error correction and bandwidth management to be used in 802.11a and 802.11b. This is critical for delay-sensitive applications such as Voice-over-Wireless-IP (VoWIP). There are two versions: Enhanced Digital Control Access (EDCA) mode, called Wireless Multimedia Extensions (WME), and HCF Coordinated Channel Access (HCCA), also known as Wireless Scheduled Multimedia (WSM). WME defines eight levels of access priority and provides more access to higher-priority packets than to lower-priority packets but provides no bandwidth guarantees, and is probably best suited for one-way audio. HCCA is a polled access method that includes WME and provides guaranteed bandwidth scheduling reservations.

802.11g   802.11g is an extension to 802.11b and operates in the 2.4 GHz band, but it will deliver data rates from 6 to 54 Mbps. 802.11g offers the throughput of 802.11a with the backward compatibility of 802.11b. 802.11g products are expected to have RF interference problems similar to 802.11b. 802.11g will have up to three non-overlapping channels. Its backward compatibility with 802.11b means that when a mobile 802.11b device joins an 802.11g access point, all connections on that point slow down to 802.11b speeds.

802.11h Defines processes that 802.11a systems can use to comply with International Telecommunications Union (ITU) recommendations for avoiding conflict with other users of the 5 GHz spectrum, such as military radar systems. These processes include Dynamic Frequency Selection (DFS), for using channels uniformly and avoiding channel conflict; and Transmit Power Control (TPC), for reducing the radio transmit power of Wi-Fi devices.

802.11i A standard approved in June 2004 that provides security enhancements based on WPA, TKIP, and AES. AES is the new U.S. Government data encryption standard and is far more secure than WPA, the previous 802.11 security mechanism. 802.11i incorporates key management and authentication, and may eventually replace WEP and WPA for WLAN security. The Wi-Fi Alliance planned to start certifying 802.11i products in September 2004 under the name WPA2, indicating that the security is enhanced relative to WPA.

802.11n A standard in development to provide WLANs with at least 100 Mbps throughput, measured at the interface between the 802.11 media access control (MAC) and higher layers. 802.11n is expected to be based on Multiple-Input Multiple-Output technology (MIMO).

802.11p A working group that is developing extensions applicable to automobiles in the 5.9 GHz spectrum allocated to vehicles. Considerations include better security, mobile operation, identification, and a more sophisticated handoff system. 802.11p will be the basis of Dedicated Short Range Communications (DSRC), a system intended for communications from one vehicle to another or to a roadside network.

802.15 An Institute of Electrical and Electronics Engineers (IEEE) standard for Wireless Personal Area Networks (WPANs). It has four subsets:

- 802.15.1 (Bluetooth) is a standard defining wireless networking with a 1 Mbps data rate that operates at 2.4 GHz over a range of up to 10 m. The 1 Mbps data rate is a serious limitation that prevents this technology from acting as a USB replacement except for very-low-speed peripherals such as keyboards.
- 802.15.2 deals with recommended practices on how 802.11 WLANs and 802.15 WPANs can coexist in the 2.4 GHz band. It is mainly working on the interference problem between Bluetooth and 802.11.
- 802.15.3 deals with higher-speed WPANs from 10 to 55 Mbps at distances less than 10 m.

■ 802.15.4 (ZigBee) deals with simple, low-cost, low-speed WPANs. Data ranges from 2 to 200 kbps and uses Direct Sequence Spread Spectrum (DSSS) modulation in the 2.4 and 915 MHz ranges.

802.16 — W iMax (W orldwide Inter operability for Micr owave Access) This IEEE standard defines broadband wireless for the metropolitan area to address the "last mile" problem of providing connections to individual homes and offices. The initial version operates in the 10 to 66 GHz frequency band with line-of-sight towers to fixed locations. The 802.16a extension does not require line-of-sight transmission and allows use of lower 2 to 11 GHz frequencies for both fixed and portable applications. 802.16a claims up to a 30 mi range and 75 Mbps data transfer that can support thousands of users, plus improved latency and per-connection QoS features. 802.16a provides selectable channel bandwidths from 1.25 to 20 MHz with up to 16 logical subchannels. A typical cell radius is probably 3 to 5 mi. WiMax was planned from the beginning to be compatible with European standards. The WiMax Forum of over 100 companies was established in 2001 by Nokia, Ensemble Communications, and the Orthogonal Frequency Division Multiplexing Forum and now works to promote deployment of broadband wireless access networks based on 802.16 and to certify product interoperability. 802.16d will update 802.16a to incorporate the many amendments associated with it. 802.16e, planned for late 2005, will feature regional roaming for broadband wireless applications up to 15 Mbps with a typical cell radius of 1 to 3 mi.

A

A5/1/2/3/8X Encryption algorithms for GSM networks.

Access Burst (AB) Used for random access and characterized by a longer guard period to allow for burst transmission from a mobile station (MS) that does not know the correct timing advance when first contacting a network.

Access Grant Channel (AGCH) Used for downlink only. The Base Transceiver Station (BTS) allocates a Traffic Channel (TCH) or Stand-Alone Dedicated Control Channel (SDCCH) to the mobile station (MS), which allows it access to the network.

Access Point (AP) An access point can be either a piece of hardware or software that connects wireless users to a wired LAN. This typically acts like a bridge. Access points use the MAC address to forward packets. Wireless devices, such as laptops or PDAs, connect to a wired LAN via an AP, which is a hardware device or a computer's software that acts as a communication hub. APs provide heightened wireless security and extend the physical range of a wireless LAN.

Adaptive Dif fer ential Pulse Code Modulation (ADPCM)   A form of voice compression that typically uses 32 kbps.

Adaptive Fr equency Hopping (AFH)   Adaptive Frequency Hopping improves resistance to radio interference from other unrelated communication devices or from microwave ovens or cordless phones. For example, when two Bluetooth devices connect under normal circumstances, they establish a frequency hopping scheme across 79 frequency channels in the 2.4 GHz ISM band. AFH aims to improve the performance of a Bluetooth connection by identifying channels with high error rates and excluding the use of these channels.

Adaptive Multirate codec (AMR)   A coder/decoder that was developed in 1999 for use in Global System for Mobile Telecommunications (GSM) networks, the AMR has been adopted by 3rd Generation Partnership Project for 3G.

Ad Hoc Mode An 802.11 WLAN configuration where clients communicate directly with other clients without the use of an AP.

Advanced Communications T   echnologies and Services (ACTS)   A European technology initiative.

Advanced Encryption Standar   d (AES) AES is the U.S. government's next-generation cryptography algorithm, which will replace Data Encryption Standard (DES) and Triple DES (3DES).

Advanced Mobile Phone System (AMPS)   An analog mobile phone technology used in North and South America and in around 35 other countries. AMPS operates in the 800 MHz band using Frequency Division Multiple Access (FDMA) technology.

A-Inter face The interface between the Mobile Switching Center (MSC) and Basic Service Set (BSS) in a GSM network.

Air Inter face In a mobile phone network it is the radio transmission path between the base station and the mobile terminal.

Air Jacking See war jacking.

Amber Alert   A method of kidnap recovery (and deterrence) whereby law enforcement officers inform broadcast media of critical details, including a description of the suspect and the vehicle. Radio and TV stations typically use the Emergency Alert System to interrupt their programming with the emergency information.

American National Standar   ds Institute (ANSI) A nonprofit, U.S. organization that does not carry out standardization work but reviews the work of standards bodies and assigns them category codes and numbers.

Analog The representation of information by a continuously variable physical quantity such as voltage.

ANSI-136 See Digital-AMPS (D-AMPS).

Association A binding between the client and an AP.

Asymmetric T ransmission Data transmissions where the traffic from the network to the subscriber is at a higher rate than that from the subscriber to the network.

Asynchr onous T ransfer Mode (A TM) A multiplexed infor mation transfer and switching method in which the data is organized into fixed-length 53-octet cells and transmitted according to each application's instantaneous need.

Authentication The process of verifying who is at the other end of the link.

Authentication Center (AUC) The element within a GSM network that generates the parameters for subscriber authentication.

B

Bandit A technically sophisticated thief who has free access to anything being transmitted over the air waves. Typically used when describing cell phone fraud.

Bandwidth A term meaning both the width of a transmission channel in terms of hertz (Hz) and the maximum transmission speed in bits per second that it will support.

Base Station Contr oller (BSC) The network entity controlling a number of Base Transceiver Stations (BTS).

Base Station System/Subsystem (BSS) The central radio transmitter/receiver that maintains communications with a mobile radio telephone within a given range.

Base Transceiver Station (BTS) The network entity that communicates with the mobile station.

Basic Service Set (BSS) An operating mode in which a BSS Master, usually an AP, acts as a gateway between the wireless and wired backbone. BSS clients gain access to the network by establishing communications with the BSS master.

Binary Runtime Envir onment for W ir eless (BREW) Developed by Qualcomm, BREW is an open source application development platform for wireless devices. BREW developers can create portable applications that work on CDMA and GSM handsets. Applications include SMS, e-mail, location positioning, games, and Internet radio. BREW and Java 2 Mobile Edition (J2ME) are competing head to head for the wireless application development market.

Bit A bit is the smallest unit of information. As bits are manipulated using the binary number system, all multiples of bits must be powers of two. A kilobit is actually 1024 bits and a megabit 1,048,576 bits. Transmission speeds are given in bits per second (bps).

Bit Error Rate (BER) The percentage of received bits in error compared to the total number of bits received.

BlackBerry A small mobile handheld device designed to allow wireless e-mail access as well as basic PDA functions such as address book, calendar, tasks, etc.

Blip A small, wireless gadget developed by Ericsson that allows anyone to broadcast information to Bluetooth devices such as mobile phones or PDAs within a radius of about 10 m.

Bluetooth A wireless technology developed by Ericsson, Intel, Nokia, and Toshiba that specifies how mobile phones, computers, and PDAs interconnect with each other, with computers, and with office or home phones. Bluetooth technology enables data connections between electronic devices in the 2.4 GHz range. Bluetooth's purpose is to replace cable or infrared connections for such devices.

Breeder Documents A term used in identity theft referring to the 240 valid forms of driver's licenses in the United States, and 10,000 different agencies that can issue birth certificates.

Bridge Type (Access Point) Connects a wireless network to a wired network transparently.

Broadcast Channels (BCH) Carry only downlink information and are mainly responsible for synchronization and frequency correction.

Broadcast Control Channel (BCCH) The logical channel used in cellular networks to broadcast signaling and control information to all mobile phones within the network.

Buffer An area of memory, often referred to as a *cache*, used to speed up access to devices. It is used for temporary storage of the data read from or waiting to be sent to a device such as a hard disk, CD-ROM, printer, or tape drive.

Busy Hour Call Attempts (BHCA) The number of call attempts made during a network's busiest hour of the day.

C

Cache See Buffer

Call Detail Record (CDR) The record made within the cellular network of all details of both incoming and outgoing calls made by subscribers. The CDR is passed to the billing system.

Capacity A measure of a cellular network's ability to support simultaneous calls.

cdmaOne The first commercial Code Division Multiple Access(CDMA) cellular system; deployed in North America and Korea; also known as IS-95.

CDMA2000 A member of the IMT-2000 3G family. CDMA2000 is backward compatible with cdmaOne. CDMA2000 includes CDMA2000 1X and CDMA2000 1XEV. CDMA2000 1XEV includes 1XEV-DO and 1xEV-DV. CDMA2000 services are being implemented in North America and Asia, but not in Europe.

CDMA 1X The first generation of CDMA2000.

CDMA 1X EV-DO A variant of CDMA 1X that delivers data only.

Cell The area covered by a cellular base station. Also, the facility housing the transmitters and receivers, antennas, and associated equipment.

Cell Splitting The process of converting a single cell to multiple cells by sectorizing the antennas in the cell site or constructing additional cells within a cell site.

Cell Yell The act of having a loud phone conversation in a public place.

Cellular Digital Packet Data (CDPD) A specification for supporting wireless access to the Internet and other public packet-switched networks. The service is largely deployed in the United States and uses idle analog channels to carry the packetized information.

Cellular Telecommunications and Internet Association (CTIA) An international trade group representing all elements of wireless communication. CTIA serves the interests of mobile operators, software developers, and manufacturers.

Centrino A technology package from Intel that provides built-in wireless support for laptop computers while making it possible to run a laptop for several hours without a battery recharge.

Channel Data Format (CDF) A system used to prepare information for Webcasting.

Circuit Switching A method used in telecommunications where a temporary dedicated circuit of constant bandwidth is established between two distant endpoints in a network. Mainly used for voice traffic; the opposite of packet switching.

Code Division Multiple Access (CDMA) A digital wireless technology that uses a spread spectrum technique to scatter a radio signal across a wide range of frequencies. These systems utilize a single frequency band for all traffic, differentiating between the individual transmissions by assigning them unique codes before transmission. CDMA is a 2G technology. Wideband Code Division Multiple Access (WCDMA) is a 3G technology based on CDMA. CDMA has multiple variants, including CDMA 1X, CDMA2000, CDMA2000 1X, CDMA2000 1xEV-DO, and cdmaOne.

Code Excited Linear Pr ediction (CELP) An analog-to-digital voice coding scheme. There are a number of variants used in cellular systems.

Code Domain Power (CDP) Measuring code domain power means verifying the distribution of power in the code channels. This verifies that the various channels are at expected power levels and determines when one code channel is leaking energy into the other channels. The correctness of the transmitted code channel numbers, their powers, and their code lengths should be verified.

Codec A word formed by combining coder and decoder. The codec is a device that encodes and decodes signals. The voice codec in a cellular network converts voice signals into bit strings and back. In GSM networks, in addition to the standard voice codec, it is possible to implement Half Rate (HR) codecs and Enhanced Full Rate (EFR) codecs.

Comfort Noise To assure the receiver that the connection is not dead, "comfort noise" is created at the receiving end by trying to match the characteristics of the transmitting end's background noise.

Common Air Inter face (CAI) A standard developed for the United Kingdom's public second-generation cordless telephony (CT2) networks that enabled the same handset to be used on different networks.

Common Contr ol Channels (CCCH) A group of uplink and downlink channels between the MS and the BTS.

Communicator A generic name for an information-centric mobile phone that combines a fully featured PDA and mobile phone in one unit.

Compact HTML (cHTML) A scaled-down version of HTML for small information devices, such as smart phones and PDAs. cHTML is derived from regular HTML. cHTML does not support JPEG images, tables, image maps, multiple fonts and styles of fonts, background colors and images, and frames. In many environments, XHTML is replacing cHTML.

Complementary Metal Oxide Semiconductor (CMOS) This is a low-power version of a chip. It commonly holds the BIOS preference of the computer through power-off with the aid of a battery.

Confer ence of Eur opean Posts and T elecommunications (CEPT) An organization of national posts, telegraphs, and telephone administrations. Operational until 1988, when this work was taken over by ETSI, the main European body for telecommunications standardization. CEPT established the original GSM standardization group.

Connected Limited Device Confi guration (CLDC) CLDC outlines the basic set of libraries and Java virtual machine features that must be present in each implementation of a J2ME environment.

Connection Management (CM) A method used to set up, maintain, and take down call connections.

Contr ol Signal A signal sent to a cellular phone from a base station or vice versa that carries information essential to the call. The control signal does not include the audio portion of a conversation in the transmission.

Cryptography The process of securing private information that is sent through public networks by encrypting it in a way that makes it unreadable to anyone except the person or persons holding the mathematical key/knowledge to decrypt the information.

CT0 Zero-generation cordless telephony; the earliest domestic cordless phones, which used analog technology and which had severe limitations in terms of range and security.

CT1 First-generation cordless telephony; improved analog phones with greater range and security. A number of European nations produced CT1 standards.

CT2 Second-generation cordless telephony. Using digital technology CT2 phones offered greater range, improved security, and a wide range of new functionalities. Used in both domestic and cordless private automatic branch exchange (PABX) deployments, CT2 was standardized as an interim European Telecommunications Standard (ETS) but was superseded by Digitally Enhanced Cordless Telecommunications (DECT).

CT2-CAI Second-generation cordless telephony-common air interface.

Customer Pr emises Equipment (CPE) All the equipment on the end user's side of the network interface.

Customized Application for Mobile Network Enhanced Logic (CAMEL) An Intelligent Network (IN) feature in GSM networks that enables users to carry personal services with them when roaming into other networks that support CAMEL.

Cyclic Redundancy Check (CRC) A common technique for detecting data transmission errors.

D

Dedicated Contr ol Channels (DCCH) Channels that are responsible for roaming, handovers, encryption, etc. Essentially a channel for communications between a mobile phone and the network.

Deleted Files Data on a hard drive that is marked to be overwritten by the file system. If a subject knows there are incriminating files on the computer, he or she may delete them in an effort to eliminate evidence.

Depending on how the files are deleted, in many instances a forensic examiner is able to recover all or part of the original data.

Denial-of-Service Attack (DoS) An attack that is aimed at specific Web sites. The attacker floods the Web server with endlessly repeated messages. This ties up the system and denies access to legitimate users.

Digital A method of representing information as numbers with discrete values; usually expressed as a sequence of bits.

Digital AMPS (D-AMPS) A U.S. wireless standard also known as IS-136.

Digital Short Range Radio (DSRR) A U.K. standard for a low-power, short-range radio system designed for small voice and data networks.

Digital Signatur e A code used to guarantee that an e-mail was sent by a particular sender.

Digitally Enhanced Cor dless T elecommunications (DECT) DECT is a digital wireless technology that originated in Europe for cordless telephones. DECT is seeing increasing adoption worldwide, including use in wireless offices and wireless telephone lines to homes. It is a radio access technology, not a complete system architecture. DECT interoperates with other network types such as the PSTN, ISDN, and GSM.

Dir ect Sequence Spr ead Spectrum (DSSS) (802.11b) A transmission signal that is spread over an allowed frequency band; a random binary string is used to modulate the transmitted signal. This random signal is called the spreading code. The data bits are mapped into a pattern of "chips" and mapped back into a bit at the destination. The number of chips that represents a bit is the spreading ratio. The higher the spreading ratio, the more the signal is resistant to interference. Recovery is faster in DSSS systems because of the ability to spread the signal over a wider band. DSSS systems provide a wireless network with both a 1 and 2 Mbps data payload communication capability.

Discontinuous T ransmission (DTX) A method that takes advantage of the fact that a person speaks less that 40 percent of the time in normal phone conversation and thereby turns the transmitter off during silent periods.

DoCoMo In Japanese, DoCoMo means "anywhere." DoCoMo is Japan's largest mobile service provider. DoCoMo's i-mode allows subscribers continuous access to the Internet via mobile telephone. The service lets users send and receive e-mail, exchange photographs, do online shopping and banking, download ringtones for their phones, and navigate specially formatted Web sites.

Drive-By Spamming A variation of drive-by hacking in which the perpetrators gain access to a vulnerable wireless local area network (WLAN) and use that access to send huge volumes of spam. Using the drive-by method allows spammers to save themselves the considerable bandwidth costs required to send that many messages legitimately, and makes it very difficult for anyone to trace the spam back to its source.

Dual Band The capability of GSM infrastructure elements and handsets to work across both the 900 and 1800 MHz bands. The capability to seamlessly handover between the two bands offers operators major capacity gains.

Dual Tone Multifr equency (DTMF) Better known as "touch tone." The tones generated by touching the keys on the phone are used for a variety of purposes including voice mail systems and voice messaging.

Dummy Burst (DB) A transmission that is used as a filler in unused timeslots of the carrier.

Duplex The wireless technique in which one frequency band is used for traffic from the network to the subscriber (the downlink) and another widely separated band is used for traffic from the subscriber to the network (the uplink).

E

E911 Short for Enhanced 911, a location technology advanced by the FCC that will enable mobile, or cellular, phones to process 911 emergency calls and enable emergency services to locate the geographic position of the caller.

Echelon An officially unacknowledged global spy network that operates an automated system for the interception and relay of electronic communications.

Electr onic Serial Number (ESN) A 32-bit number that uniquely identifies a mobile phone.

E-Mail Header An e-mail is composed of two parts — the body and the header. Normal header information gives the recipient details of time, date, sender, and subject. All e-mails also come with extended headers — information that is added by e-mail programs and transmitting devices — which shows more information about the sender that is in many circumstances traceable to an individual computer on the Internet.

Encryption The process of "scrambling" a message so that it cannot be intercepted and easily read by unauthorized parties. Messages from a digital phone or from a laptop are often encrypted in a wireless environment.

Enhanced Data GSM Envir onment (EDGE) EDGE is effectively the final stage in the evolution of the GSM standard. It uses a new modulation scheme to increase theoretical data speeds to 384 kbps within the existing GSM spectrum. EDGE is an alternative upgrade path toward 3G services for operators, such as those in the United States, without access to new spectrum.

Enhanced Full Rate (EFR) An alternative voice codec that provides improved voice quality in a GSM network.

Enhanced Radio Messaging System (ERMES) A paging technology developed by the European Telecommunications Standards Institute (ETSI) that was intended to allow users to roam throughout Europe. Adopted by a number of European and Middle Eastern countries, ERMES, like paging in general, was overtaken by the ubiquity of GSM.

EPOC EPOC is a 32-bit operating environment comprising a suite of applications, customizable user interfaces, connectivity options, and a range of development tools. Developed by Symbian for small, portable computer-telephones with wireless access to phone and other information services, EPOC is based on an earlier operating system from Psion, the first major manufacturer of personal digital assistants (PDAs).

Equipment Identity Register (EIR) A database that contains a list of all valid mobile stations within a network based on their International Mobile Equipment Identity (IMEI).

Erlang A dimensionless unit of average traffic density in a telecommunications network.

European T elecommunications Standar   ds Institute (ETSI) The European group responsible for defining telecommunications standards.

Evil Twin Attack An attack where a black hat sets an SSID to be the same as an access point at the local hotspot or corporate wireless network. The black hat disrupts or disables the legitimate AP by disconnecting it, directing a denial-of-service against it, or creating RF interference around it. Users lose their connections to the legitimate AP and reconnect to the "evil twin," allowing the hacker to intercept all the traffic to that device.

Evolution Data Only (EvDO) A wireless broadband data protocol being adopted by many CDMA mobile phone providers in both Korea and the United States. EvDO is considerably faster than other protocols, allowing users to download information at speeds up to 500 kbps.

Extended Service Set (ESS) A physical subnet that contains more than one AP. This allows APs to communicate with each other and thus allows authenticated users to "roam" between APs, handing off IP information as the clients move about.

Extensible Authentication Pr   otocol (EAP) EAP is an 802.1x standard that allows developers to pass security authentication data between RADIUS and the AP and wireless client. EAP has a number of variants, including: EAP MD5, EAP-Tunneled TLS (EAP-TTLS), Lightweight EAP (LEAP), and Protected EAP (PEAP).

F

Family Radio Service (FRS)   Often referred to as the "UHF Citizens Band."

Fast Associated Contr ol Channel (F ACCH) Similar to a Stand-alone Dedicated Control Channel (SDCCH) but used in parallel for operation of the Traffic Channel (TCH). If the data rate of the Slow Associated Control Channel (SACCH) is insufficient, borrowing mode is used.

Federal Communications Commission (FCC)   The U.S. regulatory body for telecommunications.

Fixed Satellite Service (FSS)   The interface between the PCU and the SGSN in a GSM/GPRS network.

Freedom of Mobile Multimedia Access (FOMA)   The Japan NTT DoCoMo brand name for 3G services based on W-CDMA.

Frequency Corr ection Burst (FB)   Used for frequency synchronization of the mobile unit.

Frequency Corr ection Channel (FCCH)   Used in downlinks, the correction of Mobile Station (MS) frequencies, transmission of a frequency standard to an MS, etc.

Frequency Division Duplex (FDD)   A radio technique that uses paired spectrum; the Universal Mobile Telecommunications System (UMTS) has an FDD element.

Frequency Division Multiple Access (FDMA)   A transmission technique in which the assigned frequency band for a network is divided into subbands that are allocated to a subscriber for the duration of their calls.

Frequency Hopping Spr ead Spectrum (FHSS) (802.11)   Frequency Hopping Spread Spectrum works by splitting the frequency band into many small subchannels (1 MHz). The signal then hops from subchannel to subchannel, transmitting short bursts of data on each channel for a set period of time, called *dwell time*. The hopping sequence must be synchronized at the sender and the receiver, or information will be lost. Frequency hopping is less susceptible to interference because the frequency is constantly shifting. This makes frequency hopping systems extremely difficult to intercept and harder to jam.

Frequency Shift Keying (FSK)   A method of using frequency modulation to send digital information.

Friend Finder (fr om OpenW ave 50) A service that enables mobile users to locate their friends and coworkers via their mobile phones.

Full-Duplex Pr otocol Uses two separate frequencies simultaneously so you can send and receive at the same time.

Futur e Public Land Mobile T elecommunications System (FPLMTS) The original title of the International Telecommunications Union's (ITU) third-generation concept, now known as *IMT-2000*.

G

Gateway GPRS Support Node (GGSN)   The gateway between a cellular network and an IP network.

Gateway Mobile Services Switching Center (GMSC)   The gateway between two mobile networks.

Gaussian-Filter ed Minimum Shift Keying (GMSK)   A refinement of Frequency Shift Keying (FSK), which minimizes adjacent channel interference.

Gbit/s A unit of data transmission rate equal to one billion bits per second.

Gc The inter face between the GGSN and the HLR in a GSM/GPRS network.   **Gd** The interface between the SGSN and the SMSC in a GSM/GPRS network.

General Mobile Radio Service (GMRS)   Also known as the "Class A Citizens Band."

General Packet Radio Service (GPRS)   Standardized as part of GSM Phase 2+, GPRS represents the first implementation of packet switching within GSM. GPRS enables high-speed wireless Internet and other data communications offering theoretical data speeds of up to 115 kbps. GPRS is an essential precursor for 3G as it introduces the packet-switched core required for UMTS. GPRS networks can deliver Short Message Service (SMS), Multimedia Messaging Service (MMS), e-mail, games, and Wireless Application Protocol (WAP) applications.

Geocaching   A hi-tech version of hide-and-seek that involves looking for and planting caches — usually a logbook to record visits and trinkets such as maps, toys, and food. The point of the game isn't what you find in the cache but simply finding it, using GPS (global positioning system) information supplied by the cacher.

Geostationary   Refers to a satellite in equatorial orbit above the Earth that appears from the surface to be stationary.

Gf The interface between the Serving GPRS Support Node (SGSN) and the Equipment Identity Register (EIR) in a GSM/GPRS network.

GHz A unit of frequency equal to 1 billion Hertz per second.

Gi The interface between the Gateway GPRS Support Node (GGSN) and the Internet in a General Packet Radio Service (GPRS) network.

Global Positioning System (GPS)   A location system based on a constellation of U.S. Department of Defense satellites. GPS is now being incorporated as a key feature in an increasing number of mobile handsets. GPS systems are used by "stumblers" to accurately remember the position of a hotspot for future reference.

Global System for Mobile T elecommunications (GSM)   GSM, a 2G technology, is the de facto European standard for digital cellular telephone service. GSM is also available in the Americas and claims 71 percent of the world market. GSM is the most widely used of the three digital wireless telephone technologies and supports voice, data, text messaging, and cross-border roaming. The SIM (Subscriber Identification Module), a removable plastic card that contains a user's data, is an essential element in a GSM network. GSM originally stood for Groupe Speciale Mobile, the committee that began the GSM standardization process.

Gn The interface between the GGSN and the SGSN in a GPRS network.

Gp The interfaces between the GGSN/SGSN and the Border Gateway in a GPRS network.

Gr The interface between the SGSN and the HLR in a GPRS network.

Gs The interface between the SGSN and the MSC in a GSM/GPRS network.

GSM-EDGE Radio Access Network (GERAN) The name for the evolution of GSM toward 3G based on EDGE.

GSM MoU The GSM Memorandum of Understanding, an agreement signed between all the major European operators to work together to promote GSM. The precursor of the GSM Association.

GSM-R (GSM-Railway) A variant of GSM designed to meet the special communications needs of international train operators.

H

H.323 H.323 is the standard for interoperability in audio, video, and data transmissions, as well as Internet phone and Voice-over-IP. The standard addresses call control and management for point-to-point and multipoint conferences, as well as gateway administration of media traffic, bandwidth, and user participation.

Half-Duplex Pr otocol A protocol that uses one frequency to send or receive, but not both at the same time.

Handheld Device Markup Language (HDML) Handheld Device Markup Language is used to format content for Web-enabled mobile phones. HDML allows Internet access from wireless devices and is derived from HTML. Openwave created this proprietary language, and it can only be viewed on mobile phones that use Openwave browsers. HDML was created before a WAP standard was defined. It uses Openwave's Handheld Device Transport Protocol (HDTP) instead of WAP.

Handheld Device T ransport Pr otocol (HDTP) This protocol is optimized for HDML. It presents the HDML to the HDML interpreter in an appropriate format.

Handoff The transfer of control of a cellular phone call in progress from one cell to another, without any discontinuity.

Hands-Free The operation of a cellular phone without using the handset; usually installed in vehicles.

Hierarchical Cell Structure (HCS) The architecture of a multilayered cellular network in which subscribers are handed over from the macro to the micro to the pico layer depending on the current network capacity and the needs of the subscriber.

High Performance Radio Local Access Network (HIPERLAN) A wireless local area network being standardized by the European Telecommunications Standards Institute (ETSI) specifying a broadband wireless LAN that supports data rates of 25 to 54 Mbps on a carrier frequency of 5 GHz.

High Speed Circuit-Switched Data (HSCSD) A special mode in GSM networks that provides higher data throughput by concatenating a number of timeslots, each delivering 14.4 kbps. By using this method much higher data speeds can be achieved.

High Speed Packet-Switched Data (HSPSD) The interface between the Node B and the Radio Network Controller (RNC) in a UMTS network.

High Speed Wireless Access Network Type a (HiSW ANa) An ARIB standard "ARIB STD-T70" that uses the 5.15 to 5.25 GHz band with a variable transmission rate from 6 to 36 Mbps. This system guarantees bandwidth usage and can manage bandwidth for each user.

Home Area Network (HAN) A home-based network that provides data transfer and device automation. HANs can use existing phone and electrical wiring.

Home Location Register (HLR) The database within a GSM network that stores all the subscriber data. An important element in the roaming process.

Home Phone Network Alliance (HPNA) HPNA is the high-speed, reliable, networking (LAN) technology that uses the existing phone wires in your home to share a single Internet connection with several PCs in your home.

HomePlug A device that used the electric wiring of your home or building to share data at speeds up to 14 Mbps over distances up to 1000 ft. HomePlug effectively puts a network connection at every electrical outlet.

Hotspot An area in which an AP provides public wireless broadband network services to mobile visitors through a WLAN. Hotspots are often located in heavily populated places such as airports, hotels, coffee shops, libraries, and convention centers.

Hybrid NAT Router + Bridge (Access Point) A hybrid NAT router + bridge device connects your wired and wireless networks, then routes them both to the Internet using a single IP address. This is good for sharing an Internet connection when you have both wired and wireless computers in your home.

Hyper coor dination The speeding up of urban activities through the use of mobile devices.

I

Imaging The process used to obtain all of the data present on a storage media (e.g., hard disk), whether it is active data or data in free space, in such a way as to allow it to be examined as if it were the original data.

i-mode A service developed by Japanese operators of DoCoMo, i-mode delivers a huge range of services to subscribers.

IMT-2000 The family of third-generation technologies approved by the ITU. There are five members of the family: IMT-DS, a direct sequence Wideband Code Division Multiple Access (WCDMA) FDD solution; IMT-TC, a WCDMA TDD solution; IMT-MC, a multicarrier solution developed from CDMA2000; IMT-SC, a single carrier solution developed from IS-136/UWC-136; and IMT-FT, a TDMA/TDD solution derived from Digitally Enhanced Cordless Telecommunications (DECT).

Independent Basic Service Set (IBSS) Often referred to as Ad-Hoc or Peer-to-Peer mode. In this mode, no hardware AP is required.

Industrial, Scientifi c and Medical Band (ISM) A part of the radio spectrum that can be used by anybody without a license in most countries.

Infrar ed Data Association (IrDA) This association defined a suite of protocols for infrared (IR) exchange of data between two devices. IrDA devices typically have throughput of up to 115.2 kbps or 4 Mbps. Symbian OS phones, many PDAs, printers, and laptop computers use IrDA protocols.

Infrastructur e Mode An 802.11 WLAN configuration comprising client stations and APs.

In-Phase and Quadratur e (I/Q) I/Q modulators are 90° out of phase with each other. I/Q modulation combines two channels of information into one signal and then separates them later.

Institute of Electrical and Electr onics Engineers (IEEE) The organization of scientists and engineers that develops the 802.11 and other standards.

Integrated Digital Enhanced Network (iDEN) A specialized wireless technology from Motorola combining the capabilities of a digital cellular telephone, two-way radio, alphanumeric pager, and data/fax modem in a single network.

Interim Standar d 54 (IS-54) The first evolution in the United States from analog to digital technology. IS-54 used a hybrid of analog and digital technology. It was superseded by IS-136.

Interim Standar d 136 (IS-136) IS-136, an evolved version of IS-54, is the U.S. standard for TDMA for both the cellular and PCS spectrums. Unlike IS-54, IS-136 utilizes time division multiplexing for transmitting both voice and the control channel. The Digital Control Channel (DCCH) is a key element of IS-136.

Interim Standar d 95 (IS-95) A TIA/EIA standard that was the first widely used CDMA system, and is heavily installed in North America. The initial specification, known as IS-95A, was later upgraded to IS-95B. IS-95B combines cellular and PCS systems. In addition to voice, IS-95A is able to carry data at rates up to 14.4 kbps, and IS-95B supports data rates up to 115 kbps.

Inter national Mobile Equipment Identity (IMEI) The unique number given to every single mobile phone.

Inter national Mobile Subscriber Identity (IMSI) An internal subscriber identity used only by the network.

Inter net A loose confederation of autonomous databases and networks. Originally developed for military and academic use, the Internet is now a global structure of millions of sites accessible by anyone.

Intranet A private network that utilizes the same techniques as the Internet but is accessible only by authorized users.

IPv6 The next generation of IP addressing designed to replace the current system IPv4, which uses a 32-bit address code that limits the number of possible addresses. IPv6 uses a 128-bit code, ensuring that the possible number of IP addresses will be virtually limitless.

Iridium A low-earth orbit satellite communications system developed initially by Motorola.

J

Java A programming language developed by Sun Microsystems, Java is characterized by the fact that programs written in Java do not rely on an operating system.

Java 2 Micr o Edition (J2ME) Java 2 Platform, Micro Edition (J2ME) is the edition of the Java platform that is targeted at cellular phones and PDAs. The J2ME technology consists of a virtual machine and a set of application program interfaces (APIs) suitable for tailored runtime environments for these devices.

JavaPhone A Java application program interfaces (API) specification controlling contacts, power management, call control, and phone book management. It is intended specifically for the programming requirements of mobile phones.

Java Telephony API (JT API) The Java Telephony application program interfaces (API) is an extensible application program interfaces that offers an interface to all call control services. The services include those needed in a consumer device up to those of enterprise call centers. JTAPI is part of the JavaPhone API.

L

Location-Based Technology Wireless programs that work only in limited areas. The availability of location information that can enable service providers to target services and information to users relative to their current location.

Low-Earth Orbit (LEO) LEO refers to satellites which orbit the Earth at around 1000 km.

M

Mbps Megabits per second, a unit of data transmission speed equal to 100,000 bps.

MD5 Hash An algorithm created in 1991 by Professor Ronald Rivest that is used to create digital fingerprints of storage media such as a computer hard drive. When this algorithm is applied to a hard drive, it creates a unique value. Changing the data on the disk in any way will change the MD5 value.

Media Access Control (MAC) The lower sublayer of the OSI system that is concerned with sharing the physical connection to the network among several computers.

Media Access Control (MAC) Filtering MAC filtering is a way to help secure your AP. Although it can be easily spoofed, MAC filtering attempts to restrict your AP only to certain MAC addresses (unique hardware addresses).

Megahertz (MHz) A unit of frequency equal to one million Hertz.

Messaging Defined by four types in the mobile and wireless environment:

- SMS is a feature available with some wireless phones that allows users to send and receive short alphanumeric messages.
- Picture Messaging allows users to send and receive picture messages along with text. Users can choose from several preset or received pictures stored in their phones. Some phones also contain a picture editor.
- Chat Messaging lets users "talk" using SMS messages.
- MMS (Multimedia Messaging Service) is a new standard that is being defined for use in advanced wireless terminals. The service allows for non-real-time transmission of various kinds of multimedia content, such as images, audio, and video clips.

Microbrowser Also called a minibrowser. A mircobrowser is software built into a wireless device that allows users to access and display specially formatted Internet content, such as stock reports, news, and sports scores.

mMode Music Store An AT&T initiative which enables its mobile phone subscribers to browse and purchase song downloads over the phone and then retrieve them online using a personal computer.

Mobile Commerce (mCommerce) Mobile commerce refers to transactions using a wireless device and data connection that result in the transfer of value in exchange for information, services, or goods. Mobile commerce, facilitated generally by mobile phones, includes services such as banking, payment, and ticketing.

Mobile Execution Environment (MeXe) MeXe is a framework to ensure a predictable environment for third-party applications in GSM or UMTS. MeXe enables WAP-enabled devices to offer a wider range of features with greater security and flexibility, as well as greater control of telephony features.

Mobile Information Device Profile (MIDP) A set of Java APIs that is generally implemented on the Connected Limited Device Configuration (CLDC). The MIDP specification addresses issues such as user interface, persistent storage, networking, and application model.

Mobile Switching Center (MSC) The switching center of a mobile phone network, the MSC has interfaces to the Base Station Controller (BSC), Home Location Register **(HLR),** Visitor Location Register (VLR), and other MSCs.

Mobile System A mobile phone network or system that consists of a network of cells. A radio base station serves each cell, where calls are forwarded to and received from a mobile phone by wireless radio signals.

Mobilization The process by which mobile technologies fold themselves into the fabric of our economies, social lives, and communities. Considered more of a social phenomenon than a political or technological one.

Modulation The process of imposing an information signal on a carrier. This can be done by changing the amplitude (AM), the frequency (FM) or the phase, or any combination of these.

"Money Stack" Locator A bank robbery deterrent and recovery device. A money stack locator is a wireless transmitter that is placed within a stack of bills in a bank's drawer. In the event of a robbery, the teller hands the tagged cash to the thief so that the authorities can then track the cash.

Motion Pictur e Experts Gr oup (MPEG) MPEG4 is a technology for compressing voice and video so that the information can be transmitted over normally difficult links such as mobile radio.

mTerr orism Acts of terrorism in which the wireless computer network infrastructure is disrupted or destroyed.

Multimedia Messaging Service (MMS) MMS allows for non-real-time transmission of various kinds of multimedia contents, such as images, audio, and video clips.

Multiple-Input Multiple-Output (MIMO) A process in which information is sent over two or more antennas. The signals reflect off objects and create multiple paths that cause interference and fading in conventional radios. MIMO uses these paths to carry more information, which is recombined on the receiving side based on MIMO algorithms. MIMO is expected to greatly increase performance and range but handle existing 802.11a/b/g radios with only a slight cost increase. Some form of MIMO may be used by the IEEE 802.11n Task Group, which is creating a specification for WLANs having at least 100 Mbps throughput (see 802.11), and for WiMax/802.16 wireless "last mile" access.

Multiplexing A telecommunications technique in which several channels can be combined to share the same transmission medium. The most common forms are Time Division Multiplexing (TDM) and Frequency Division Multiplexing (FDM).

N

NAT Router Type (Access Point) NAT router type routes traffic from your wireless network to an Ethernet wired network, but it will not route traffic back. This type can be used to share an Internet connection.

.NET Compact Framework (.NET CF) The .NET Compact framework is a smaller version of the .NET Common Language Runtime, optimized for the deployment of mobile applications running on resource-constrained devices such as PDAs. .NET CF supports only devices running Microsoft operating systems — specifically, Windows CE 3.0.

Node B The element in a UMTS network that interfaces with the mobile station, analogous to a BTS in a GSM network.

Noppa A Finnish Government project that combines cell phones, wireless Internet, GPS, and voice technology to help the blind move freely in cities.

Normal Burst (NB) Used to carry traffic and control channels except the Random Access Channel (RACH).

NS Basic A development environment for programming in BASIC for handheld devices. NS Basic allows a programmer to develop and test programs in a desktop environment and then download them to handheld devices. NS Basic is currently available for development with Palm OS, Windows CE and the discontinued Apple Newton.

O

Object Exchange (OBEX) Object Exchange is a set of protocols allowing objects such as vCard contact information and vCalendar schedule entries to be exchanged using either IrDA or Bluetooth. Symbian OS implements IrDA for exchange of vCards.

Open Spectrum Technology Open Spectrum Technology permits anyone to send signals across any range of spectrum without permission, with the minimum set of rules required to enable the success of a "wireless commons."

Open System Interconnection (OSI) A seven-layer model for protocols defined by the International Standards Organization (ISO).

Orthogonal Frequency Division Multiplexing (OFDM) OFDM is a method of digital modulation in which a signal is split into several narrowband channels at different frequencies.

P

Packet Switching A communication system in which the information is transmitted in packets of a set size. These packets have address headers and find their way to their destination by the most efficient route through the network. Compared to circuit switching, in which a connection is occupied until the traffic exchange is completed, packet switching offers considerable efficiencies as connections can be used by a number of users simultaneously

Paging Paging is a single-direction radio service for alerting subscribers and leaving messages.

Paging Channel (PCH) Used for downlinks only; the MS is informed of incoming calls by the BTS via the Paging Channel (PCH).

Palm OS Palm OS is the operating system that provides a software platform for the PalmPilot series of handheld PDAs made by Palm Computing. Palm OS was designed to fit into a handheld device of a specific size and with a specific display size.

Pan Eur opean Digital Communications (PEDC) A designation occasionally used in the early 1990s to describe GSM. The term is no longer in use.

Peabody Peabody is a GSM and GPRS mobile phone platform by Microsoft offered under a partnership with Flextronics. It is based on Windows Mobile software and will be designed and integrated for OEMs by Flextronics.

Penetration The percentage of the total population that owns a mobile phone.

Personal Access Communication System (P ACS) A digital cordless technology developed initially by Bell Labs in the United States, PACS was designed to compete with Digitally Enhanced Cordless Telecommunications (DECT).

Personal Communications Network (PCN) A designation initially used in the United Kingdom to refer to networks operating in the 1800 MHz band. The term is no longer in use.

Personal Communications Service (PCS) Personal Communications Service is a generic term for a mass-market mobile phone service. PCS communications use modern digital cellular technologies.

Personal Communications Systems 1900 MHz (PCS 1900) The terminology used in the United States to describe the new digital networks being deployed in the 1900 MHz band; rarely used today.

Personal Computer Memory Car d Inter face Association (PCMCIA) The association was originally responsible for defining the standards and formats for memory expansion cards for laptop computers and PDAs. The PCMCIA standard has been extended several times to cover cards for various devices, including mobile phones.

Personal Digital Communications (PDC) A digital cellular technology developed and deployed uniquely in Japan. A Time Division Multiple Access (TDMA) technology, PDC is incompatible with any other digital cellular standard.

Personal HandyPhone System/Phone (PHS/PHP) A digital cordless technology developed in Japan. Deployed by DoCoMo and other Japanese operators, PHS offered two-way communications, data services, and Internet access. Now in decline as cellular's wide area capabilities offer better service.

PersonalJava A Java platform optimized for the requirements and constraints of mobile devices.

Personal Operating Space (POS) As it relates to Personal Area Networks (PANs), it is the space that typically extends up to 10 m in all directions around a person and envelops the person. This POS "bubble" is present whether stationary or in motion. As you go through your daily activities, there are many opportunities for information to be exchanged between you and others or between your POS "bubble" and currently existing applications or devices.

Personal Wireless Telecommunications (PWT) A variant of Digitally Enhanced Cordless Telecommunications (DECT) developed for use in the United States.

Phishing Phishing is a scam in which the perpetrator sends out legitimate-looking e-mails appearing to come from some of the Web's biggest sites, including eBay, PayPal, MSN, Yahoo, BestBuy, and America Online, in an effort to phish (prounounced "fish") for personal and financial information from the recipient.

Phreaking Closely related to hacking, phreaking uses a computer or other device to trick a phone system. Typically, phreaking is used to make free calls or to have calls charged to a different account.

Picture Messaging Picture messaging allows users to send and receive picture messages along with text. Users can choose from several preset and received pictures stored in their phones. Some phones also contain a picture editor.

Pocket PC Microsoft's Pocket PC is a mobile device platform based on the Windows CE operating system. Pocket PCs are used for standard PIM functionality, games and multimedia, Web browsing, and are capable of running custom enterprise applications built in Visual C++, Embedded Visual Basic, or .NET Compact Framework.

Points of Presence (PoP) A method of measuring the value of a cellular license; the approximate number of potential customers within a geographic area.

Port The word has three possible meanings:

- Where information goes into or out of a computer, e.g., the serial port on a personal computer; where a modem would be connected.
- On the Internet, *port* often refers to a number that is part of an URL appearing after a colon (:) right after the domain name.

■ It also refers to translating a piece of software to bring it from one type of computer system to another, e.g., to translate a Windows program so that it will run on a Macintosh.

Post Office Code Standar dization Gr oup (POCSAG) A now-defunct industry grouping that standardized pager addressing systems.

Privacy-Conscious Personalization (PCP) framework A set of software tools developed by Lucent Technologies' Bell Labs that is designed to give wireless users complete control over who can and can't track them. PCP promises to give mobile users the benefits they want from sharing location information without having to buy into a wholesale surveillance mechanism.

Private Automatic Branch Exchange (P ABX) A private automatic branch exchange (PABX) is an automatic telephone switching system within a private enterprise.

Private Mobile Radiocommunications (PMR) Two-way radio technology widely used for dispatch and delivery services, taxi companies, and the like. See TETRA.

Protected Extensible Authentication Pr otocol (PEAP) PEAP is an EAP extension that enhances the security of the authentication phase. PEAP provides the security framework for mutual authentication between an EAP client and an EAP server.

Public Access Mobile Radio (P AMR) A commercial service that uses trunking techniques in which multiple groups of users can set up their own closed systems within a shared public network.

Public Land Mobile Network (PLMN) Any cellular operator's network.

Public Safety Radio Communications Pr oject (PSRCP) An initiative by the U.K. Government to standardize all emergency services communications onto a single digital technology. See TETRA.

Pulse Code Modulation (PCM) The standard digital scheme for transmitting analog voice data.

Q

Quality of Service (QoS) Quality of service is a measure of network performance that reflects the network's transmission quality and service availability. QoS can come in the form of traffic policy in which the transmission rates are limited, thereby guaranteeing a certain amount of bandwidth will be available to applications. Or QoS may take the form of traffic shaping, which are techniques that reserve bandwidth for applications but do not guarantee its availability.

R

Radio Fixed Part (RFP) The equivalent to a base station in a DECT system.

Radio Fr equency Identifi cation (RFID) An RFID system uses radio frequencies to retrieve stored identification information from a tiny object called an RFID Tag, which is typically attached unobtrusively to a product or an animal, etc. A Passive RFID Tag derives all its operation and response power from the signal it receives on its antenna, typically operates over ranges of 10 mm to 5 m, and responds with just an ID number. An Active RFID Tag has its own power source such as a small battery, a greater range, and the ability to respond with much more information. RFID systems use a wide variety of frequencies, including 125–135 kHz, 6.7 MHz, 13.5 MHz, 902–928 MHz, and 2.4 GHz.

Radio On Fiber (ROF) A system in which an optical signal modulated with a radio signal is transmitted via optical fiber to roadside receiver stations, where it is then converted back to a radio signal for broadcasting from antennas. This technique can be used to transmit wideband wireless signals with relatively low noise.

Radio Network Contr oller (RNC) The element that controls the Node B's within a UMTS network. It is roughly analogous to a BSC in a GSM network.

Random Access Channel (RACH)   Used for uplinks only, RACH allows the MS to request a Stand-alone Dedicated Control Channel (SDCCH) in response to a page or for a call. For this reason, an entire timeslot has to be dedicated to mobiles attempting to contact the network (known as the RACH in GSM).

Redfang A hacking tool that targets Bluetooth devices.

Reuse The assignment of frequencies or channels to cells so that adjoining cells do not use the same frequencies and cause interference, but more distant cells can use the same frequencies. Reuse expands the capacity of a cellular network by enabling the use of the same channels throughout the network.

Roaming A service unique to GSM that enables a subscriber to make and receive calls when outside the service area of his or her home network, e.g., when traveling abroad.

Robust Security Network (RSN)   Robust Security Network is an element in 802.11i. RSN dynamically negotiates the authentication and encryption algorithms to be used for communications between WAPs and wireless clients. This means that as new threats are discovered, new algorithms can be added.

Router A device that forwards information in a network on a connectionless basis.

S

Service Set Identification (SSID) A network name that must be specified and matched by both the AP and the clients for the client to associate with the AP.

Serving GPRS Support Node (SGSN) The gateway between the Radio Network Controller (RNC) and the core network in a GPRS/UMTS network.

Session Initiation Protocol (SIP) SIP is the real-time communication protocol for Voice-over-IP (VoIP), and it has been expanded to support video and instant messaging applications. SIP performs basic call-control tasks, such as session set up and tear down and signaling for features such as hold, caller ID, and call transferring.

Session Stealing Also called a Theft of Information Attack. This attack is performed by waiting for a valid node to authenticate itself and initiate an application session, then capturing the session by masquerading as the legitimate node. Typically, this requires the attacker to transmit numerous nuisance packets to thwart the legitimate node from recognizing that the session has been captured. This type of attack can be thwarted by using end-to-end or link-layer encryption.

Short Message Service (SMS) An SMS allows users to send and receive short text messages (up to 160 characters) via the network operator's message center or from the Internet via the operator's SMS gateway Web site. If the phone is powered off or out of range, SMS messages are stored in the network and delivered at the next opportunity.

ShotCode A software product for mobile phones that allows users to connect to Internet sites using a ShotCode interface, which is a circular type of barcode.

SIM ToolKit (STK) STK allows operators to add additional functions to the phone menu to provide new services such as mobile banking or e-mail.

Simple Object Access Protocol (SOAP) SOAP is a way for a program running in one kind of operating system to communicate with a program in the same or another kind of an operating system using HTTP and XML.

Skimming Skimming is a technique in which criminals use a PDA to load and transmit stolen credit card numbers. Typically, an unsuspecting restaurant patron hands over his credit card to pay the bill. The waiter then swipes the number into a handheld device he has secreted in his pocket, capturing the number and selling it later.

Slack Space   The unused space in a disk cluster. The DOS and Windows file systems use fixed-size clusters. Even if the actual data being stored requires less storage than the cluster size, an entire cluster is reserved for the file. The unused space is called the slack space.

Slow Associated Contr ol Channel (SACCH)   SACCH transmits continuous measurements in parallel with operation of Traffic Channel (TCH) or Stand-alone Dedicated Control Channel (SDCCH). SACCH is needed for handover decisions.

Smart Mob   The creation of a group through use of mobile Internet access, allowing people who don't know each other to act in concert.

Smartcar d   Plastic cards, typically with an electronic chip embedded, that contain electronic value tokens. Such value is disposable at both physical retail outlets and online shopping locations.

Smartphone   A generic name for a voice-centric mobile phone with information capabilities.

SMS Center (SMSC)   The network entity that switches Short Message Service (SMS) traffic.

Sniffing   Sniffing is the act of looking for and monitoring signals being sent and received to capture data.

Social Engineering   Social engineering occurs when an attacker attempts to spoof his or her identity, e.g., by pretending to be someone who is authorized to have access to network information, and tricks a user out of that information, such as the user's username and password.

Space-Time Delocalization   A sociological manifestation; the idea that a disembodied voice on the other end of a mobile phone is impossible to contextualize. New mobile devices may change this because a person will be able to request a picture, video, or other location-based proof of where the person he or she is talking with actually is.

Spear Phishing   A variant of traditional "phishing" in which black hats glean as much information about a specific identity as they can for potential use in cybercrime.

Specialized Mobile Radio (SMR)   The U.S. term for private mobile radio.

Speech Application Language T ags (SALT)   The Speech Application Language Tags specification largely overlaps the VoiceXML specification. Both specifications share some common functionality, but SALT includes multimodal capabilities for inputting and outputting data, making speech and traditional data I/O more interchangeable. Microsoft, Phillips, Intel, and many others support the SALT specification.

Stand-Alone Dedicated Contr ol Channel (SDCCH)   The communications channel between the MS and the BTS. Used for signaling during call setup before a Traffic Channel (TCH) is allocated.

Str eaming An Internet-derived expression for the one-way transmission of video and audio content.

Stumble To stumble is to find and connect to insecure APs other than your own.

Subscriber Identity Module (SIM) A SIM is the smart card inside a GSM phone that identifies the user account to the network, handles authentication, and provides data storage for user data such as phone numbers and network information. It may contain applications that run on the phone. A user's SIM card can be moved from phone to phone as it contains all the key information required to activate the phone.

Symbian A joint venture among Ericsson, Motorola, Nokia, and Psion to develop new operating systems for wireless devices such as phones and handhelds. The Symbian OS is based on Psion's EPOC32 platform. The first operating system, called EPOC, was released in 2001. Symbian's operating system for data-enabled mobile phones includes a multitasking multithreaded core, a user interface framework, data services enablers, application engines, and integrated PIM (Personal Information Manager) functionality and wireless communications.

Symbian Connect The PC-based Symbian Connect is a system for data synchronization, file management, printing via PC, application installation from a PC, and other utility functions that enable Symbian OS phones to integrate effectively with PC and server-based data.

Synchr onization Burst (SB) Used for time synchronization of a mobile device.

Synchr onization Channel (SCH) Used for downlink only, SCH is used for frame synchronization and identification of the base station.

SyncML SyncML, which is based on XML, enables data synchronization between mobile devices and networked services. SyncML is transport, data type, and platform independent. SyncML works on a wide variety of transport protocols, including HTTP and WSP (part of WAP), and with data formats ranging from personal data (such as vCard and vCalendar) to relational data and XML documents. The SyncML consortium was set up by IBM, Nokia, and Psion and is sponsored by Symbian.

T

Telecommunications and Inter net Pr otocol Har monization over Networks (TIPHON) An European Telecommunications Standards Institute (ETSI) project designed to support the market for voice communications and voice band communications. In particular,

TIPHON ensures that users on IP-based networks can communicate with those on circuit-switched networks.

Telematics A wireless communications system designed for the collection and dissemination of information, particularly with vehicle-based electronic systems, vehicle tracking and positioning, online vehicle navigation, and information systems and emergency assistance.

Temporal Key Integrity Pr otocol (TKIP) The Temporal Key Integrity Protocol is part of the IEEE 802.11i encryption standard for wireless LANs. TKIP is the next generation of the Wired Equivalency Protocol (WEP), which is used to secure 802.11 wireless LANs. TKIP provides per-packet key mixing, a message integrity check, and a rekeying mechanism, thus fixing the flaws of WEP.

Temporary Mobile Subscriber Identity (TMSI) Covers the International Mobile Subscriber Identity (IMSI) to prevent over-the-air interception and tracing.

Terr estrial T runked Radio (TETRA) A European-developed digital private mobile radio technology that is now being extensively deployed worldwide.

Tetrapol A digital Private Mobile Radiocommunications (PMR) technology developed by French vendors that competes with Terrestrial Trunked Radio (TETRA).

Time Division Duplex (TDD) A radio technology for use in the unpaired spectrum.

Time Division Multiple Access (TDMA) A technology used in digital cellular telephone communication to divide each cellular channel into three time slots to increase the amount of data that can be carried. GSM and Digital AMPS (D-AMPS) use TDMA in one form or another. TDMA is also known as IS-136.

Time Division-Synchr onous CDMA (TD-SCDMA) A Code Division Multiple Access (CDMA) variant developed by Chinese vendors that is claimed to offer high data rates and greater coverage.

Timeslot A frame within a Time Division Multiple Access (TDMA) schema that has a time interval of 576 μs. The physical content of a timeslot is also known as a burst. Five different burst types exist; they are distinguished by different TDMA frame divisions.

Total Access Communications System (T ACS) An Advanced Mobile Phone System (AMPS) variant deployed in a number of countries, principally the United Kingdom.

Transcoder Rate Adapter Unit (TRAU) The transport unit for a 16 kbps traffic channel on the A-bis interface.

Transferr ed Account Pr ocedur e (TAP) The essential charging methodology for international GSM roaming. There have been four TAP standards: TAP1, TAP2, TAP2+, and TAP3. The latter offers variable record length and is sufficiently flexible to support all future requirements arising from the move to 3G.

Tri-band Refers to a mobile phone able to operate on the three internationally designated GSM frequencies: 900, 1800, and 1900 MHz.

TrueSync A technology that enables the optimal synchronization of calendars, address books, action lists, and memoranda. It enables multipoint, one-step synchronization of wireless and wireline devices, desktop computers, and server-based applications and services.

U

Ultrawideband (UWB) Also called digital pulse wireless, UWB is a wireless technology used for transmitting large amounts of digital data over a wide spectrum of frequency bands with very low power for a short distance.

Um The air interface between the BTS and the MS in a GSM network.

Unifor m Resour ce Locator (URL) The addressing system of the Internet.

Universal Mobile T elecommunications System (UMTS) The European standard for 3G. UMTS supports a theoretical data throughput of up to 2 Mbps.

Universal T err estrial Radio Access (UTRA) The air interface component of Wideband Code Division Multiple Access (WCDMA).

Universal T err estrial Radio Access Network (UTRAN) The UMTS radio access network comprising the Radio Network Controller (RNC), Node B, and the air interface.

Universal Subscriber Identity Module (USIM) The 3G equivalent of the GSM SIM.

Uu The air interface between the Node B and the MS in a UMTS network.

V

VeriChip An implantable computer chip the size of a grain of rice used for storing medical information. The chip itself contains no medical records, but codes that can be used by a doctor to unlock parts of a secure medical database as needed.

Virtual Private Network (VPN) A VPN works by using the shared public infrastructure while maintaining privacy through security procedures and tunneling protocols. Currently a VPN is the most secure way to log onto a wireless network and gain access to a LAN and WAN (typically the Internet).

Vocoded Vocoded, a name derived from *voice coder,* means the sound is not only digitized, but compressed as well. Its primary use is for secure radio communication. Vocoders are also often used to create the sound of a robot talking.

Voice Extensible Markup Language (V   oiceXML) VoiceXML is a specification designed to make applications more usable by allowing input and output of data using voice recognition, synthesized speech, digitized audio, and more. It uses voice recognition and response to let users interact more easily and naturally with telephony applications using a voice browser. AT&T, IBM, Lucent Technologies, and Motorola created VoiceXML 1.0 in a joint effort.

Voice-over-IP (V oIP) VoIP is a set of technologies that enables voice to be sent over a packet network. Although few corporations use VoIP today, over the next several years, companies will deploy VoIP in conjunction with 802.11 wireless LANs, enabling workers to have WLAN-based mobile phones when in the office.

Voice-over-W ireless-IP (V oWIP) VoWIP combining VoIP with 802.11 wireless LANs to create a wireless telephone system for offices is an emerging market segment. VoWIP enables businesses to leverage their wireless LANs to add voice communications, enabling companies to deploy and manage voice and data over a single wireless backbone.

W

WAP Identity Module (WIM)   WIM is the security module implemented in the SIM card for WAP applications. WIM provides security services for WAP applications, and allows you to use digital signatures. SIM cards with security module are provided by the SIM card issuer.

War-Chalking The systematic practice of marking and mapping nonsecured Wi-Fi 802.11b wireless APs. It involves the act of making chalk marks on outdoor surfaces (walls, sidewalks, buildings, sign posts, trees) to indicate the existence of an open wireless network connection, usually offering an Internet connection so that others can benefit from the free wireless access. There are three basic designs that are currently used: a pair of back-to-back semicircles, which denotes an open node; a closed circle, which denotes a closed node; a closed circle with a "W" inside, which denotes a node equipped with WEP.

War-Driving A computer-cracking technique that involves driving through a neighborhood with a wireless-enabled notebook computer and mapping houses and businesses that have wireless APs. War-driving is also called *whacking.*

War Flying A computer technique of sniffing for wireless networks from the air. The same equipment is used as for war-driving, but from an aircraft.

War Jacking Knocking out a real AP with a DoS attack and then setting up a new AP to serve as a new hub to devices that homed on the legitimate AP.

War Spamming Taking over a network connected to an unsecured AP and using it to inject spam into the Internet, typically from people's home accounts.

War Walking This is war-driving performed on foot instead of in a car. War walkers often like to use MiniStumbler and Pocket PCs to sniff shopping malls and big-box retail stores.

Wideband Code Division Multiple Access (WCDMA) Wideband CDMA is the 3G standard for GSM in Europe, Japan, and the United States. It's also the principal alternative being discussed in Asia. It supports very high-speed multimedia services such as full-motion video, Internet access, and videoconferencing. It uses one 5 MHz channel for both voice and data, offering data speeds up to 2 Mbps.

Wi-Fi Stands for wireless fidelity. Wi-Fi is the term for wireless Internet technology, otherwise currently known as the 802.11 standard.

Wi-Fi Alliance The Wi-Fi Alliance is a nonprofit international association formed in 1999 to certify interoperability of wireless Local Area Network products based on IEEE 802.11 specification. The goal of the Wi-Fi Alliance's members is to enhance user experience through product interoperability.

Wi-Fi Meshes In Wi-Fi mesh topology, each wireless node (workstation or other device) is connected directly to each of the others. In the partial mesh topology, some nodes are connected to all the others, but some of the nodes are connected only to those other nodes with which they exchange the most data.

Wi-Fi Protected Access (WP A) WPA is meant to be an interim solution and will try to fill the security void until the 802.11i draft is standardized. WPA proposes two security enhancements. The first is the Temporal Key Integrity Protocol (TKIP) to provide better data encryption. The second enhancement is EAP to authenticate the users. It provides a two-way authentication, so that it does not fall victim to man-in-the-middle attacks.

Wired Equivalent Privacy (WEP) WEP was a data encryption method used to protect the transmission between 802.11 wireless clients and APs. However, it used the same key among all communicating devices. WEP's problems are well known, including insufficient key length and lack of an automated method for distributing the keys. WEP can be easily cracked in a couple of hours with off-the-shelf tools.

Wireless Access Point See Access Point.

Wireless Application Protocol (WAP) WAP is an open specification that supports Internet protocols on wireless devices such as mobile phones, pagers, two-way radios, smart phones, and communicators to easily access and interact with Internet-based services. Simply put, WAP is a special way of formatting content so that it can appear on small screens, like those on mobile phones. WAP is designed to work with most wireless networks.

Wireless Internet Service Provider (WISP) A WISP is a service provider that specializes in offering users wireless access to the Internet. Many WISPs offer hotspot access.

Wireless IP The packet data protocol standard for sending wireless data over the Internet.

Wireless Local Area Network (WLAN) Local area networks using wireless transmissions such as radio or infrared instead of phone lines or fiber-optic cable to connect data devices. WLAN enables suitably equipped users to access the fixed network wirelessly, providing high-speed access to distant servers.

Wireless Local Loop (WLL) A technique for providing telephony and low-speed data services to fixed customers using wireless. Regarded as having considerable potential for rapidly addressing the telecommunications gap in developing countries. A number of different WLL solutions have been marketed based on cellular and cordless technologies.

Wireless Markup Language (WML) An XML language that's used to specify content and the user interface for WAP devices. WML is supported by almost every mobile phone browser in the world. It allows the text portions of Web pages to be presented on mobile phones and PDAs via a wireless connection. WML pages are requested and served in the same way as HDML pages. For Web servers to serve WML pages, they must contain the `text/vnd.wap.wml` mime type.

Wolfpack This technology would deny the enemy the use of all radio communications, including mobile phones, on the battlefield.

World Administration Radio Conference (WARC) An ITU conference held at regular intervals to determine the allocation of spectrum for various services.

Worldwide Geodetic System 1984 (WGS-84) A GPS standard. The system provides a built-in frame of reference allowing receivers from different vendors to provide the same positioning information.

Worldwide Interoperability for Microwave Access (Wi-Max) See 802.16.

X

XOR The XOR (exclusive-OR) gate provides an "either/or" function. The output is 1 if the inputs are different, but 0 if the inputs are the same.

eXtensible Hypertext Markup Language (xHTML)   xHTML is a family of document types that reproduce, subset, and extend HTML. xHTML family document types are XML based and designed to work in conjunction with XML-based user agents.

eXtensible Markup Language (XML)   XML is a markup language that describes data. XML is an open standard intended to make it easy to define, author, and manage document types. It is an extremely simple dialect of SGML. It can be used for Web pages or to store any kind of structure information or to encapsulate information to pass it between computers that would otherwise be unable to communicate.

Appendix A: Computer Fraud and Abuse Act 1986 (US) 18 USC 1030

Computer Fraud and Abuse Act 1986 (US) 18 USC 1030(a) 1030. Fraud and Related Activity in Connection With Computers

(a) Whoever

(1) knowingly accesses a computer without authorization or exceeds authorized access, and by means of such conduct obtains information that has been determined by the United States Government pursuant to an Executive order or statute to require protection against unauthorized disclosure for reasons of national defense or foreign relations, or any restricted data, as defined in paragraph r. of section 11 of the Atomic Energy Act of 1954, with the intent or reason to believe that such information so obtained is to be used to the injury of the United States, or to the advantage of any foreign nation;

(2) intentionally accesses a computer without authorization or exceeds authorized access, and thereby obtains information contained in a financial record of a financial institution, or of a card issuer as defined in section 1602(n) of title 15, or contained in a file of a consumer reporting agency on a consumer, as such terms are defined in the Fair Credit Reporting Act (15 U.S.C. 1681 et seq.);

(3) intentionally, without authorization to access any computer of a department or agency of the United States, accesses such a computer of that department or agency that is exclusively for the use of the Government of the United States or, in the case of a computer not exclusively for such use, is used by or for the Government of the United States and such conduct affects the use of the Government's operation of such computer;

(4) knowingly and with intent to defraud, accesses a Federal interest computer without authorization, or exceeds authorized access, and by means of such conduct furthers the intended fraud and obtains anything of value, unless the object of the fraud and the thing obtained consists only of the use of the computer;

(5) intentionally accesses a Federal interest computer without authorization and by means of one or more instances of such conduct alters, damages, or destroys information in any such Federal interest computer, or prevents authorized use of any such computer or information, and thereby

    (A) causes loss to one or more others of a value aggregating $1,000 or more during any one year period; or

    (B) modifies or impairs, or potentially modifies or impairs the medical examination, medical diagnosis, medical treatment, or medical care of one or more individuals; or

(6) knowingly and with intent to defraud traffics (as defined in section 1029) in any password or similar information through which a computer may be accessed without authorization, if

    (A) such trafficking affects interstate or foreign commerce; or

    (B) such computer is used by or for the Government of the United States; shall be punished as provided in subsection (c) of this section.

Computer Fraud and Abuse Act 1986 (US) 18 USC 1030(b)

(b) Whoever attempts to commit an offense under subsection (a) of this section shall be punished as provided in subsection (c) of this section.

Computer Fraud and Abuse Act 1986 (US) 18 USC 1030(c)

(c) The punishment for an offense under subsection (a) or (b) of this section is –

(1)(A) a fine under this title or imprisonment for not more than ten years or both, in the case of an offense under subsection (a)(1) of this section which does not occur after a conviction for another offense under such subsection, or an attempt to commit an offense punishable under this subparagraph; and

(B) a fine under this title or imprisonment for not more than twenty years, or both, in the case of an offense under subsection (a)(1) of this section which occurs after a conviction for another offense under such subsection, or an attempt to commit an offense punishable under this subparagraph; and

(2)(A) a fine under this title or imprisonment for not more than one year, or both, in the case of an offense under subsection (a)(2), (a)(3) or (a)(6) of this section which does not occur after a conviction for another offense under such subsection, or an attempt to commit an offense punishable under this subparagraph; and

(B) a fine under this title or imprisonment for not more than ten years, or both, in the case of an offense under subsection (a)(2), (a)(3) or (a)(6) of this section which occurs after a conviction for another offense under such subsection, or an attempt to commit an offense punishable under this subparagraph; and

(3)(A) a fine under this title or imprisonment for not more than five years or both, in the case of an offense under subsection (a)(4) or (a)(5) of this section which does not occur after a conviction for another offense under such subsection, or an attempt to commit an offense punishable under this subparagraph; and

(B) a fine under this title or imprisonment for not more than ten years, or both, in the case of an offense under subsection (a)(4) or (a)(5) of this section which occurs after a conviction for another offense under such subsection, or an attempt to commit an offense punishable under this subparagraph.

Computer Fraud and Abuse Act 1986 (US) 18 USC 1030(d)

(d) The United States Secret Service shall, in addition to any other agency having such authority, have the authority to investigate offenses under this section. Such authority of the United States Secret Service shall be exercised in accordance with an agreement which shall be entered into by the Secretary of the Treasury and the Attorney General.

Computer Fraud and Abuse Act 1986 (US) 18 USC 1030(e)

(e) As used in this section

(1) the term **"computer"** means an electronic, magnetic, optical, electrochemical, or other high speed data processing device performing logical, arithmetic, or storage functions, and includes any data storage facility or communications facility directly related to or operating in conjunction with such device, but such term does not include an automated typewriter or typesetter, a portable hand held calculator, or other similar device;

(2) the term **"Federal interest computer"** means a computer

    (A) exclusively for the use of a financial institution or the United States Government, or, in the case of a computer not exclusively for such use, used by or for a financial institution or the United States Government and the conduct constituting the offense affects the use of the financial institution's operation or the Government's operation of such computer; or

    (B) which is one of two or more computers used in committing the offense, not all of which are located in the same State;

(3) the term **"State"** includes the District of Columbia, the Commonwealth of Puerto Rico, and any other possession or territory of the United States;

(4) the term **"financial institution"** means

    (A) an institution with deposits insured by the Federal Deposit Insurance Corporation;

    (B) the Federal Reserve or a member of the Federal Reserve including any Federal Reserve Bank;

    (C) a credit union with accounts insured by the National Credit Union Administration;

    (D) a member of the Federal home loan bank system and any home loan bank;

    (E) any institution of the Farm Credit System under the Farm Credit Act of 1971;

    (F) a broker-dealer registered with the Securities and Exchange Commission pursuant to section 15 of the Securities Exchange Act of 1934; and

    (G) the Securities Investor Protection Corporation;

(5) the term **"financial record"** means information derived from any record held by a financial institution pertaining to a customer's relationship with the financial institution;

(6) the term **"exceeds authorized access"** means to access a computer with authorization and to use such access to obtain or alter information in the computer that the assessor is not entitled so to obtain or alter; and

(7) the term **"department of the United States"** means the legislative or judicial branch of the government or one of the executive departments enumerated in section 101 of title 5.

Computer Fraud and Abuse Act 1986 (US) 18 USC 1030(f)

(f) This section does not prohibit any lawfully authorized investigative, protective, or intelligence activity of a law enforcement agency of the United States, a State, or a political subdivision of a State, or of an intelligence agency of the United States.

Appendix B: Communications Interception Act

Section 2510. Definitions

As used in this chapter

(1) "wire communication" means any aural transfer made in whole or in part through the use of facilities for the transmission of communications by the aid of wire, cable, or other like connection between the point of origin and the point of reception (including the use of such connection in a switching station) furnished or operated by any person engaged in providing or operating such facilities for the transmission of interstate or foreign communications or communications affecting interstate or foreign commerce;

(2) "oral communication" means any oral communication uttered by a person exhibiting an expectation that such communication is not subject to interception under circumstances justifying such expectation, but such term does not include any electronic communication;

(3) "State" means any State of the United States, the District of Columbia, the Commonwealth of Puerto Rico, and any territory or possession of the United States;

(4) "intercept" means the aural or other acquisition of the contents of any wire, electronic, or oral communication through the use of any electronic, mechanical, or other device.

(5) "electronic, mechanical, or other device" means any device or apparatus which can be used to intercept a wire, oral, or electronic communication other than

    (a) any telephone or telegraph instrument, equipment or facility, or any component thereof,

        (i) furnished to the subscriber or user by a provider of wire or electronic communication service in the ordinary course of its business and being used by the subscriber or user in the ordinary course of its business or furnished by such subscriber or user for connection to the facilities of such service and used in the ordinary course of its business; or

        (ii) being used by a provider of wire or electronic communication service in the ordinary course of its business, or by an investigative or law enforcement officer in the ordinary course of his duties;

    (b) a hearing aid or similar device being used to correct subnormal hearing to not better than normal;

(6) "person" means any employee, or agent of the United States or any State or political subdivision thereof, and any individual, partnership, association, joint stock company, trust, or corporation;

(7) "Investigative or law enforcement officer" means any officer of the United States or of a State or political subdivision thereof, who is empowered by law to conduct investigations of or to make arrests for offenses enumerated in this chapter, and any attorney authorized by law to prosecute or participate in the prosecution of such offenses;

(8) "contents", when used with respect to any wire, oral, or electronic communication, includes any information concerning the substance, purport, or meaning of that communication;

(9) "Judge of competent jurisdiction" means

    (a) a judge of a United States district court or a United States court of appeals; and

    (b) a judge of any court of general criminal jurisdiction of a State who is authorized by a statute of that State to enter orders authorizing interceptions of wire, oral, or electronic communications;

(10) "communication common carrier" shall have the same meaning which is given the term "common carrier" by section 153(h) of title 47 of the United States Code;

(11) "aggrieved person" means a person who was a party to any intercepted wire, oral, or electronic communication or a person against whom the interception was directed;

(12) "electronic communication" means any transfer of signs, signals, writing, images, sounds, data, or intelligence of any nature transmitted in whole or in part by a wire, radio, electromagnetic, photoelectronic or photooptical system that affects interstate or foreign commerce, but does not include

    (A) any wire or oral communication;

    (B) any communication made through a tone-only paging device;

    (C) any communication from a tracking device (as defined in section 3117 of this title); or

    (D) electronic funds transfer information stored by a financial institution in a communications system used for the electronic storage and transfer of funds;

(13) "user" means any person or entity who

    (A) uses an electronic communication service; and

    (B) is duly authorized by the provider of such service to engage in such use;

(14) "electronic communications system" means any wire, radio, electromagnetic, photooptical or photoelectronic facilities for the transmission of wire or electronic communications, and any computer facilities or related electronic equipment for the electronic storage of such communications;

(15) "electronic communication service" means any service which provides to users thereof the ability to send or receive wire or electronic communications;

(16) "readily accessible to the general public" means, with respect to a radio communication, that such communication is not

    (A) scrambled or encrypted;

    (B) transmitted using modulation techniques whose essential parameters have been withheld from the public with the intention of preserving the privacy of such communication;

    (C) carried on a subcarrier or other signal subsidiary to a radio transmission;

    (D) transmitted over a communication system provided by a common carrier, unless the communication is a tone only paging system communication; or

    (E) transmitted on frequencies allocated under part 25, subpart D, E, or F of part 74, or part 94 of the Rules of the Federal Communications Commission, unless, in the case of a communication transmitted on a frequency allocated under part 74 that is not exclusively allocated to broadcast auxiliary services, the communication is a two-way voice communication by radio;

(17) "electronic storage" means

(A) any temporary, intermediate storage of a wire or electronic communication incidental to the electronic transmission thereof; and

(B) any storage of such communication by an electronic communication service for purposes of backup protection of such communication;

(18) "aural transfer" means a transfer containing the human voice at any point between and including the point of origin and the point of reception;

(19) "foreign intelligence information", for purposes of section 2517(6) of this title, means

(A) information, whether or not concerning a United States person, that relates to the ability of the United States to protect against

  (i) actual or potential attack or other grave hostile acts of a foreign power or an agent of a foreign power;

  (ii) sabotage or international terrorism by a foreign power or an agent of a foreign power; or

  (iii) clandestine intelligence activities by an intelligence service or network of a foreign power or by an agent of a foreign power; or

(B) information, whether or not concerning a United States person, with respect to a foreign power or foreign territory that relates to

  (i) the national defense or the security of the United States; or

  (ii) the conduct of the foreign affairs of the United States;

(20) "protected computer" has the meaning set forth in section 1030; and

(21) "computer trespasser"

(A) means a person who accesses a protected computer without authorization and thus has no reasonable expectation of privacy in any communication transmitted to, through, or from the protected computer; and

(B) does not include a person known by the owner or operator of the protected computer to have an existing contractual relationship with the owner or operator of the protected computer for access to all or part of the protected computer.

Section 2511. Interception and Disclosure of Wire, Oral, or Electronic Communications Prohibited

(1) Except as otherwise specifically provided in this chapter any person who

   (a) intentionally intercepts, endeavors to intercept, or procures any other person to intercept or endeavor to intercept, any wire, oral, or electronic communication;

   (b) intentionally uses, endeavors to use, or procures any other person to use or endeavor to use any electronic, mechanical, or other device to intercept any oral communication when

      (i) such device is affixed to, or otherwise transmits a signal through, a wire, cable, or other like connection used in wire communication; or

      (ii) such device transmits communications by radio, or interferes with the transmission of such communication; or

      (iii) such person knows, or has reason to know, that such device or any component thereof has been sent through the mail or transported in interstate or foreign commerce; or

      (iv) such use or endeavor to use

         (A) takes place on the premises of any business or other commercial establishment the operations of which affect interstate or foreign commerce; or

         (B) obtains or is for the purpose of obtaining information relating to the operations of any business or other commercial establishment the operations of which affect interstate or foreign commerce; or

      (v) such person acts in the District of Columbia, the Commonwealth of Puerto Rico, or any territory or possession of the United States;

   (c) intentionally discloses, or endeavors to disclose, to any other person the contents of any wire, oral, or electronic communication, knowing or having reason to know that the information was obtained through the interception of a wire, oral, or electronic communication in violation of this subsection;

   (d) intentionally uses, or endeavors to use, the contents of any wire, oral, or electronic communication, knowing or having reason to know that the information was obtained through the interception of a wire, oral, or electronic communication in violation of this subsection; or

(e)

    (i) intentionally discloses, or endeavors to disclose, to any other person the contents of any wire, oral, or electronic communication, intercepted by means authorized by sections 2511(2)(a)(ii), 2511(2)(b)–(c), 2511(2)(e), 2516, and 2518 of this chapter,

    (ii) knowing or having reason to know that the information was obtained through the interception of such a communication in connection with a criminal investigation,

    (iii) having obtained or received the information in connection with a criminal investigation, and

    (iv) with intent to improperly obstruct, impede, or interfere with a duly authorized criminal investigation, shall be punished as provided in subsection (4) or shall be subject to suit as provided in subsection (5).

(2)

  (a)

    (i) It shall not be unlawful under this chapter for an operator of a switchboard, or an officer, employee, or agent of a provider of wire or electronic communication service, whose facilities are used in the transmission of a wire or electronic communication, to intercept, disclose, or use that communication in the normal course of his employment while engaged in any activity which is a necessary incident to the rendition of his service or to the protection of the rights or property of the provider of that service, except that a provider of wire communication service to the public shall not utilize service observing or random monitoring except for mechanical or service quality control checks.

    (ii) Notwithstanding any other law, providers of wire or electronic communication service, their officers, employees, and agents, landlords, custodians, or other persons, are authorized to provide information, facilities, or technical assistance to persons authorized by law to intercept wire, oral, or electronic communications or to conduct electronic surveillance, as defined in section 101 of the Foreign Intelligence Surveillance Act of 1978, if such provider, its officers, employees, or agents, landlord, custodian, or other specified person, has been provided with

      (A) a court order directing such assistance signed by the authorizing judge, or

(B) a certification in writing by a person specified in section 2518(7) of this title or the Attorney General of the United States that no warrant or court order is required by law, that all statutory requirements have been met, and that the specified assistance is required, setting forth the period of time during which the provision of the information, facilities, or technical assistance is authorized and specifying the information, facilities, or technical assistance required. No provider of wire or electronic communication service, officer, employee, or agent thereof, or landlord, custodian, or other specified person shall disclose the existence of any interception or surveillance or the device used to accomplish the interception or surveillance with respect to which the person has been furnished a court order or certification under this chapter, except as may otherwise be required by legal process and then only after prior notification to the Attorney General or to the principal prosecuting attorney of a State or any political subdivision of a State, as may be appropriate. Any such disclosure, shall render such person liable for the civil damages provided for in section 2520. No cause of action shall lie in any court against any provider of wire or electronic communication service, its officers, employees, or agents, landlord, custodian, or other specified person for providing information, facilities, or assistance in accordance with the terms of a court order or certification under this chapter.

(b) It shall not be unlawful under this chapter for an officer, employee, or agent of the Federal Communications Commission, in the normal course of his employment and in discharge of the monitoring responsibilities exercised by the Commission in the enforcement of chapter 5 of title 47 of the United States Code, to intercept a wire or electronic communication, or oral communication transmitted by radio, or to disclose or use the information thereby obtained.

(c) It shall not be unlawful under this chapter for a person acting under color of law to intercept a wire, oral, or electronic communication, where such person is a party to the communication or one of the parties to the communication has given prior consent to such interception.

(d) It shall not be unlawful under this chapter for a person not acting under color of law to intercept a wire, oral, or electronic communication where such person is a party to the communication or where one of the parties to the communication has given prior consent to such interception unless such communication is intercepted for the purpose of committing any criminal or tortious act in violation of the Constitution or laws of the United States or of any State.

(e) Notwithstanding any other provision of this title or section 705 or 706 of the Communications Act of 1934, it shall not be unlawful for an officer, employee, or agent of the United States in the normal course of his official duty to conduct electronic surveillance, as defined in section 101 of the Foreign Intelligence Surveillance Act of 1978, as authorized by that Act.

(f) Nothing contained in this chapter or chapter 121 or 206 of this title, or section 705 of the Communications Act of 1934, shall be deemed to affect the acquisition by the United States Government of foreign intelligence information from international or foreign communications, or foreign intelligence activities conducted in accordance with otherwise applicable Federal law involving a foreign electronic communications system, utilizing a means other than electronic surveillance as defined in section 101 of the Foreign Intelligence Surveillance Act of 1978, and procedures in this chapter or chapter 121 and the Foreign Intelligence Surveillance Act of 1978 shall be the exclusive means by which electronic surveillance, as defined in section 101 of such Act, and the interception of domestic wire, oral, and electronic communications may be conducted.

(g) It shall not be unlawful under this chapter or chapter 121 of this title for any person

   (i)   to intercept or access an electronic communication made through an electronic communication system that is configured so that such electronic communication is readily accessible to the general public;

   (ii) to intercept any radio communication which is transmitted

      (I)   by any station for the use of the general public, or that relates to ships, aircraft, vehicles, or persons in distress;

      (II) by any governmental, law enforcement, civil defense, private land mobile, or public safety communications system, including police and fire, readily accessible to the general public;

(III) by a station operating on an authorized frequency within the bands allocated to the amateur, citizens band, or general mobile radio services; or

(IV) by any marine or aeronautical communications system;

(iii) to engage in any conduct which

(I) is prohibited by section 633 of the Communications Act of 1934; or

(II) is excepted from the application of section 705(a) of the Communications Act of 1934 by section 705(b) of that Act;

(iv) to intercept any wire or electronic communication the transmission of which is causing harmful interference to any lawfully operating station or consumer electronic equipment, to the extent necessary to identify the source of such interference; or

(v) for other users of the same frequency to intercept any radio communication made through a system that utilizes frequencies monitored by individuals engaged in the provision or the use of such system, if such communication is not scrambled or encrypted.

(h) It shall not be unlawful under this chapter

(i) to use a pen register or a trap and trace device (as those terms are defined for the purposes of chapter 206 (relating to pen registers and trap and trace devices) of this title); or

(ii) for a provider of electronic communication service to record the fact that a wire or electronic communication was initiated or completed in order to protect such provider, another provider furnishing service toward the completion of the wire or electronic communication, or a user of that service, from fraudulent, unlawful or abusive use of such service.

(i) It shall not be unlawful under this chapter for a person acting under color of law to intercept the wire or electronic communications of a computer trespasser transmitted to, through, or from the protected computer, if

(I) the owner or operator of the protected computer authorizes the interception of the computer trespasser's communications on the protected computer;

(II) the person acting under color of law is lawfully engaged in an investigation;

(III) the person acting under color of law has reasonable grounds to believe that the contents of the computer trespasser's communications will be relevant to the investigation; and

(IV) such interception does not acquire communications other than those transmitted to or from the computer trespasser.

(3)

(a) Except as provided in paragraph (b) of this subsection, a person or entity providing an electronic communication service to the public shall not intentionally divulge the contents of any communication (other than one to such person or entity, or an agent thereof) while in transmission on that service to any person or entity other than an addressee or intended recipient of such communication or an agent of such addressee or intended recipient.

(b) A person or entity providing electronic communication service to the public may divulge the contents of any such communication

(i) as otherwise authorized in section 2511(2)(a) or 2517 of this title;

(ii) with the lawful consent of the originator or any addressee or intended recipient of such communication;

(iii) to a person employed or authorized, or whose facilities are used, to forward such communication to its destination; or

(iv) which were inadvertently obtained by the service provider and which appear to pertain to the commission of a crime, if such divulgence is made to a law enforcement agency.

(4)

(a) Except as provided in paragraph (b) of this subsection or in subsection (5), whoever violates subsection (1) of this section shall be fined under this title or imprisoned not more than five years, or both.

(b) If the offense is a first offense under paragraph (a) of this subsection and is not for a tortious or illegal purpose or for purposes of direct or indirect commercial advantage or private commercial gain, and the wire or electronic communication with respect to which the offense under paragraph (a) is a radio communication that is not scrambled, encrypted, or transmitted using modulation techniques the essential parameters of which have been withheld from the public with the intention of preserving the privacy of such communication, then

(i) if the communication is not the radio portion of a cellular telephone communication, a cordless telephone communication that is transmitted between the cordless telephone handset and the base unit, a public land mobile radio service communication or a paging service communication, and the conduct is not that described in subsection (5), the offender shall be fined under this title or imprisoned not more than one year, or both; and

(ii) if the communication is the radio portion of a cellular telephone communication, a cordless telephone communication that is transmitted between the cordless telephone handset and the base unit, a public land mobile radio service communication or a paging service communication, the offender shall be fined under this title.

(c) Conduct otherwise an offense under this subsection that consists of or relates to the interception of a satellite transmission that is not encrypted or scrambled and that is transmitted

(i) to a broadcasting station for purposes of retransmission to the general public; or

(ii) as an audio subcarrier intended for redistribution to facilities open to the public, but not including data transmissions or telephone calls, is not an offense under this subsection unless the conduct is for the purposes of direct or indirect commercial advantage or private financial gain.

(5)

(a)

(i) If the communication is

(A) a private satellite video communication that is not scrambled or encrypted and the conduct in violation of this chapter is the private viewing of that communication and is not for a tortious or illegal purpose or for purposes of direct or indirect commercial advantage or private commercial gain; or

(B) a radio communication that is transmitted on frequencies allocated under subpart D of part 74 of the rules of the Federal Communications Commission that is not scrambled or encrypted and the conduct in violation of this chapter is not for a tortious or illegal purpose or for purposes of direct or indirect commercial advantage or private commercial gain, then the person who engages in such conduct shall be subject to suit by the Federal Government in a court of competent jurisdiction.

(ii) In an action under this subsection

(A) if the violation of this chapter is a first offense for the person under paragraph (a) of subsection (4) and such person has not been found liable in a civil action under section 2520 of this title, the Federal Government shall be entitled to appropriate injunctive relief; and

(B) if the violation of this chapter is a second or subsequent offense under paragraph (a) of subsection (4) or such person has been found liable in any prior civil action under section 2520, the person shall be subject to a mandatory $500 civil fine.

(b) The court may use any means within its authority to enforce an injunction issued under paragraph (ii)(A), and shall impose a civil fine of not less than $500 for each violation of such an injunction

Section 2512. Manufacture, Distribution, Possession, and Advertising of Wire, Oral, or Electronic Communication Intercepting Devices Prohibited

(1) Except as otherwise specifically provided in this chapter, any person who intentionally

(a) sends through the mail, or sends or carries in interstate or foreign commerce, any electronic, mechanical, or other device, knowing or having reason to know that the design of such device renders it primarily useful for the purpose of the surreptitious interception of wire, oral, or electronic communications;

(b) manufactures, assembles, possesses, or sells any electronic, mechanical, or other device, knowing or having reason to know that the design of such device renders it primarily useful for the purpose of the surreptitious interception of wire, oral, or electronic communications, and that such device or any component thereof has been or will be sent through the mail or transported in interstate or foreign commerce; or

(c) places in any newspaper, magazine, handbill, or other publication any advertisement of

(i) any electronic, mechanical, or other device knowing or having reason to know that the design of such device renders it primarily useful for the purpose of the surreptitious interception of wire, oral, or electronic communications; or

>   (ii) any other electronic, mechanical, or other device, where such advertisement promotes the use of such device for the purpose of the surreptitious knowing or having reason to know that such advertisement will be sent through the mail or transported in interstate or foreign commerce, shall be fined under this title or imprisoned not more than five years, or both.

(2) It shall not be unlawful under this section for
   (a) a provider of wire or electronic communication service or an officer, agent, or employee of, or a person under contract with, such a provider, in the normal course of the business of providing that wire or electronic communication service, or
   (b) an officer, agent, or employee of, or a person under contract with, the United States, a State, or a political subdivision thereof, in the normal course of the activities of the United States, a State, or a political subdivision thereof, to send through the mail, send or carry in interstate or foreign commerce, or manufacture, assemble, possess, or sell any electronic, mechanical, or other device knowing or having reason to know that the design of such device renders it primarily useful for the purpose of the surreptitious interception of wire, oral, or electronic communications.

(3) It shall not be unlawful under this section to advertise for sale a device described in subsection (1) of this section if the advertisement is mailed, sent, or carried in interstate or foreign commerce solely to a domestic provider of wire or electronic communication service or to an agency of the United States, a State, or a political subdivision thereof which is duly authorized to use such device.

Section 2513. Confiscation of Wire, Oral, or Electronic Communication Intercepting Devices

Any electronic, mechanical, or other device used, sent, carried, manufactured, assembled, possessed, sold, or advertised in violation of section 2511 or section 2512 of this chapter may be seized and forfeited to the United States. All provisions of law relating to

(1) the seizure, summary and judicial forfeiture, and condemnation of vessels, vehicles, merchandise, and baggage for violations of the customs laws contained in title 19 of the United States Code,
(2) the disposition of such vessels, vehicles, merchandise, and baggage or the proceeds from the sale thereof,

(3) the remission or mitigation of such forfeiture,

(4) the compromise of claims, and

(5) the award of compensation to informers in respect of such forfeitures, shall apply to seizures and forfeitures incurred, or alleged to have been incurred, under the provisions of this section, insofar as applicable and not inconsistent with the provisions of this section; except that such duties as are imposed upon the collector of customs or any other person with respect to the seizure and forfeiture of vessels, vehicles, merchandise, and baggage under the provisions of the customs laws contained in title 19 of the United States Code shall be performed with respect to seizure and forfeiture of electronic, mechanical, or other intercepting devices under this section by such officers, agents, or other persons as may be authorized or designated for that purpose by the Attorney General.

Section 2515. Prohibition of Use as Evidence of Intercepted Wire or Oral Communications

Whenever any wire or oral communication has been intercepted, no part of the contents of such communication and no evidence derived therefrom may be received in evidence in any trial, hearing, or other proceeding in or before any court, grand jury, department, officer, agency, regulatory body, legislative committee, or other authority of the United States, a State, or a political subdivision thereof if the disclosure of that information would be in violation of this chapter.

Section 2516. Authorization for Interception of Wire, Oral, or Electronic Communications

(1) The Attorney General, Deputy Attorney General, Associate Attorney General, or any Assistant Attorney General, any acting Assistant Attorney General, or any Deputy Assistant Attorney General or acting Deputy Assistant Attorney General in the Criminal Division specially designated by the Attorney General, may authorize an application to a Federal judge of competent jurisdiction for, and such judge may grant in conformity with section 2518 of this chapter an order authorizing or approving the interception of wire or oral communications by the Federal Bureau of Investigation, or a Federal agency having responsibility for the investigation of the

offense as to which the application is made, when such interception may provide or has provided evidence of

(a) any offense punishable by death or by imprisonment for more than one year under sections 2274 through 2277 of title 42 of the United States Code (relating to the enforcement of the Atomic Energy Act of 1954), section 2284 of title 42 of the United States Code (relating to sabotage of nuclear facilities or fuel), or under the following chapters of this title: chapter 37 (relating to espionage), chapter 90 (relating to protection of trade secrets), chapter 105 (relating to sabotage), chapter 115 (relating to treason), chapter 102 (relating to riots), chapter 65 (relating to malicious mischief), chapter 111 (relating to destruction of vessels), or chapter 81 (relating to piracy).

(b) a violation of section 186 or section 501(c) of title 29, United States Code (dealing with restrictions on payments and loans to labor organizations), or any offense which involves murder, kidnapping, robbery, or extortion, and which is punishable under this title.

(c) any offense which is punishable under the following sections of this title: section 201 (bribery of public officials and witnesses), section 215 (relating to bribery of bank officials), section 224 (bribery in sporting contests), subsection (d), (e), (f), (g), (h), or (i) of section 844 (unlawful use of explosives), section 1032 (relating to concealment of assets), section 1084 (transmission of wagering information), section 751 (relating to escape), section 1014 (relating to loans and credit applications generally; renewals and discounts), sections 1503, 1512, and 1513 (influencing or injuring an officer, juror, or witness generally), section 1510 (obstruction of criminal investigations), section 1511 (obstruction of State or local law enforcement), section 1751 (Presidential and Presidential staff assassination, kidnapping, and assault), section 1951 (interference with commerce by threats or violence), section 1952 (interstate and foreign travel or transportation in aid of racketeering enterprises), section 1958 (relating to use of interstate commerce facilities in the commission of murder for hire), section 1959 (relating to violent crimes in aid of racketeering activity), section 1954 (offer, acceptance, or solicitation to influence operations of employee benefit plan), section 1955 (prohibition of business enterprises of gambling), section 1956 (laundering of monetary instruments), section 1957 (relating to engaging in monetary transactions in property derived from specified unlawful activity), section 659 (theft from interstate shipment), section 664 (embezzlement from pension and welfare funds), section 1343 (fraud by wire, radio, or television), section 1344 (relating to bank fraud), sections 2251 and 2252 (sexual exploitation of children), sections 2312, 2313, 2314, and 2315 (interstate transportation of stolen property), section 2321 (relating to trafficking in certain motor vehicles or motor vehicle parts), section 1203 (relating to hostage taking), section 1029 (relating to fraud and related activity in connection with access devices), section 3146 (relating to penalty for failure to appear), section 3521(b)(3) (relating to witness relocation and assistance), section 32 (relating to destruction of aircraft or aircraft facilities), section 38 (relating to aircraft parts fraud), section 1963 (violations with respect to racketeer influenced and corrupt organizations), section 115 (relating to threatening or retaliating against a Federal official), section 1341 (relating to mail fraud), a felony violation of section 1030 (relating to computer fraud and abuse), section 351 (violations with respect to congressional, Cabinet, or Supreme Court assassinations, kidnapping, and assault), section 831 (relating to prohibited transactions involving nuclear materials), section 33 (relating to destruction of motor vehicles or motor vehicle facilities), section 175 (relating to biological weapons), section 1992 (relating to wrecking trains), a felony violation of section 1028 (relating to production of false identification documentation), section 1425 (relating to the procurement of citizenship or nationalization unlawfully), section 1426 (relating to the reproduction of naturalization or citizenship papers), section 1427 (relating to the sale of naturalization or citizenship papers), section 1541 (relating to passport issuance without authority), section 1542 (relating to false statements in passport applications), section 1543 (relating to forgery or false use of passports), section 1544 (relating to misuse of passports), or section 1546 (relating to fraud and misuse of visas, permits, and other documents).

(d) any offense involving counterfeiting punishable under section 471, 472, or 473 of this title;

(e) any offense involving fraud connected with a case under title 11 or the manufacture, importation, receiving, concealment, buying, selling, or otherwise dealing in narcotic drugs, marihuana, or other dangerous drugs, punishable under any law of the United States;

(f) any offense including extortionate credit transactions under sections 892, 893, or 894 of this title.

(g) a violation of section 5322 of title 31, United States Code (dealing with the reporting of currency transactions;

(h) any felony violation of sections 2511 and 2512 (relating to interception and disclosure of certain communications and to certain intercepting devices) of this title;

(i) any felony violation of chapter 71 (relating to obscenity) of this title;

(j) any violation of section 60123(b) (relating to destruction of a natural gas pipeline) or section 46502 (relating to aircraft piracy) of title 49;

(k) any criminal violation of section 2778 of title 22 (relating to the Arms Export Control Act);

(l) the location of any fugitive from justice from an offense described in this section;

(m) a violation of section 274, 277, or 278 of the Immigration and Nationality Act (8 U.S.C. 1324, 1327, or 1328) (relating to the smuggling of aliens);

(n) any felony violation of sections 922 and 924 of title 18, United States Code (relating to firearms);

(o) any violation of section 5861 of the Internal Revenue Code of 1986 (relating to firearms);

(p) a felony violation of section 1028 (relating to production of false identification documents), section 1542 (relating to false statements in passport applications), section 1546 (relating to fraud and misuse of visas, permits, and other documents) of this title or a violation of section 274, 277, or 278 of the Immigration and Nationality Act (relating to the smuggling of aliens); or

(q) any criminal violation of section 229 (relating to chemical weapons); or sections 2332, 2332a, 2332b, 2332d, 2339A, or 2339B of this title (relating to terrorism); or

(r) any conspiracy to commit any offense described in any sub-paragraph of this paragraph.

(2) The principal prosecuting attorney of any State, or the principal prosecuting attorney of any political subdivision thereof, if such attorney is authorized by a statute of that State to make application to a State court judge of competent jurisdiction for an order authorizing or approving the interception of wire, oral, or electronic communications, may apply to such judge for, and such judge may grant in conformity with section 2518 of this chapter and with the applicable State statute an order authorizing, or approving the interception of wire, oral, or electronic communications by investigative or law enforcement officers having responsibility for the

investigation of the offense as to which the application is made, when such interception may provide or has provided evidence of the commission of the offense of murder, kidnapping, gambling, robbery, bribery, extortion, or dealing in narcotic drugs, marihuana or other dangerous drugs, or other crime dangerous to life, limb, or property, and punishable by imprisonment for more than one year, designated in any applicable State statute authorizing such interception, or any conspiracy to commit any of the foregoing offenses.

(3) Any attorney for the Government (as such term is defined for the purposes of the Federal Rules of Criminal Procedure) may authorize an application to a Federal judge of competent jurisdiction for, and such judge may grant, in conformity with section 2518 of this title, an order authorizing or approving the interception of electronic communications by an investigative or law enforcement officer having responsibility for the investigation of the offense as to which the application is made, when such interception may provide or has provided evidence of any Federal felony.

Section 2517. Authorization for Disclosure and Use of Intercepted Wire, Oral, or Electronic Communications

(1) Any investigative or law enforcement officer who, by any means authorized by this chapter, has obtained knowledge of the contents of any wire, oral, or electronic communication, or evidence derived therefrom, may disclose such contents to another investigative or law enforcement officer to the extent that such disclosure is appropriate to the proper performance of the official duties of the officer making or receiving the disclosure.

(2) Any investigative or law enforcement officer who, by any means authorized by this chapter, has obtained knowledge of the contents of any wire, oral, or electronic communication or evidence derived therefrom may use such contents to the extent such use is appropriate to the proper performance of his official duties.

(3) Any person who has received, by any means authorized by this chapter, any information concerning a wire, oral, or electronic communication, or evidence derived therefrom intercepted in accordance with the provisions of this chapter may disclose the contents of that communication or such derivative evidence while giving testimony under oath or affirmation in any proceeding held

under the authority of the United States or of any State or political subdivision thereof.

(4) No otherwise privileged wire, oral, or electronic communication intercepted in accordance with, or in violation of, the provisions of this chapter shall lose its privileged character.

(5) When an investigative or law enforcement officer, while engaged in intercepting wire, oral, or electronic communications in the manner authorized herein, intercepts wire, oral, or electronic communications relating to offenses other than those specified in the order of authorization or approval, the contents thereof, and evidence derived therefrom, may be disclosed or used as provided in subsections (1) and (2) of this section. Such contents and any evidence derived therefrom may be used under subsection (3) of this section when authorized or approved by a judge of competent jurisdiction where such judge finds on subsequent application that the contents were otherwise intercepted in accordance with the provisions of this chapter. Such application shall be made as soon as practicable.

(6) Any investigative or law enforcement officer, or attorney for the Government, who by any means authorized by this chapter, has obtained knowledge of the contents of any wire, oral, or electronic communication, or evidence derived therefrom, may disclose such contents to any other Federal law enforcement, intelligence, protective, immigration, national defense, or national security official to the extent that such contents include foreign intelligence or counterintelligence (as defined in section 3 of the National Security Act of 1947 (50 U.S.C. 401a)), or foreign intelligence information (as defined in subsection (19) of section 2510 of this title), to assist the official who is to receive that information in the performance of his official duties. Any Federal official who receives information pursuant to this provision may use that information only as necessary in the conduct of that person's official duties subject to any limitations on the unauthorized disclosure of such information.

Section 2518. Procedure for Interception of Wire, Oral, or Electronic Communications

(1) Each application for an order authorizing or approving the interception of a wire, oral, or electronic communication under this chapter shall be made in writing upon oath or affirmation to a judge of competent jurisdiction and shall state the applicant's

authority to make such application. Each application shall include the following information:

(a) the identity of the investigative or law enforcement officer making the application, and the officer authorizing the application;

(b) a full and complete statement of the facts and circumstances relied upon by the applicant, to justify his belief that an order should be issued, including

    (i) details as to the particular offense that has been, is being, or is about to be committed,

    (ii) except as provided in subsection (11), a particular description of the nature and location of the facilities from which or the place where the communication is to be intercepted,

    (iii) a particular description of the type of communications sought to be intercepted,

    (iv) the identity of the person, if known, committing the offense and whose communications are to be intercepted;

(c) a full and complete statement as to whether or not other investigative procedures have been tried and failed or why they reasonably appear to be unlikely to succeed if tried or to be too dangerous;

(d) a statement of the period of time for which the interception is required to be maintained. If the nature of the investigation is such that the authorization for interception should not automatically terminate when the described type of communication has been first obtained, a particular description of facts establishing probable cause to believe that additional communications of the same type will occur thereafter;

(e) a full and complete statement of the facts concerning all previous applications known to the individual authorizing and making the application, made to any judge for authorization to intercept, or for approval of interceptions of, wire, oral, or electronic communications involving any of the same persons, facilities or places specified in the application, and the action taken by the judge on each such application; and

(f) where the application is for the extension of an order, a statement setting forth the results thus far obtained from the interception, or a reasonable explanation of the failure to obtain such results.

(2) The judge may require the applicant to furnish additional testimony or documentary evidence in support of the application.

(3) Upon such application the judge may enter an ex parte order, as requested or as modified, authorizing or approving interception of wire, oral, or electronic communications within the territorial jurisdiction of the court in which the judge is sitting (and outside that jurisdiction but within the United States in the case of a mobile interception device authorized by a Federal court within such jurisdiction), if the judge determines on the basis of the facts submitted by the applicant that
   (a) there is probable cause for belief that an individual is committing, has committed, or is about to commit a particular offense enumerated in section 2516 of this chapter;
   (b) there is probable cause for belief that particular communications concerning that offense will be obtained through such interception;
   (c) normal investigative procedures have been tried and have failed or reasonably appear to be unlikely to succeed if tried or to be too dangerous;
   (d) except as provided in subsection (11), there is probable cause for belief that the facilities from which, or the place where, the wire, oral, or electronic communications are to be intercepted are being used, or are about to be used, in connection with the commission of such offense, or are leased to, listed in the name of, or commonly used by such person.
(4) Each order authorizing or approving the interception of any wire, oral, or electronic communication under this chapter shall specify
   (a) the identity of the person, if known, whose communications are to be intercepted;
   (b) the nature and location of the communications facilities as to which, or the place where, authority to intercept is granted;
   (c) a particular description of the type of communication sought to be intercepted, and a statement of the particular offense to which it relates;
   (d) the identity of the agency authorized to intercept the communications, and of the person authorizing the application; and
   (e) the period of time during which such interception is authorized, including a statement as to whether or not the interception shall automatically terminate when the described communication has been first obtained.
   An order authorizing the interception of a wire, oral, or electronic communication under this chapter shall, upon request of the applicant, direct that a provider of wire or electronic communication service, landlord, custodian or other person shall furnish the applicant forthwith all information,

facilities, and technical assistance necessary to accomplish the interception unobtrusively and with a minimum of interference with the services that such service provider, landlord, custodian, or person is according the person whose communications are to be intercepted. Any provider of wire or electronic communication service, landlord, custodian or other person furnishing such facilities or technical assistance shall be compensated therefor by the applicant for reasonable expenses incurred in providing such facilities or assistance. Pursuant to section 2522 of this chapter, an order may also be issued to enforce the assistance capability and capacity requirements under the Communications Assistance for Law Enforcement Act.

(5) No order entered under this section may authorize or approve the interception of any wire, oral, or electronic communication for any period longer than is necessary to achieve the objective of the authorization, nor in any event longer than thirty days. Such thirty-day period begins on the earlier of the day on which the investigative or law enforcement officer first begins to conduct an interception under the order or ten days after the order is entered. Extensions of an order may be granted, but only upon application for an extension made in accordance with subsection (1) of this section and the court making the findings required by subsection (3) of this section. The period of extension shall be no longer than the authorizing judge deems necessary to achieve the purposes for which it was granted and in no event for longer than thirty days. Every order and extension thereof shall contain a provision that the authorization to intercept shall be executed as soon as practicable, shall be conducted in such a way as to minimize the interception of communications not otherwise subject to interception under this chapter, and must terminate upon attainment of the authorized objective, or in any event in thirty days. In the event the intercepted communication is in a code or foreign language, and an expert in that foreign language or code is not reasonably available during the interception period, minimization may be accomplished as soon as practicable after such interception. An interception under this chapter may be conducted in whole or in part by Government personnel, or by an individual operating under a contract with the Government, acting under the supervision of an investigative or law enforcement officer authorized to conduct the interception.

(6) Whenever an order authorizing interception is entered pursuant to this chapter, the order may require reports to be made to the judge

who issued the order showing what progress has been made toward achievement of the authorized objective and the need for continued interception. Such reports shall be made at such intervals as the judge may require.

(7) Notwithstanding any other provision of this chapter, any investigative or law enforcement officer, specially designated by the Attorney General, the Deputy Attorney General, the Associate Attorney General, or by the principal prosecuting attorney of any State or subdivision thereof acting pursuant to a statute of that State, who reasonably determines that

    (a) an emergency situation exists that involves

        (i) immediate danger of death or serious physical injury to any person,

        (ii) conspiratorial activities threatening the national security interest, or

        (iii) conspiratorial activities characteristic of organized crime, that requires a wire, oral, or electronic communication to be intercepted before an order authorizing such interception can, with due diligence, be obtained, and

    (b) there are grounds upon which an order could be entered under this chapter to authorize such interception, may intercept such wire, oral, or electronic communication if an application for an order approving the interception is made in accordance with this section within forty-eight hours after the interception has occurred, or begins to occur. In the absence of an order, such interception shall immediately terminate when the communication sought is obtained or when the application for the order is denied, whichever is earlier. In the event such application for approval is denied, or in any other case where the interception is terminated without an order having been issued, the contents of any wire, oral, or electronic communication intercepted shall be treated as having been obtained in violation of this chapter, and an inventory shall be served as provided for in subsection (d) of this section on the person named in the application.

(8)

    (a) The contents of any wire, oral, or electronic communication intercepted by any means authorized by this chapter shall, if possible, be recorded on tape or wire or other comparable device. The recording of the contents of any wire, oral, or electronic communication under this subsection shall be done in such a way as will protect the recording from editing or other alterations. Immediately upon the expiration of the period of the order, or extensions thereof, such recordings shall be made available to the judge issuing such order and sealed under his directions. Custody of the recordings shall be wherever the judge orders. They shall not be destroyed except upon an order of the issuing or denying judge and in any event shall be kept for ten years. Duplicate recordings may be made for use or disclosure pursuant to the provisions of subsections (1) and (2) of section 2517 of this chapter for investigations. The presence of the seal provided for by this subsection, or a satisfactory explanation for the absence thereof, shall be a prerequisite for the use or disclosure of the contents of any wire, oral, or electronic communication or evidence derived therefrom under subsection (3) of section 2517.

(b) Applications made and orders granted under this chapter shall be sealed by the judge. Custody of the applications and orders shall be wherever the judge directs. Such applications and orders shall be disclosed only upon a showing of good cause before a judge of competent jurisdiction and shall not be destroyed except on order of the issuing or denying judge, and in any event shall be kept for ten years.

(c) Any violation of the provisions of this subsection may be punished as contempt of the issuing or denying judge.

(d) Within a reasonable time but not later than ninety days after the filing of an application for an order of approval under section 2518(7)(b) which is denied or the termination of the period of an order or extensions thereof, the issuing or denying judge shall cause to be served, on the persons named in the order or the application, and such other parties to intercepted communications as the judge may determine in his discretion that is in the interest of justice, an inventory which shall include notice of

(1) the fact of the entry of the order or the application;

(2) the date of the entry and the period of authorized, approved or disapproved interception, or the denial of the application; and

(3) the fact that during the period wire, oral, or electronic communications were or were not intercepted.

The judge, upon the filing of a motion, may in his discretion make available to such person or his counsel for inspection such portions of the intercepted communications, applications and orders as the judge determines to be in the interest of justice. On an ex parte showing of good cause to a judge of competent jurisdiction the serving of the inventory required by this subsection may be postponed.

(9)   The contents of any wire, oral, or electronic communication intercepted pursuant to this chapter or evidence derived therefrom shall not be received in evidence or otherwise disclosed in any trial, hearing, or other proceeding in a Federal or State court unless each party, not less than ten days before the trial, hearing, or proceeding, has been furnished with a copy of the court order, and accompanying application, under which the interception was authorized or approved. This ten-day period may be waived by the judge if he finds that it was not possible to furnish the party with the above information ten days before the trial, hearing, or proceeding and that the party will not be prejudiced by the delay in receiving such information.

(10)

(a) Any aggrieved person in any trial, hearing, or proceeding in or before any court, department, officer, agency, regulatory body, or other authority of the United States, a State, or a political subdivision thereof, may move to suppress the contents of any wire or oral communication intercepted pursuant to this chapter, or evidence derived therefrom, on the grounds that

(i)   the communication was unlawfully intercepted;

(ii) the order of authorization or approval under which it was intercepted is insufficient on its face; or

(iii) the interception was not made in conformity with the order of authorization or approval. Such motion shall be made before the trial, hearing, or proceeding unless there was no opportunity to make such motion or the person was not aware of the grounds of the motion. If the motion is granted, the contents of the intercepted wire or oral communication, or evidence derived therefrom, shall be treated as having been obtained in violation of this chapter. The judge, upon the filing of such motion by the aggrieved person, may in his discretion make available to the aggrieved person or his counsel for inspection such portions of the intercepted communication or evidence derived therefrom as the judge determines to be in the interests of justice.

(b) In addition to any other right to appeal, the United States shall have the right to appeal from an order granting a motion to suppress made under paragraph (a) of this subsection, or the denial of an application for an order of approval, if the United States attorney shall certify to the judge or other official granting such motion or denying such application that the appeal is not taken for purposes of delay. Such appeal shall be taken within thirty days after the date the order was entered and shall be diligently prosecuted.

(c) The remedies and sanctions described in this chapter with respect to the interception of electronic communications are the only judicial remedies and sanctions for nonconstitutional violations of this chapter involving such communications.

(11) The requirements of subsections (1)(b)(ii) and (3)(d) of this section relating to the specification of the facilities from which, or the place where, the communication is to be intercepted do not apply if

(a) in the case of an application with respect to the interception of an oral communication

(i) the application is by a Federal investigative or law enforcement officer and is approved by the Attorney General, the Deputy Attorney General, the Associate Attorney General, an Assistant Attorney General, or an acting Assistant Attorney General;

(ii) the application contains a full and complete statement as to why such specification is not practical and identifies the person committing the offense and whose communications are to be intercepted; and

(iii) the judge finds that such specification is not practical; and

(b) in the case of an application with respect to a wire or electronic communication

(i) the application is by a Federal investigative or law enforcement officer and is approved by the Attorney General, the Deputy Attorney General, the Associate Attorney General, an Assistant Attorney General, or an acting Assistant Attorney General;

(ii) the application identifies the person believed to be committing the offense and whose communications are to be intercepted and the applicant makes a showing that there is probable cause to believe that the person's actions could have the effect of thwarting interception from a specified facility;

(iii) the judge finds that such showing has been adequately made; and

(iv) the order authorizing or approving the interception is limited to interception only for such time as it is reasonable to presume that the person identified in the application is or was reasonably proximate to the instrument through which such communication will be or was transmitted.

(12) An interception of a communication under an order with respect to which the requirements of subsections (1)(b)(ii) and (3)(d) of this section do not apply by reason of subsection (11)(a) shall not begin until the place where the communication is to be intercepted is ascertained by the person implementing the interception order. A provider of wire or electronic communications service that has received an order as provided for in subsection (11)(b) may move the court to modify or quash the order on the ground that its assistance with respect to the interception cannot be performed in a timely or reasonable fashion. The court, upon notice to the government, shall decide such a motion expeditiously.

Section 2519. Reports Concerning Intercepted Wire, Oral, or Electronic Communications

(1) Within thirty days after the expiration of an order (or each extension thereof) entered under section 2518, or the denial of an order approving an interception, the issuing or denying judge shall report to the Administrative Office of the United States Courts

   (a) the fact that an order or extension was applied for;

   (b) the kind of order or extension applied for (including whether or not the order was an order with respect to which the requirements of sections 2518(1)(b)(ii) and 2518(3)(d) of this title did not apply by reason of section 2518(11) of this title);

   (c) the fact that the order or extension was granted as applied for, was modified, or was denied;

   (d) the period of interceptions authorized by the order, and the number and duration of any extensions of the order;

   (e) the offense specified in the order or application, or extension of an order;

   (f) the identity of the applying investigative or law enforcement officer and agency making the application and the person authorizing the application; and

   (g) the nature of the facilities from which or the place where communications were to be intercepted.

(2) In January of each year the Attorney General, an Assistant Attorney General specially designated by the Attorney General, or the principal prosecuting attorney of a State, or the principal prosecuting attorney for any political subdivision of a State, shall report to the Administrative Office of the United States Courts

(a) the information required by paragraphs (a) through (g) of subsection (1) of this section with respect to each application for an order or extension made during the preceding calendar year;

(b) a general description of the interceptions made under such order or extension, including

(i) the approximate nature and frequency of incriminating communications intercepted,

(ii) the approximate nature and frequency of other communications intercepted,

(iii) the approximate number of persons whose communications were intercepted,

(iv) the number of orders in which encryption was encountered and whether such encryption prevented law enforcement from obtaining the plain text of communications intercepted pursuant to such order, and

(v) the approximate nature, amount, and cost of the manpower and other resources used in the interceptions;

(c) the number of arrests resulting from interceptions made under such order or extension, and the offenses for which arrests were made;

(d) the number of trials resulting from such interceptions;

(e) the number of motions to suppress made with respect to such interceptions, and the number granted or denied;

(f) the number of convictions resulting from such interceptions and the offenses for which the convictions were obtained and a general assessment of the importance of the interceptions; and

(g) the information required by paragraphs (b) through (f) of this subsection with respect to orders or extensions obtained in a preceding calendar year.

(3) In April of each year the Director of the Administrative Office of the United States Courts shall transmit to the Congress a full and complete report concerning the number of applications for orders authorizing or approving the interception of wire, oral, or electronic communications pursuant to this chapter and the number of orders and extensions granted or denied pursuant to this chapter during the preceding calendar year. Such report shall include a summary and analysis of the data required to be filed with the Administrative Office by subsections (1) and (2) of this section. The Director of the Administrative Office of the United States Courts is authorized to issue binding regulations dealing with the content and form of the reports required to be filed by subsections (1) and (2) of this section.

Section 2520. Recovery of Civil Damages Authorized

(a) In General.

Except as provided in section 2511(2)(a)(ii), any person whose wire, oral, or electronic communication is intercepted, disclosed, or intentionally used in violation of this chapter may in a civil action recover from the person or entity, other than the United States, which engaged in that violation such relief as may be appropriate.

(b) Relief.

In an action under this section, appropriate relief includes

  (1) such preliminary and other equitable or declaratory relief as may be appropriate;

  (2) damages under subsection (c) and punitive damages in appropriate cases; and

  (3) a reasonable attorney's fee and other litigation costs reasonably incurred.

(c) Computation of Damages.

  (1) In an action under this section, if the conduct in violation of this chapter is the private viewing of a private satellite video communication that is not scrambled or encrypted or if the communication is a radio communication that is transmitted on frequencies allocated under subpart D of part 74 of the rules of the Federal Communications Commission that is not scrambled or encrypted and the conduct is not for a tortious or illegal purpose or for purposes of direct or indirect commercial advantage or private commercial gain, then the court shall assess damages as follows:

    (A) If the person who engaged in that conduct has not previously been enjoined under section 2511(5) and has not been found liable in a prior civil action under this section, the court shall assess the greater of the sum of actual damages suffered by the plaintiff, or statutory damages of not less than $50 and not more than $500.

    (B) If, on one prior occasion, the person who engaged in that conduct has been enjoined under section 2511(5) or has been found liable in a civil action under this section, the court shall assess the greater of the sum of actual damages suffered by the plaintiff, or statutory damages of not less than $100 and not more than $1000.

  (2) In any other action under this section, the court may assess as damages whichever is the greater of

   (A) the sum of the actual damages suffered by the plaintiff and any profits made by the violator as a result of the violation; or

   (B) statutory damages of whichever is the greater of $100 a day for each day of violation or $10,000.

(d) Defense.

   A good faith reliance on

   (1) a court warrant or order, a grand jury subpoena, a legislative authorization, or a statutory authorization;

   (2) a request of an investigative or law enforcement officer under section 2518(7) of this title; or

   (3) a good faith determination that section 2511(3) of this title permitted the conduct complained of; is a complete defense against any civil or criminal action brought under this chapter or any other law.

(e) Limitation.

   A civil action under this section may not be commenced later than two years after the date upon which the claimant first has a reasonable opportunity to discover the violation.

(f) Administrative Discipline.

   If a court or appropriate department or agency determines that the United States or any of its departments or agencies has violated any provision of this chapter, and the court or appropriate department or agency finds that the circumstances surrounding the violation raise serious questions about whether or not an officer or employee of the United States acted willfully or intentionally with respect to the violation, the department or agency shall, upon receipt of a true and correct copy of the decision and findings of the court or appropriate department or agency promptly initiate a proceeding to determine whether disciplinary action against the officer or employee is warranted. If the head of the department or agency involved determines that disciplinary action is not warranted, he or she shall notify the Inspector General with jurisdiction over the department or agency concerned and shall provide the Inspector General with the reasons for such determination.

(g) Improper Disclosure Is Violation.

   Any willful disclosure or use by an investigative or law enforcement officer or governmental entity of information beyond the extent permitted by section 2517 is a violation of this chapter for purposes of section 2520(a).

Section 2521. Injunction Against Illegal Interception

Whenever it shall appear that any person is engaged or is about to engage in any act which constitutes or will constitute a felony violation of this chapter, the Attorney General may initiate a civil action in a district court of the United States to enjoin such violation. The court shall proceed as soon as practicable to the hearing and determination of such an action, and may, at any time before final determination, enter such a restraining order or prohibition, or take such other action, as is warranted to prevent a continuing and substantial injury to the United States or to any person or class of persons for whose protection the action is brought. A proceeding under this section is governed by the Federal Rules of Civil Procedure, except that, if an indictment has been returned against the respondent, discovery is governed by the Federal Rules of Criminal Procedure.

Section 2522. Enforcement of the Communications Assistance for Law Enforcement Act

(a) Enforcement by Court Issuing Surveillance Order.
   If a court authorizing an interception under this chapter, a State statute, or the Foreign Intelligence Surveillance Act of 1978 (50 U.S.C. 1801 et seq.) or authorizing use of a pen register or a trap and trace device under chapter 206 or a State statute finds that a telecommunications carrier has failed to comply with the requirements of the Communications Assistance for Law Enforcement Act, the court may, in accordance with section 108 of such Act, direct that the carrier comply forthwith and may direct that a provider of support services to the carrier or the manufacturer of the carrier's transmission or switching equipment furnish forthwith modifications necessary for the carrier to comply.

(b) Enforcement Upon Application by Attorney General.
   The Attorney General may, in a civil action in the appropriate United States district court, obtain an order, in accordance with section 108 of the Communications Assistance for Law Enforcement Act, directing that a telecommunications carrier, a manufacturer of telecommunications transmission or switching equipment, or a provider of telecommunications support services comply with such Act.

(c) Civil Penalty. –

(1) In general.

A court issuing an order under this section against a telecommunications carrier, a manufacturer of telecommunications transmission or switching equipment, or a provider of telecommunications support services may impose a civil penalty of up to $10,000 per day for each day in violation after the issuance of the order or after such future date as the court may specify.

(2) Considerations.

In determining whether to impose a civil penalty and in determining its amount, the court shall take into account

(A) the nature, circumstances, and extent of the violation;

(B) the violator's ability to pay, the violator's good faith efforts to comply in a timely manner, any effect on the violator's ability to continue to do business, the degree of culpability, and the length of any delay in undertaking efforts to comply; and

(C) such other matters as justice may require.

(d) Definitions.

As used in this section, the terms defined in section 102 of the Communications Assistance for Law Enforcement Act have the meanings provided, respectively, in such section.

Appendix C: Acronyms

3G	Third Generation Mobile
3GPP	Third Generation Partnership Project
4G	Fourth Generation Mobile
AAL	ATM Adaptation Layer
AB	Access Burst
ABR	Available Bit Rate
A-bis	Interface between the BSC and BTS in a GSM network
ACU	Antenna Combining Unit
AFC	Automatic Frequency Control
AM	Amplitude Modulation
AMPS	Advanced Mobile Phone System
AMR	Adaptive Multi-Rate codec
AoC	Advice of Charge
API	Application Program Interface
ARPU	Average Revenue Per User
ASCII	American Standard Code for Information Interchange
ASIC	Application Specific Integrated Circuit
ASP	Application Service Provider
A-TDMA	Advanced Time Division Multiple Access
BCCH	Broadcast Control Channel
BCH	Broadcast Channels

B-CDMA	Broadband Code Division Multiple Access
BERT	Bit Error Rate Test
BHCA	Busy Hour Call Attempts
B-ISDN	Broadband ISDN
BPSK	Binary Phase Shift Keying
BREW	Binary Runtime Environment for Wireless
BSC	Base Station Controller
BSS	Base Station System/Subsystem
BTS	Base Transceiver Station
CAI	Common Air Interface
CB	Cell Broadcast
CC	Call Control
CCB	Customer Care and Billing
CCK	Complementary Code Keying
CCS7	Common Channel Signaling No. 7
CDF	Channel Data Format
CDMA	Code Division Multiple Access
CDPD	Cellular Digital Packet Data
CDPSK	Coherent Differential Phase Shift Keying
CDR	Call Detail Record
CELP	Code Excited Linear Prediction
CF	Call Forwarding
CGALIES	Coordination Group on Access to Location Information by Emergency Services
cHTML	Compact Hypertext Markup Language
CI	Carrier to Interference Ratio
CIBER	Cellular Intercarrier Billing Exchange Roamer Record
CID	Caller Identification
CLDC	Connected Limited Device Configuration
CLID	Calling Line Identification
CLIP	Calling Line Identification Presentation
CLIR	Calling Line Identification Restriction
CM	Connection Management
CMOS	Complementary Metal Oxide Substrate
CPE	Customer Premises Equipment
CPU	Central Processing Unit
CRC	Cyclic Redundancy Check
CRM	Customer Relationship Management
CSE	CAMEL Service Environment

CSMA	Carrier Sense Multiple Access
CSS	Customer Support System
CT	Cordless Telephony
CTA	Cordless Terminal Adaptor
CTIA	Cellular Telecommunications and Internet Association
CTM	Cordless Terminal Mobility
CTR	Common Technical Regulation
CUG	Closed User Group
D-AMPS	Digital AMPS
D/A	Digital to Analog Conversion
DAC	Digital to Analog Converter
DAMA	Demand Assigned Multiple Access
DAN	DECT Access Node
DB	Dummy Burst
DBPSK	Differential Binary Phase Shift Keying
DCA	Dynamic Channel Assignment
DCCH	Dedicated Control Channels
DCE	Data Communications Equipment
DCH	Data Clearing House
DCS1800	Digital Cellular System at 1800 MHz
DECT	Digitally Enhanced Cordless Telecommunications
DEPSK	Differential Encoded Phase Shift Keying
DES	Digital Encryption Standard
DFSK	Double Frequency Shift Keying
DHCP	Dynamic Host Configuration Protocol
DoS	Denial-of-Service
DPCM	Differential Pulse Code Modulation
DPSK	Differential Phase Shift Keying
DQPSK	Differential Quadrature Phase Shift Keying
DSRR	Digital Short Range Radio
DSSS	Direct Sequence Spread Spectrum
DS-CDMA	Direct Sequence CDMA
DSP	Digital Signal Processing
DTE	Data Terminal Equipment
DTMF	Dual Tone Multifrequency
DTX	Discontinuous Transmission
DVB	Digital Video Broadcasting

EAP	Extensible Authentication Protocol
EDGE	Enhanced Data Rates for GSM Evolution
EEPROM	Electrically Erasable Programmable Read Only Memory
EFR	Enhanced Full Rate
EFT	Electronic Funds Transfer
EGSM	Extended (frequency range) GSM
EIR	Equipment Identity Register
EIRP	Effective Isotropic Radiated Power
EOTD	Enhanced Observed Time Difference
EPROM	Erasable Programmable Read-Only Memory
ERMES	Enhanced Radio Messaging System
ERO	European Radiocommunications Office
ERP	Effective Radiated Power
ESMR	Enhanced Special Mobile Radio
ESN	Electronic Serial Number
ESPRIT	European Strategic Programme for Research and Development in Information Technology
ETACS	Extended TACS
ETS	European Telecommunications Standard
ETSI	European Telecommunications Standards Institute
EvDO	Evolution Data Only
FACCH	Fast Associated Control Channel
FB	Frequency Correction Burst
FCC	Federal Communications Committee
FDD	Frequency Division Duplex
FDMA	Frequency Division Multiple Access
FEC	Forward Error Correction
FH	Frequency Hopping
FH-CDMA	Frequency Hopping CDMA
FHSS	Frequency Hopping Spread Spectrum
FMC	Fixed Mobile Convergence
FMI	Fixed Mobile Integration
FRA	Fixed Radio Access
FRS	Family Radio Service
FSDPSK	Filtered Symmetric Differential Phase Shift Keying
FSK	Frequency Shift Keying
FSOQ	Frequency Shift Offset Quadrature Modulation
FSS	Fixed Satellite Service

GAP	Generic Access Profile
GCF	Global Certification Forum
GERAN	GSM-EDGE Radio Access Network
GGRF	GSM Global Roaming Forum
GGSN	Gateway GPRS Support Node
GMPCS	Global Mobile Personal Communications by Satellite
GMSC	Gateway Mobile Switching Center
GMSK	Gaussian Minimum Shift Keying
GPRS	Generalized Packet Radio System
GPS	Global Positioning System
GRX	GPRS Roaming Exchange
GSM	Global System for Mobile Telecommunications
HDLC	High-Level Data Link Control
HR/DSSS	High Rate Direct Sequence Spread Spectrum
HAN	Home Area Network
HIPERLAN	High Performance Radio LAN
HIPERMAN	High Performance Radio Metropolitan-Area Network
HIPERPAN	High Performance Radio Personal-Area Network
HIPERACCESS	High Performance Radio Access
HLR	Home Location Register
HSPSD	High Speed Packet Switched Data
IBSS	Independent Basic Service Set
iDEN	Integrated Digital Enhanced Network
IDS	Intrusion Detection System
IEEE	Institute of Electrical and Electronics Engineers
IETF	Internet Engineering Task Force
I-ETS	Interim European Telecommunications Standard
IMEI	International Mobile Equipment Identity
IMSI	International Mobile Subscriber Identity
IN	Intelligent Network
INAP	Intelligent Network Application Part
IP	Internet Protocol
IPR	Intellectual Property Rights
IrDA	Infrared Data Association
ISDN	Integrated Services Digital Network
ISM	Industrial, Scientific and Medical (Frequency range)
ISO	International Standards Organization
ISP	Internet Service Provider

ITU	International Telecommunications Union
ITU-R	ITU Telecommunications Radio Sector
ITU-T	ITU Telecommunications Standardization Sector
IWF	Interworking Function
IV	Initialization Vector
J2ME	Java 2 Mobile Edition
JPEG	Joint Photographic Experts Group
LAN	Local Area Network
LANS	Local Area Network Services
LAP	Link Access Protocol
LEO	Low Earth Orbit
LMSS	Land Mobile Satellite Service
LOS	Line of Sight
MAC	Media Access Control
MAN	Metropolitan Area Network
MAP	Mobile Application Part
MCPA	Multi Carrier Power Amplifier
MeXe	Mobile Execution Environment
MFSK	Multiple Frequency Shift Keying
MHz	Megahertz
MIDP	Mobile Information Device Profile
MMI	Man Machine Interface
MMS	Multimedia Messaging Service
MMSK	Modified Minimum Shift Keying
MNO	Mobile Network Operator
MS	Mobile Station
MSC	Mobile Switching Center
MSISDN	Mobile Station International ISDN Number
MSK	Minimum Shift Keying (also called FFSK)
MVPN	Mobile Virtual Private Network
N-AMPS	Narrowband AMPS
NB	Normal Burst
NET	Norme Europeenne de Telecommunications
NMT	Nordic Mobile Telephone
OBEX	Object Exchange

OFDM	Orthogonal Frequency Division Multiplexing
OTA	Over the Air Activation (of services and tariff changes)
OTDOA	Observed Time Difference of Arrival
O&M	Operations and Maintenance
OMC	Operations and Maintenance Center
OMC-R	The Radio OMC
OMC-S	The Switching OMC
OSI	Open Systems Interconnection
PABX	Private Automatic Branch Exchange
PAN	Personal Area Network
PAP	Public Access Profile
PBCC	Packet Binary Convolutional Coding
PCU	Packet Control Unit
PCH	Paging Channel
PCM	Pulse Code Modulation
PCMCIA	Personal Computer Memory Card Interface Association
PCN	Personal Communications Network
PCS 1900	Personal Communications Systems 1900 MHz
PDA	Personal Digital Assistant
PDC	Personal Digital Communications
PEAP	Protected Extension Authentication Protocol
PEDC	Pan European Digital Communications
PHS/PHP	Personal HandyPhone System/Phone
PHY	Physical (layer)
PIN	Personal Identifier Number
PKI	Public Key Infrastructure
PLMN	Public Land Mobile Network
PMR	Private Mobile Radiocommunications
POCSAG	Post Office Code Standardization Advisory Group
PoP	Points of Presence
POTS	Plain Old Telephone Service
PRNG	Pseudo Random Number Generator
PROM	Programmable Read Only Memory
PSK	Phase Shift Keying
PSDN	Public Switched Data Network
PSPDN	Public Switched Packet Data Network
PSTN	Public Switched Telephone Network

PSU	Power Supply Unit
PTO	Public Telecommunication Operator
PTT	Postal Telegraph and Telephone
PTT	Push-to-Talk
PoP	Points of Presence
PSRCP	Public Safety Radio Communications Project
PWT	Personal Wireless Telecommunications
QAM	Quadrature Amplitude Modulation
QAPSK	Quadrature Amplitude Phase Shift Keying
QCELP	Quadrature Code Excited Linear Prediction
QoS	Quality of Service
QPSK	Quadrature Phase Shift Keying
RACE	Research in Advanced Communications in Europe
RACH	Random Access Channel
RADIUS	Remote Authentication Dial-In User Service
RAM	Random Access Memory
RCC	Radio Common Carrier
RELP	Residual Excited Linear Prediction
RF	Radio Frequency
RFID	Radio Frequency Identification Device
RFP	Radio Fixed Part
RNC	Radio Network Controller
RP	Radio Part
RRM	Radio Resource Management
RT	Remote Terminal
SACCH	Slow Associated Control Channel
SAR	Specific Absorption Rate
SAT	SIM Application Toolkit
SB	Synchronization Burst
S-CDMA	Synchronous CDMA
SCH	Synchronization Channel
SCP	Switching/Service Control Point
SDCCH	Stand-Alone Dedicated Control Channel
SDLC	Synchronous Data Link Control
SDMA	Spatial Division Multiple Access
SDR	Software Defined Radio
SGSN	Serving GPRS Support Node

SIM	Subscriber Identity Module
SoHo	Small Office/Home Office
SMR	Specialized Mobile Radio
SMS	Short Message Service
SMSC	SMS Center
SMSCB	SMS Cell Broadcast
SMS-MO	SMS Mobile Originated
SMS-MT	SMS Mobile Terminated
SMS-PP	SMS Point to Point
SP	Service Provider
SQAM	Staggered Quadrature Amplitude Modulation
SQPSK	Staggered Quadrature Phase Shift Keying
SS	Supplementary Service
SS7	Signaling System Number 7
SSID	Server Set ID
SSP	Service Switching Point
STK	SIM ToolKit
STM	Synchronous Transfer Mode
TACS	Total Access Communications System
TAP	Transferred Account Procedure
TBR	Technical Basis for Regulation
TCH	Traffic Channel
TD-CDMA	Time Division CDMA
TDD	Time Division Duplex
TDMA	Time Division Multiple Access
TDOA	Time Difference of Arrival
TD-SCDMA	Time Division-Synchronous Code Division Multiple Access
TETRA	Terrestrial Trunked Radio
TFTS	Terrestrial Flight Telephone System
TIPHON	Telecommunications and Internet Protocol Harmonization over Networks
TKIP	Temporal Key Integrity Protocol
TMN	Telecommunications Management Network
TMSI	Temporary Mobile Subscriber Identity
TRAU	Transcoder Rate Adapter Unit
TRX	Transmitter/Receiver (transceiver)
TTLS	Tunneled Transport Layer Security

UI	User Interface
UMTS	Universal Mobile Telecommunications System
UPN	Universal Personal Number
UPT	Universal Personal Telecommunications
URL	Uniform Resource Locator
USIM	Universal Subscriber Identity Module
USO	Universal Service Obligation
UTRA	Universal Terrestrial Radio Access
UTRAN	Universal Terrestrial Radio Access Network
UWB	Ultrawideband
VAS	Value Added Services
VBR	Variable Bit Rate
VHE	Virtual Home Environment
VLR	Visitor Location Register
Vocoder	Voice Coder
VoIP	Voice over Internet Protocol
VPN	Virtual Private Network
VSAT	Very Small Aperture Terminal
VSELP	Vector Sum Excited Linear Prediction
WAP	Wireless Application Protocol
WARC	World Administration Radio Conference
WCDMA	Wideband Code Division Multiple Access
WEP	Wired Equivalent Privacy
WLAN	Wireless Local Area Network
WLL	Wireless Local Loop
WML	Wireless Mark-up Language
WPA	Wi-Fi Protected Access
WQAM	Weighted Quadrature Amplitude Modulation
xHTML	eXtensible Hypertext Markup Language

Appendix D: The 802.11 Alphabet

802.11a

802.11a uses 5.725 GHz U-NII Orthogonal Frequency-Division Multiplexing (OFDM) and has data transfer rates of 6, 9, 12, 18, 24, 36, 48, and 54 Mbps. Its security includes 168-bit key Wired Equivalency Protocol (WEP).

Typically 802.11a is used for:

- Corporate business environments
- Limited small office home/office deployments
- Point-to-point bridged networks
- High-speed digital content delivery

802.11b

802.11b uses 2.4 GHz Direct Sequence Spread Spectrum (DSSS), 2.4 GHz Frequency Hopping Spread Spectrum (FHSS) or Infrared (850 nm – 960 nm IR) and has data transfer rates of 1, 2, 5.5, and 11 Mbps. Its security includes 64-bit and 128-bit key Wired Equivalency Protocol (WEP).

Typically 802.11b is used for:

- Corporate campus environments
- Small office home office (SOHO) networks
- Industrial and manufacturing
- Point-to-point bridged networks

802.11d

802.11d is the standard for multicountry roaming. It is a way for WLAN access points to broadcast what country they're in and what country-specific rules client network interface cards have to follow. Basically, this means you could fly from Los Angeles to Sydney, walk into your office or hotel, power up your wireless laptop, and expect to connect with whatever WLAN is open.

802.11e

802.11e is the extensible quality of service (QoS) standard. 802.11e is implemented at the MAC layer and is to be used in implementations of Voice-over-IP (VoIP), streaming video distribution, and other media delivery systems.

802.11g

802.11g is intended to directly replace 802.11b. 802.11g uses 2.4 GHz Direct Sequence Spread Spectrum (DSSS), 2.4 GHz Frequency Hopping Spread Spectrum (FHSS), or Infrared (850–960 nm IR) and has data transfer rates of 6, 9, 12, 18, 24, 36, 48, and 54 Mbps. Its security will include Wi-Fi Protected Access (WPA).

802.11h

802.11h is the dynamic frequency selection and transmission power control standard. 802.11h creates a set of management messages for access points and clients in the European 5 GHz band to coordinate efforts to avoid interfering with radar and satellite communications in the same band. The WLAN devices select another channel and adjust power output if needed, but these same actions can be used to improve WLAN efficiency. Some elements of this work are also being carried out in the 802.11k standard as well.

802.11i

802.11i is the approved standard to improve wireless security. 802.11i implements the use of the TKIP (Temporal Key Integrity Protocol) protocol to improve security with legacy hardware and RSN (Robust Security

Network) for new hardware deployments. It is important to note that 802.11i is not a radio specification; rather, it is a security specification.

802.11j

802.11j uses the 4.9 to 5 Ghz spectrum and is set aside solely for public safety and Homeland Security in the United States.

802.11k

802.11k is the radio resource management standard. This project standardizes an array of radio measurements, roaming requests, data about the radio channel, and data about the client devices. This will also standardize how they make decisions on when to roam from one access point (AP) to another. Currently, the decision to roam between access points is based on vendor criteria and isn't standardized. Additionally, this data can be made available to higher-level WLAN management applications, where the information can be used in tasks such as optimizing performance and balancing traffic loads.

802.11ma

802.11ma corrects and makes enhancements to the 802.11 MAC and physical functions that have generally been adopted by vendors, but not solidified into a standard.

802.11n

802.11n is the standard for enhanced throughput for 802.11 networks. It offers a new physical layer standard allowing for longer range and improved throughput using MIMO (multiple-input, multiple-output) technology. 802.11n networks are designed to achieve greater than 100 Mbps real throughput.

802.11p

802.11p, also referred to as Wireless Access in Vehicular Environments (WAVE), is a new physical layer specification using the licensed 5.9 GHz band for transactions between the roadside and moving vehicles. It will be used for toll-debit services for cars on the highway and could also be used for voice conversations in cars, eventually replacing cellular technology.

802.11r

802.11r, also referred to as Fast Roaming, is designed to reduce the amount of time to roam between access points, eliminating the short loss of service to which real-time streaming protocols, such as VoIP calls, are incredibly sensitive. The goal is to create a standard for fast roaming so that users don't have to reauthenticate at each new access point or have their calls disrupted.

802.11s

802.11s, also referred to as Extended Service Set Mesh (ESS Mesh), is meant to provide peer-to-peer connectivity using other stations as routers for wireless data, forwarding traffic to neighboring access points as Internet nodes do today with a series of multi-hop transmissions. This application of wireless technology would allow organizations to cover large areas without a significant investment in infrastructure.

802.11t

802.11t is the Wireless Performance Prediction (WPP) standard. 802.11t tests methods and metrics. This will open the testing standards and processes for wireless equipment.

802.11u

802.11u is the standard designed for interworking with non-802 networks. 802.11u will utilize techniques that can be used to internetwork 802.11 networks with other wireless networks (e.g. cellular, GSM, etc.).

802.11v

802.11v is the wireless network management standard. 802.11v technology will be able to manage access points in a distributed or a centralized fashion and identify the failures in SNMP (Simple Network Management Protocol).

Index

Find Friends service, 32
Firewalls, 22
First responders
    roles and responsibilities of in
        cybercrime investigation, 55
Flash random-access memory. *See* FRAM
Forensic analysts
    roles and responsibilities of in
        cybercrime investigation, 56
Forensic Card Reader, 98
Forensic evidence
    looking into WLANs for, 58
    obtaining from BlackBerry devices, 83
    obtaining from cell phones, 94
        rules for, 99
    obtaining from Palm PDAs, 72
    obtaining from Windows CE/Pocket PC
        devices, 79
Forensic examiners
    roles and responsibilities of in
        cybercrime investigation, 56
Forensic fingerprints, 56
Forensic principles, 51
ForensicSIM, 98
FRAM, 93
Fraud, 53
    detection, 29
Fraud Task Force, 29
Free space optics. *See* FSO
Frequency division multiple access. *See*
    FDMA
Frequency hopping spread spectrum. *See*
    FHSS
Friendships
    mobile phones and, 139
FSO, 7

G

Gambling
    future wireless technologies for, 148
Gap fillers, 136
General Packet Radio Service. *See* GPRS
Global System for Mobile Communications.
    See GSM
GPRS, 9
GPS
    jamming, 35
    use of for agriculture, 149
Grafedia, 131, 133

Graph Theoretic Anomaly Detection. *See*
    GTAD
Grocery shopping
    use of RFID for, 129
GSM, 8
GSM.XRY, 96
GTAD, 38
Guidance Software's EnCase, 63

H

Hacking
    cell phones
        tracking people by, 31
Harassment, 52
Hardware
    wireless
        finding, 58
Healthcare
    use of wireless technologies in, 149
Hi-tech
    crime, 51
    patrol cars, 44
HLR, 57
Home Location Register. *See* HLR
Honeyd, 48
Honeypots, 47
HotSpots
    city-sized, 144
HotSync process, 67, 69
HTTPS, 23

I

Identity theft, 35, 54
    virtual, 36
    wireless, 37
Identity Theft Resource Center. *See* ITRC
iMode, 10
Information revolution, 135
Infrared. *See* IrDA
Infrared Financial Messaging. *See* IrFM
Initialization Vectors. *See* IVs
Insiders, 39
Intel Centrino, 10
Internet crime, 51
Investigators